INTERVIEWS WITH CONTEMPORARY NOVELISTS

INTERVIEWS WITH
CONTEMPORARY
NOVELISTS

Diana Cooper-Clark

St. Martin's Press   New York

© Diana Cooper-Clark 1986

Printed in Hong Kong
Published in the United Kingdom by The Macmillan Press Ltd.
First published in the United States of America in 1986

ISBN 0–312–42534–1

Library of Congress Cataloging in Publication Data
Cooper-Clark, Diana.
Interviews with contemporary novelists.
Includes index.
1. Novelists – 20th century – Interviews.   I. Title.
PN452.C66   1986   809.3′04 [B]   85–14520
ISBN 0–312–42534–1

To Trevor, with love

Contents

Introduction

Interviews have been both damned and praised. Saul Bellow dislikes interviews because he says they are like thumbprints on his windpipe. V. S. Naipaul agrees and feels that some people are wounded by interviews and lose a part of themselves. Hans Habe recalled in his autobiography that in the thirties and forties, the successful writer was snatched up by a tornado of interviews, often to the detriment of the writer. Fortunately, for me, all writers do not feel this way. James Dickey has said that the interview is one of the great art forms of our time. I concede to those who might find my insertion of Dickey's statement self-serving; perhaps there is a middle ground. Julio Cortázar believed that an interview is like a sonata for two instruments, and it must be played equally well by both instruments if the sonata is to be beautiful. If one instrument is good and the other is not, then the sonata is a failure.

I do know I am grateful that I had not read a recent interview with Carlos Fuentes, entitled 'No More Interviews' before I invited him to participate in this book. There are those who might see interviewers in the same light as biographers. In 1946, Richard Ellmann visited Edith Sitwell to discuss W. B. Yeats for his book, *Yeats: The Man and the Masks*. Sitwell later explained to John Lehmann that Ellmann's thesis was the effect on his poetry of Yeats' relationship with Maud Gonne and others. 'Oh, oh, oh', she cried, 'is it not *awful* that every great man has got to be exhumed and nailed down at the crossroads with a stake through his heart?' That is something to consider! However, the writers in this book participated in its creation and hopefully the interviews are not stakes through their hearts or their novels.* Rightly or wrongly, when a writer excites and

---

* Sadly, after the book was completed, Julio Cortázar died. This was his last major interview and he was very pleased with it. My thanks to him and to all of the other writers.

enchants me, I want to breathe the same air, ascend the heights in conversation, and in some small measure follow the creative river to its source; it is *one* way to enter the secret garden of literature. It was in the spirit of St Augustine's lovely notion in his *Confessions*, that I began this book: 'Conversations and jokes together, mutual rendering of good services, the reading together of sweetly phrased books, the sharing of nonsense and mutual attentions.' These interviews are not the result of star-mania. In accounting for this not so new phenomenon, Hans Habe wrote:

> The . . . lack of imagination, . . . makes it necessary to see an author whose work one has read; otherwise one cannot picture him. Like so many other things, one must be able to touch him. It is the same attitude that makes Americans take their beautifully constructed motor-cars to pieces as soon as they have bought them; they are not satisfied until they have personally convinced themselves what makes them tick. Similarly they must look into the author's head.[1]

Obviously, this is not an exclusively American phenomenon. It wasn't *necessary* to meet these writers in order to enter their literary worlds and I wasn't 'symbol-sniffing'. But I did want to talk to the writers about contemporary literature in general, and their work in particular, and give them an opportunity to respond to critical interpretations of their work. The interviews also taught me a great deal about my own failings as both a reader and a critic. It was sometimes humorous in my un-intentional parody of myself. In my interview with Margaret Drabble, I pontificated about the connections between Boethius' *The Consolation of Philosophy* and her novel *The Ice Age*, pridefully secure in my own flight. She reduced my bombast to embarrassing simplicity.

To read a book is one of the most intimate ways of sharing someone's mind and heart. Writer and reader travel together. It is a personal journey for both. The writer begins as the cartographer, drawing the map, marking the lines and charting new territory. And in the best writers it is a new land because no-one has quite seen it that way before. The Indians had already seen the Pacific before Balboa first gazed from the heights of Darien at its wonder. Yet that infinite expanse of water must have given him a vision that was individual and uniquely his own. New York becomes fresh and new each time through the eyes of Saul Bellow, Jack Kerouac, Thomas Wolfe or Bernard Malamud. The reader then joins the exploration and together with the writer creates new worlds. Carlos Fuentes has said that when he reads Dickens, he is recreating his books. Fuentes becomes Charles Dickens in a way, and he believes that Dickens comes to life through his reading. Reader and writer meet each other with a 'shock of recognition'. Each is a kindred spirit to be communicated with again and again. This does not necessarily mean that reader, writer and book ingratiatingly pat each other on the back and welcome each other into the inner *sanctum sanctorum* of mutual sensibilities. Sometimes they quarrel which may or may not end in reconciliation. Julio Cortázar said that he wrote *Hopscotch* as he did to make the reader grow very angry and independent and hurl the book out of the window if he chose.

It has been said of Christ that many follow Him to the breaking of the bread, but few to drinking with Him the chalice of His passion. This statement could possibly be applied to the writer and the reader. Fuentes has joked that people teased him that one needs a sabbatical year to read *Terra Nostra*. Our culture often complains and whines about the writer's commitment to the reader, and this is fair enough. But what of the reader's commitment to the writer, his or her responsibility to meet the energy, the work, and the time which authors have put into their writing? When people accused William Faulkner of being obscure and difficult, he wondered why they would think that what he had to say could be embraced in simple language, simple techiques. This is not merely a hard-headed, élitist response. If you read to kill time, that's fine, if, as Ezra Pound said, you like your time dead. Some books require readers to reach the level of the writer's own struggle to bait his hook for Leviathan, to use Stanley Edgar Hyman's lovely metaphor. It has been suggested that a book is like a mirror; if an ass looks in, don't expect an apostle to look out. Books are like quicksilver, they change as we change, as our expectations of the narrative change, and as the words dart back and forth for the rest of our lives, from that first moment when we discover a book we love until the moment that either we die or the text dies for us.

How frustrating when readers remark, 'I didn't like the book, it's no good, it depressed me!' Don't they understand that the book *worked* if it touched and moved them? Tragedy elevates you because first it forces you to confront fear and failure and success and security and insecurity and pity and terror and glory and death and the eternal sorrows of mankind. Saul Bellow believes that: 'Art cannot and should not compete with amusement. It has business at the heart of humankind.' The artist, as Collingwood tells us, must be a prophet, 'not in the sense that he foretells things to come, but that he tells the audience, at the risk of their displeasure, the secrets of their own hearts'.[2] A book need not disturb us with the violence of Kafka's axe but it should elicit some response whether it be tears or laughter; it should be a catalyst for movement of some kind. The painter, Robert Rauschenberg, said: 'If you do not change your mind about something when you confront a picture you have not seen before, you are either a stubborn fool or the painting is not very good.' How strange it would be if at the end of Céline's *Journey to the End of the Night* or Mauriac's *Vipers' Tangle* or Ludwig Lewisohn's *The Case of Mr. Crump* a reader sighed, 'That was a nice book.' We live in a world that is described as greasy and sloppy in its expression of feeling and at the same time cold and impersonal. Certainly contemporary criticism seems to have no room for emotion. Carolyn Heilbrun admitted that 'professionally trained in the so-called New Criticism, that close attention to the text that denies the relevance of any factors outside it, I found that this criticism nicely reinforced my need for impersonality'.[3] Still I remember a student who cried during his perceptive oral presentation of Tennyson's 'The Ancient Sage' because it moved him so deeply. And I remember a marvellously coherent and articulate lecture during which the professor cried at the power and beauty of Dante. I suppose this will be considered excessive in some circles. but it is possible to be both objective and personal. Discovery *is* moving and exciting and a variety of responses are legitimate whether it is the scientist, Archimedes, running naked through the streets yelling 'Eureka', or a tear sliding down someone's cheek. Didn't tears often fall on the manuscript of *Uncle Tom's Cabin* and didn't Harriet Beecher Stowe take to her bed for two days after writing the death of Little Eva? Didn't Gertrude Stein cry in a library when she realized that she couldn't read all the books in the world which interested her? And didn't Flaubert vomit after writing the passage about Madame Bovary's poisoning? Writers and readers know that literature is not bloodless. (At this point, I can hear some voices protesting that I must have read D. H. Lawrence in my formative years.)

I am stressing the emotional response because so many people today dismiss it. Clearly, human beings do not have to have a compartmentalized involvement with a book, all one thing or another. Readers can marvel at the structural and verbal arabesques or the beauty of form, whether it is voluptuous or bone-clean in its sparsity. All of this can both thrill us and give us food for thought. I'm not talking here about colourful pyrotechnical displays that are empty and barren at their centre. Brecht has talked about artists who in striving for form, lose the content. In his essay, 'Form and Content', he tells the story of a man who tried to prune a laurel tree into the shape of a globe. After much cutting, the tree at last resembled a globe, albeit a very small one. Disappointed the gardener asked: 'Well, that is a globe, but where is the laurel?' We need not make a bonzai tree of literature. Toni Morrison would like to write a book to which one has a visceral response and which is exciting to non-readers, and at the same time has a lot of food for people of fastidious intellect.

In addition to creating new worlds, books also pull from the depths, of both reader and writer, worlds that have always existed but had never yet lived or seen the light of day. These worlds are the breath of life across our face with all of its stink, its beauty, its absurdity, its grating noise, its silence, its compassion, its indifference, its truth, its lie, its ragged edges, and its splendour. According to the Chinese poet, Lu Chi, literature is born when the poet succeeds in wrestling meaning out of the mysterious, silent, meaningless universe, and 'traps Heaven and Earth in the cage of form'. Form here is a prison that can bring us the freedom of illumination.

Henry Miller has written about 'the flight which the poet makes over the face of the earth, and then, as if he had been ordained to re-enact a lost drama, the heroic descent to the very bowels of the earth, the dark and fearsome sojourn in the belly of the whale, the bloody struggle to liberate himself, to emerge clean of the past, a bright, gory sun-god cast up'. Ideally, readers and writers are pilgrim travellers who make this journey. I would like to believe interviewers too. They travel to the sacred place of literature as an act of devotion. Literature transfigures the ordinary. Writers take us around the world and it is literal geography: Naipaul's Trinidad, Gordimer's South Africa, Hardy's Wessex (Dorset), Amado's Brazil, Laurence's Manawaka, Manitoba, or Aksyonov's Russia. Although Nadine Gordimer had never left Africa until she was thirty years' old, she had preconceived the world outside that continent through reading. When she stood in London for the first time, it was familiar because she had seen it through Virginia Woolf's eyes. But it is also aesthetic geography, a landscape of the mind, of the heart, and of the soul. Eudora Welty has written about the importance of this 'hereness' of things in her essay, 'Place in Fiction'. Place 'is the named, identified, concrete, exact and exacting, and therefore credible, gathering spot of all that has been felt, is about to be experienced. . . . Location pertains to feeling; feeling profoundly pertains to place; place in history partakes of feeling, as feeling about history partakes of place.'[4] When the elements work in literature, they speak to the deep, flowing current that resides in the hearts of all men and women. Robertson Davies has used the Russian word 'shamanstvo' to describe the function of a writer of fiction in relation to his fellow travellers. In Russia, shamanstvo is the teller of epic tales; he articulates the unconscious by way of stories. He also dreams the dreams of import for the entire community. Robertson Davies, Julio Cortázar, Carlos Fuentes, and Toni Morrison are a few of the writers in this book for whom language is sacred, incantatory and profoundly powerful.

Literature leaves 'scope for the imagination', as Anne of Green Gables would say. You don't have to agree with the world the writer creates. However, you must see it; at its best it is a world that you cannot fight. The page forces your surrender. But you do not relinquish possession of yourself; rather, you find yourself, or possibly a new self, and much more besides. As the author of *Sweetsir*, Helen Yglesias, has said: when she grew up, literature 'was no longer just a way out, but a way *in*, into itself and into myself'. You may be lucky as George Moore was when he read Huysmans: 'Huysmans goes to my soul like a gold ornament of Byzantine workmanship.' Or Eudora Welty reading Chekhov: 'Reading Chekhov was just like the angels singing to me.'

I've talked about the gifts and glory of literature. Let's talk about the pain. Read Erica Jong's interview if you want to know about the pain of critical abuse. O. H. Cheney, in his *Economic Survey of the Book Industry* (1931) asserted that 'the industry is organized around causes and effects about as related as dice throws'. It doesn't seem to have changed. A few years ago, a freelance writer, Chuck Ross, decided to see if he could get a manuscript published by an unknown author. He used the pseudonym of Erik Demos (this might alone have sent signals to an editor with a background in Greek: dêmos means 'people') and submitted a typed copy of Jerzy Kosinski's novel *Steps*, which had won the National Book award in 1969. The manuscript was rejected by fourteen publishers and thirteen literary agents. Among these were Random House (which had published *Steps* nine years before), Houghton Mifflin (which had published three Kosinski novels), Harcourt Brace Jovanovich, and William Morrow. Or look at the irritations that the master writer Robertson Davies had to deal with in his own country, Canada. When *Fifth Business* was published Davies received universal praise but it was outside Canada. Saul Bellow said that Davies' novel had taught him much; John Fowles said, 'I must express my admiration'; *The New York Times Book Review*, *Esquire* and *The New Yorker* all praised it. The major Toronto (Davies' hometown) newspapers' judgement was that the novel was 'tedious' and 'boring'. This about the writer that Anthony Burgess has said is 'one of the most elegant' novelists in North America. Davies told me that after the wonderful foreign reviews, one of the Canadian reviewers went to see him and said, 'I just don't understand it.' Is it a surprise that Davies has said: 'I have given all that I could to Canada, my love, my hate, my bitter indifference; this raw, frost-bitten place and its raw frost-bitten people have numbed my heart.' It seems to be true that Canadians are as attracted by failure as Americans are by success.

Have you ever met a writer on a promotional tour? The humourist Eric Nicol calls the promotion tour an 'all-expense paid trip to intensive care'. Betty Jane Wylie, the author of *Beginnings*, has said that you become a writer because you are by nature an introvert, content to spend hours alone, communing with paper, either printed, which you read, or blank, which you fill with words. And then, in the interests of the marketplace, you become a hustler, an extrovert ready to shoot off at the mouth to anyone who will listen, in the hopes that some other introvert will read what you have written. But 'hype' isn't new. Ibsen achieved the fame of a movie star. Cigarettes, coffee and clothes were advertised as being 'à la Ibsen'. George du Maurier's novel *Trilby* (1894) produced Trilby songs, a burlesque opera *Trilby*, a circus ringmaster made up as Svengali and a bareback rider as Trilby, a new town in Florida called Trilby with a street called 'Svengali', a new $3.00 shoe called Trilby, Trilby hams and sausages, a Trilby hearthbrush, and a patent medicine company put out the following rhyme:

> Had she spurned Svengali's offer
> When her headache made her sick
> And just taken Bromo-Seltzer,
> 'Twould have cured her just as quick.

Today, John and Bo Derek own a movie company called Svengali Productions. Added to this, a significant number of writers find writing torturous. Years ago, Carlos Fuentes said that he wrote with the nerves of his stomach, and paid for it with a duodenal ulcer and a chronic colic. Mercifully, this is no longer true. George Orwell has said: 'Writing a book is a horrible, exhausting struggle, like a long bout of some painful illness.' Joan Didion confirms that to go into her writing room is 'low dread, every morning'.

Perhaps learning to read is akin to learning to write and one process hones the other. The act of writing is many things to many people. At one point, Graham Greene realized that 'the act of writing, were ways of escape'. For Greene, writing is a form of therapy, an escape from the 'madness, the melancholia, the panic fear which is inherent in the human situation'. For Mario Vargas Llosa, the act of writing exorcises the writer's demons. For Harlan Ellison, it is self-discovery, walking on a tightrope and learning the truth about oneself that is too terrible to bear. A number of writers see the novelist as an 'imaginative historian', whose finger is closest to the pulse of contemporary life. On the contrary, there are others who are doomsayers of all kinds and who herald the Death of the Novel. This is also not new. Articles abound: 'Will the Novel Disappear?' (*North*

American Review, Sept. 1902); 'Is Present-Day Fiction Quite Ephemeral?' (*Lippincott's Magazine*, Mar. 1909); 'The Passing of the Novel' (*Independent*, Dec. 1910); 'The Break-up of the Novel' (*Yale Review*, Jan. 1923); 'Is the Novel Done For?' (*Harper*, Dec. 1942). More recently, Frank Kermode has proclaimed 'The British Novel Lives' (*Atlantic*, vol. 230, 1972). When did it die? Walter Allen has also assured us that 'the novel is not dead' (*Contemporary Novelists*, New York, 1972). Nevertheless, Gore Vidal chides us that, 'rather like priests who have forgotten the meaning of the prayers they chant, we shall go on for quite a long time talking of books and writing books, pretending all the while not to notice that the church is empty and the parishioners gone elsewhere to attend other gods, perhaps in silence or with new words'. Maybe Mary Gordon is correct in saying that Gore Vidal believes that, because he'd like to write novels, but can't. In an incisive rejoinder, John Fowles has written: 'If the novel is dead, the corpse still remains oddly fertile. We are told no one reads novels any more; so the authors of *Julian* and *The Collector* must be grateful to the two million ghosts or more who have bought copies of their respective books. . . . Surgery is what we want, not dissection. It is not only the extirpation of the mind that kills the body: the heart will do the trick as well.'[5]

To further complicate matters, there are so many theories of composition among novelists that it has been suggested that it is impossible to create a poetics of the novel. Some may see this as all to the good. For example, there is no consensus on 'plot' and why should there be? Novelists, such as John Irving, tell us that plot is everything whereas Flaubert tells us the opposite:

> The story, the plot of the novel is of no interest to me. When I write a novel I aim at rendering a colour, a shade. For instance, in my Carthaginian novel, I want to do something purple. The rest, the characters and the plot, is a mere detail. In *Madame Bovary*, all I wanted to do was to render a grey colour, the mouldy colour of a wood-louse's experience.[6]

When he was a young writer, John Hawkes said that plot, character, setting and theme are the natural enemies of fiction. He has since recanted and now believes that plot is necessary even though he says that he cannot create a plot and still doesn't know what a plot is.

To further compound what looks to be a literary Tower of Babel, is the changing face of the novel. In B. S. Johnson's *House Mother Normal* (1971), there are blank pages representing moments of blank consciousness. In *Alberto Angelo* (1964) he has separate columns for dialogue and inner dialogue. In that book, holes are cut into the pages for the reader to see what is coming. In *See the Old Lady Decently* (1975) he interrupts the narrative with photographic reproductions of documents, letters, and concrete poems, two of which are in the shape of a breast. Some readers may feel that they are wrestling with Proteus. Modern fiction can be obfuscating, an aesthetic plaything, word games, where words are more important than character. Margaret Drabble finds the 'literary games' of writers like Spark, Pynchon and Barth arid. Mary Gordon never wants to read *Finnegans Wake* because she feels that it is about language, not about people. Erica Jong tries to preserve energy and passion at the risk of technique because she hates the graduate student quality in contemporary literature where writing becomes a 'puzzle' and a 'literary game'. Isaac Bashevis Singer concludes that the 'real writer explores life all the time, not style'. In many contemporary novels the reader is urged to enter the book intellectually, not emotionally. Annie Dillard has written that contemporary modernist fiction (her term) is 'a self-lighted opacity, not a window and not a mirror. It is a painted sphere, not a crystal ball.'[7] The reader must confront the fictionality of fiction, its surfaces and structure. Modernist art declares itself as a conscious and self-conscious artifice. The following story in many ways sums it up. A visitor to Matisse's studio stated: 'M. Matisse, I have never seen a woman who looked like the one you have painted.' Matisse responded: 'Madame, that is not a woman; that is a painting.' Fiction writers today will interject, draw pictures, cut holes, leave blank pages, splinter syntax or leave the story unfinished. In Italo Calvino's *If On a Winter's Night a Traveller*, the reader and Calvino's protagonist read the first chapters of ten very different novels all in Calvino's one novel. Each novel is interrupted and is left unfinished. *If On a Winter's Night a Traveller* explores the pursuit of a lost or interrupted book. Finally, Dillard has suggested that the contemporary modernist writer 'may wish to distance readers so thoroughly that he dispenses with character and narration altogether'. The discussion is a heated one. I've heard the New Novel called 'bionic bullshit'. I agree that too often the theory of some contemporary fiction is more interesting than the product. Such fiction reminds me of Gilbert and Sullivan's *Patience*: 'The meaning doesn't matter if it's only idle chatter of a transcendental kind.' To tell a story or not to tell a story, that is the question. Robbe-Grillet has insisted that 'to tell a story has become strictly impossible'. Isaac Bashevis Singer has affirmed my own feeling that if you 'take away story-telling from literature' then 'literature has lost everything'. Julio Cortázar concurred that 'a novel must be above all a story'. But I don't want to divide modernist writers into either/or categories, one thing or the other, my theory do or die. The range of possibilities is enormous. A number of writers engage the reader emotionally as well as intellectually. Writers such as Carlos Fuentes, Vasily Aksyonov, Nadine Gordimer and Gabriel García Márquez shed new light on old possibilities. And their books create their own readers. Writers do not live in a vacuum. Their readers also share the same world. They grow together. Readers are often encouraged and invited to share in the creation of the novel. The various techniques that characterize some of the finest contemporary novels do not have to ignore, assault, bully, brutalize or alienate the reader. Writers such as Margaret Drabble talk to their readers and halt the narrative. In *The Realms of Gold*, she invites the reader to 'invent a more suitable ending if you can'. She isn't playing word games. She does not sacrifice story, clarity, or emotion. Neither does John Fowles who has asked, 'To what extent am I being a coward by writing inside the old tradition? To what extent am I being panicked into avant-gardism?'[8] We can understand Fowles' anxious questions when confronted with pronouncements such as the following:

to be serious and ambitious in the novel, the writer must create works of prose comparable to those experiments in painting which have brought us, . . . to Pop and Op-art and in music to the strategic silences of Mr. John Cage. Whether or not these experiments succeed or fail is irrelevant. It is

enough, if the artist is serious, to attempt new forms; certainly
he must not repeat old ones.[9]

You guessed it. That was Death of the Novel Vidal. How new is
'new' and how old is 'old'? Mallarmé was trying to incorporate
'silence' into his writing a hundred years ago. And yes, modern
writers know that the drama of human existence is not heard
only in the voice but in the silences as well. Silence is not merely
'aesthetic'. Mallarmé found meaning in the articulation of what
is between the signs, in the gaps and intervals created by them.
The reader would fill in the empty spaces. Mallarmé found
reality in silence. Toni Morrison has said that the writer has to
use the words she does *not* use in order to get a certain kind of
power, like a painter uses white space, or a musician uses
silence. Elie Wiesel has said that his use of 'silence' is a
metaphysical one. Seen in this way, silence is not a response to
form for form's sake (and I'm not suggesting that Vidal is being
as simple-minded as this). Not only has consciousness changed
but so has world history.

Older literary forms cannot accommodate the horror of the
Holocaust. The ineffable experience of Auschwitz lies outside
language itself. In Elie Wiesel's *Night*, the writer witnesses the
murder of a man by his own son who then stole the bread from
the man's mouth. The killer is, in turn, beaten to death by the
other prisoners. About his own reaction, Wiesel has but five
words: 'I was fifteen years old.' 'Silence, for Wiesel', says Harry
Cargas, 'is beyond language, beyond lies.'[10] Silence, indeed,
seems a viable alternative given the desecration and corruption
of language in the Third Reich. Language was used to mask the
reality. The people who remained after others had been sent to
the gas chambers were called 'preserved monuments'. 'Special
treatment' meant genocide. The square that faced the gas
chambers at Maidanek was called 'The Rose Garden'. The
Germans were not the only ones to abuse language in this way.
The A-bomb dropped on Hiroshima was called 'little boy'.
Words can bless, heal, kill, torture. Harry Levin has argued that
'art can be viewed and judged as imitation only when men are in
confident touch with the realities that have been imitated'.[11] We
are not so confident now. The Holocaust has removed us from
historical time; its events are beyond the scope and definition of

past memory. In *By Words Alone*, Sidra Dekoven Ezrahi has put it well:

> The distorted image of the human form which the artist might present as but a mirror of nature transformed can hardly be contained within the traditional perimeters of mimetic art, because although Holocaust literature is a reflection of recent history it cannot draw upon the timeless archetypes of human experience and human behaviour which can render unlived events familiar through the medium of the imagination.[12]

Metaphors strain the boundaries of the imagination in Wiesel's *Night*. After a child is hung for all to see his writhing agony, the narrator tells us that the soup eaten after 'tasted of corpses'. We are asked in Carlo Levi's Italian novel *The Watch*:

> What sort of novel do you want after Auschwitz and Buchenwald? Did you see the photographs of women weeping as they buried pieces of soap made from the bodies of their husbands and sons? That's the way the confusion ended. The individual exchanged for the whole. . . . There you are! Your *tranche de vie* – a piece of soap.[13]

If Wiesel is right that 'a novel about Auschwitz is not a novel, or else it is not about Auschwitz', then Alvin Rosenfeld is right that we lack critical maps to guide us. A series of questions arise. How can art or should art represent the inexpressible torment of the victims without transfiguring their suffering? Since, as Wiesel has told me, the reader can never 'enter the gates of the burning ghetto or the gates of the death camp', is it wrong to get aesthetic pleasure from literature such as this? Literature cannot help but order the chaos. Is dream, metaphor, fantasy, allegory, and sparse language enough to replace our previous vocabulary for what Günther Grass calls 'the quivering flesh of the reality'? Does literature best embody Solzhenitsyn's idea that 'a man can cross the threshold of death before his body is lifeless' or Jakov Lind's perception that 'death too can be a way of life'? Will contemporary fairy tales begin, 'Once upon a time there were gas chambers and crematoria and no one lived happily ever after'?

Women are also investigating new forms of creating and

responding. It is unfortunate that the weight of political history renders their genuine concerns trivial to some people when confronted with the threat of Fascism, racism, nuclear warfare, poverty and disease. It is startling to hear women writers in our time lament that if you are female, and you want to write, you'll have to have your tongue removed, like the Little Mermaid in Hans Christian Andersen's fairytale. Both Erica Jong and Mary Gordon have discussed the problems of women writers who have been trained by their society to be 'good girls'. The cultural passivity of women has been beaten to death in print. But it's true. Erica Jong has spoken of a distinguished critic who came to her creative writing class when she was a student. He told them: 'Women can't be writers. They don't know blood and guts, and puking in the streets, and fucking whores, and swaggering through Pigalle at 5 a.m.' What do you suppose the classes' reaction was? Did the women in the class protest, argue or ignore him? No, they accepted his dictum, including Jong. I once heard a professor discussing an 'anonymous' poem with his class. Casually, and without rancour, he suggested that it had been written by a woman because the lines were 'turgid', the language 'weak', and the sentiment 'soppy'. Colin Wilson also dislikes women writers because 'they think about their feelings all the time'. They are 'subjective' and 'right-brainers'. Mary Gordon has written that: 'I have been told by male but not by female critics that my work was "exquisite", "lovely", "like a watercolour". They, of course, were painting in oils. They were doing the important work. Watercolours are cheap and plentiful; oils are costly; their base must be bought!' These same people think that 'no major work can be painted in watercolours'.[14] In the same essay, she says that there are people who think that 'Hemingway writing about boys in the woods is major; Mansfield writing about girls in the house is minor.' Virginia Woolf talked about writers and critics who think it only important to write of war, leading nations etc. and look down on anything else as small, trivial, or womanly. Literary values and aesthetics need to be re-examined when looking at books by women, even if Proust was correct that there are no excuses in art. Historical events have inextricably married 'domestic concerns' such as birth, the body's rhythm (e.g. the menstrual cycle) and life as 'organic' to the catastrophes of the A-bomb and the Holocaust. Robert Jay

Lifton suspects that 'this threat of disconnected death, and therefore of disconnected life, has had much to do with the prominence of women . . . in A-bomb literature – whether as practitioners of that literature or as critics of it. In either case, women are expressing their close identification with organic life and its perpetuation as an antidote to nuclear severance.'[15] There is also a predominance of women writers in Holocaust literature. In these books, the resumption of the menstrual cycle and the birth of children in the death camps are of essential importance.

The critical response to women writers has often been non-existent or harsh. It has pretty well been a no-win situation. In the nineteenth century, women writers were criticized because of their delicacy, modesty and fragility while in the nineteen-sixties and seventies they have been criticized for the opposite; their lack of delicacy, modesty and fragility. There is a long list of sins. They talk about their bodies too much. If their stories are gentle and sweet, they are not 'powerful' enough; if their stories are full of rage, they are 'castrating'. Words like 'emotional, vague, weak, tremulous, pastel, nervous, and subjective' are just some of the words I've seen used to describe books by women. Male writers, on the other hand, are described as 'strong, grand, bold, forceful, clear, vigorous, muscular, tough and objective'. It has been said that a Toni Morrison novel generally resembles a 'beautifully patterned quilt'. Morrison remarks that the critics would never have used that image for a male writer, they probably would have suggested a 'chess game'. Too many reviews of novels and poems by women refer to their sex for no relevant purpose. Norman Podheretz attacked Mary McCarthy's *The Group* as 'this trivial lady-writer's book'; in Hollywood, Pauline Kael reported that McCarthy herself was regarded as 'poison . . . she's competitive'. A study done at York University, Ontario, on sexual bias in reviewing in the seventies revealed the following results: *none* of the male writers answered 'yes' to the bias but half of the women writers said 'yes' and one-quarter said 'maybe'. I can confirm that I'm always sent books by women to review unless I point out that I read books by men too. Feminist literary critics are not without their bias all the same. On several occasions, both Margaret Drabble and Erica Jong have been severely reprimanded because the critics felt that they should have created superhuman models instead of women who are confused, who have not transcended all conflict, who are torn between the past and the future, trapped between their mothers' frustrations and their extraordinary hopes for their daughters' lives.

Among the many changes in fiction that have occurred, one of the most intriguing is the blurring of genres and the appearance of new hybrid forms. Elie Wiesel hates the term 'genre'. Colin Wilson believes in 'deliberately using different genres as exercises'. He has written 'spoof pornography', science fiction, and detective novels. Italo Calvino's *If On a Winter's Night a Traveller* runs the gamut from thriller, neo-gothic fabulism, to a take-off on the Japanese erotic novel. Vasily Aksyonov has written a novel that he says is 'a thriller, part realism, and part an excursion into fairytale'. Writers such as John Fowles in 'The Enigma', Julio Cortázar in *The Blow-Up and Other Stories*, and Heinrich Böll in *The Lost Honour of Katherina Blum*, used the established form of the detective story to pursue their own complex literary purposes. Julio Cortázar observed that a lot of current poetry is put into novels and becomes a part of these novels. He said that '*The Odyssey* and *The Iliad* are at the same time novels as well as poems. The form is a poem and the content is a novel.' In our time, 'this is reversed; the form is prose but the content of many novels is deeply poetic'.

The influence of the East has also changed both structure and content in Western art. It has introduced new 'ways of seeing' and given Western artists possibilities for crystallizing ideas, attitudes and feelings that already existed and were searching for expression. There can be major gaps, however, between that kind of art and the critical response to it. For some time Doris Lessing has been a student of Sufism and its impact on her work cannot be underestimated. In her book review of Idries Shah's 'What Looks Like an Egg and Is an Egg?', she cited a Sufi maxim: 'Wisdom is not in books – only some of the ways to search for it.' In other words, we cannot reach enlightenment through the intellect but only through experience. In some of her earlier fiction, we can see her emphasis on the development of the human being and the search for self-knowledge which is essential to Sufism. She uses Nasrudin's teaching-stories in *Landlocked*; a Dervish teaching-story in *The Four-Gated City*; and a passage quoted from Sage Mahmoud Shabistari's 'The Secret Garden' in *Briefing for a Descent into Hell*. These teaching-stories encourage new paths of thought to replace established ways of thinking. Now here's the problem. If I suggest that her novels are incoherent, hasn't Lessing thwarted me already by writing that the nature of Sufism is its variety and lack of coherence? This makes me uninformed. If I accuse her of self-indulgence, hasn't she explained that in our culture we need to move beyond 'our formulas for exegetics', our rational modes of thought, into new ways of using the mind? This makes me one of her small-minded scholars, 'fed too long on the pieties of academia'. If I try to describe her version of the Sufi's 'teaching-story', hasn't she clarified that there is 'no word in modern languages which has been set aside to describe them'? This makes me pitifully obtuse. There is no point in looking to the critics for a guideline. They both chastise and admire her for the same thing. Michael L. Magie deplores her 'irrationalism' and her 'indulgence' while Nancy Hardin praises this saving vision that will awaken us 'from the roles to which we have been so skillfully programmed'. Any response seems up for grabs.

Another major contribution to contemporary literature has come from the Latin American authors. Latin American literature became prominent in the sixties for readers outside of the Spanish-speaking world. This was due in part to the excellent translations being done, most notably by Gregory Rabassa. This was also a time of great virtuosity and originality as writers such as Carlos Fuentes, Julio Cortázar, Gabriel García Márquez, Miguel Asturias and Vargas Llosa created and shared their worlds of wonder. They fed a hungry part of the contemporary spirit. Webster Schott wrote in 1967, that these writers, south of the Rio Grande, brought 'a quality of imagination now missing from the closed U.S. circle of writers preoccupied with black humour, gray sex, white guilt. They want to know everything – the causes of man's tragic reach beyond his grasp, the mysteries of time, space and consciousness, the alchemy of their art itself.' This is true. But it is not necessary to denigrate the literary gifts of American writers in order to understand the immense impact of the Latin American writers. Several characteristics mark contemporary Latin American literature. The reader is often invited to participate in the composition and creation of the novel. There is an interest in having both reader and writer observe the author in the act of creating fiction. These writers also extend the modernist tradition of challenging our comprehension of reality and the language that defines it, what we know and how we know it. Technique often points to a truer reality than the content. In a world that demands explanation, conclusion and definition, these writers refuse to capitulate. Let us make no mistake, however. These books are difficult and demanding. Myth melds with reality. Realism is 'magic'. The marvellous is indeed an aspect of the real, as Robertson Davies says. The fantastic is a part of the commonplace world. Nobel prize winner Miguel Asturias has said: 'Between the "real" and the "magic" there is a third sort of reality. It is a melting of the visible and the tangible, the hallucination and the dream.' American writer Tim O'Brien, among others, enters this world in his novel *Going after Cacciato*. Time is telescoped, simultaneous and circular, rather than linear; miltiple times or multiple places may appear as a single time or a single place. Life is a multiple point of view.

As for the standards, aesthetics and criticism to deal with all of these new approaches, we are as far from the philosopher's stone as ever. The battle over what constitutes artistic 'good' and the best method to pan for its gold has been carried on in a cheerfully savage manner by critics and writers of all persuasions. Article counters article, letter refutes letter in the learned journals; occasionally a book is written to 'correct' current errors; this unites the critics and writers in attack, and the flurry of publication continues, each one hoist by his own canard. The same passages are quoted by different critics to different ends; and, apart from the gratuitous swipes at earlier critics, the commonest feature of these 'analyses' is the clause, 'It seems to me.' Whether it is the Republican point of view that every moron has the right to be a moron or the élitist position (the details of which probably couldn't be contained in this whole book much less an introduction), we have a maelstrom of literary values, opinions, and methods, and they are not scientifically verifiable nor do I want them to be. Actually, I enjoy the diversity of ideas. I suppose that I am a child of my time – I am comfortable with being uncomfortable. It is inevitable that individuals will develop their own sense of the 'aesthetically' good. That's fine. We're not in an aesthetic poker game, winner take all. What better adventure is there than to wander and roam, stop and start, poke and probe, lose and find.

We probably all try to cover our tracks in order to sound the sanest, or the least conspicuous, of all. So I'll go for broke and look at a few tantalizing questions. Somerset Maugham said that his novel *Of Human Bondage* was an 'easel picture' and not a 'fresco'. He was well known for denigrating his talents and he meant that his novel was not as good as a 'fresco' novel. We're back to Mary Gordon's discussion of the distinction between 'oils' and 'water colours', major and minor art. Did Maugham mean that an easel painting is a lesser achievement than a fresco? Would the criteria for that judgement be a question of size, scope, difficulty in handling the materials, the length of time it would take, the larger visual breadth of the fresco? Is there any value in comparing a Rembrandt painting to Michelangelo's ceiling of the Sistine Chapel at the expense of Rembrandt?

Is there any point in comparing Charlotte Brontë's *Jane Eyre* with Rosemary Rogers' *Wicked Loving Lies*? Well, no, not if it's only to say that one is better than the other. But it can be an interesting comparison for other reasons. If, in fact, the great novel is the popular novel transformed, what alchemical process has occurred? Let me head you off at the pass and say that, of course, I prefer *Jane Eyre*, and yes, I do think Brontë is the greater writer. However, if it is true that *Jane Eyre* is the great-great-grandmother of modern Harlequin & Avon and Mills & Boon romances, why don't we take a look at the two? If we reduce the Rochester story line in *Jane Eyre* to its simplest and crudest plot, listen to what we have:

A greedy father wills all of his property to his eldest son in order to keep it intact and sends his second son to the West Indies to marry a rich, potentially degenerate, insane, and sexually depraved Creole heiress for her dowry of thirty thousand pounds. The taint in her family becomes evident in her soon after the wedding. The bridegroom's father and brother die and he becomes a rich man. But he is doomed to unhappiness because his wife has now been medically pronounced insane thus making the divorce legally impossible. The young man returns to England with his wife and secretly imprisons her in his secluded Yorkshire house, where she is taken care of by a former wardress of an asylum. The man spends the next years on the Continent where he is profligate, has mistresses, has an alleged illegitimate daughter and fights a duel with the second lover of his unfaithful mistress. He returns to England and courts his child's governess while trying to make her jealous with another woman. Throughout all of this his wife prowls about the house by night, sets fire to his bed and stabs and attempts to drink the blood of her own brother when he tries to visit. Finally, the man of the house attempts a bigamous marriage with the innocent governess but this is foiled by his wife's brother who stops the ceremony. The governess runs away, although she desperately loves him, and has her own adventures. Eventually, his wife sets fire to the house and is killed. He is blinded and maimed. In his anguish and loneliness the man cries out for his love, the governess, who returns to his arms guided by his supernatural call.

Put like that, *Jane Eyre* sounds like pure Gothic at its basest level. You could do the same with Jane's story line.

Both *Jane Eyre* and *Wicked Loving Lies* have male heroes who are dark, Byronic, and melancholy. Both female heroines are orphaned and thrown to the mercy of the world and relatives. Both books have women from the West Indies involved with men in the Old World. Both books are written by women. But here the comparison stops. In *Wicked Loving Lies*, the sado-masochism pays off. The heroine, Marisa, falls for her tormentor, a man who has raped her too many times to count. Why do readers see that as a happy ending? Dena Justin rightly states that: 'So subtly have our nerve ends been twisted against our own reason that we accept the resolution of the *Arabian Nights* as a routine happy ending. The virtuous and talented Scheherazade has won her reward. She will share the bed of a psychotic sex-killer forever after. The sultan who rapes a different maiden nightly and murders her at dawn has become Prince Charming.'[16] Jane, on the other hand, never gives in to Rochester's *attempts* at seduction. And here marks a significant difference in the male characters of both books. Domenic Challenger (*Wicked Loving Lies*) thinks 'all women are whores' and treats them as such. Rochester only attempts to seduce Jane and while he seeks to dominate her, he never succeeds. This does not incite him, however, to physical violence. Jane also has more control over her own life than Rogers' heroine. We are told that Marisa is 'a strange mixture of defiant child and mysterious woman'. Jane refuses the child in the woman. We might reasonably believe that Rogers lived in the nineteenth century and Brontë in the twentieth century instead of the reverse. The authors control their stories differently. As I said, Marisa goes off happily into the sunset with her rapist (shades of *General Hospital*). Rochester has a different fate. He must be punished and crippled for trying to exert his power over Jane before she is psychologically and socially able to marry him (no wonder D. H. Lawrence despised the book). A chasm separates the craftsmanship of the two writers. Rogers uses a pen and pencil, shovel and trowel symbolism. What I mean by this is that her attempts to insert symbols are textually gratuitous. She gives you a bare-boned description of a man and a woman on a horse or a fire and assumes that the Freudian and the mythical are so much a part of our cultural currency that they will do her work for her. They don't. Brontë's symbols live because of their deeply-felt passion, inner knowledge and organic connection to the rest of the book. The language and ultimate statements of these books couldn't differ more. Rogers is an adequate writer but hers is a wingless realism. She caters to the worst notions of what the 'women's' novel is about and what women want to read, all the while cultivating dangerous, soft-porn, stereotyped fantasies. Brontë has written that she wanted her work to win a place by the 'hearts' very hearthstone'. I believe her in a way that I cannot believe Rogers and this is not only the result of differing ideological positions. It is as Virginia Woolf said; we read Brontë for her poetry, and at the end of *Jane Eyre*, we are 'steeped through and through with the genius, the vehemence, the indignation of Charlotte Brontë'. Her voice may not be the truth but it is true.

This is all very well and good but there are those who would like a more *definitive* response to literature. For those people, there are a variety of old and new critical methodologies. Contemporary criticism ranges from semiotics, linguistics, structuralism, post-structuralism, computer analyses of, for example, James Joyce, Robertson Davies and Margaret Atwood, revisionism (of all kinds), deconstruction, hermeneutics, phenomenology, structural fabulation, paracriticism, metacriticism, feminist literary criticism, to neo-Imagism. Some novels are reduced to mathematical equations, or what looks like a reasonable facsimile to the layman. In his semiotic analysis of Agatha Christie's novels, I. I. Revzin drew a table (see Figure 1) to show her various types of characters and the way some of these types 'fuse together'.[17]

In order to read many of the critical methodologies listed above, one should be conversant with forbidding words like 'asyndetic', 'maieutic', 'recontextualization', 'paranomasia', 'allegoresis', 'extended catachresis' and 'semantic overdetermination'.

It is not hard to find negative diatribes against literary criticism. The critic has often been seen as a bloodless parasite,

	a	b	c	d	e	f	g	h
a								
b								2
c					3	1		
d								
e		3						
f		1						
g								
h		2						

Key:
1. *The Murder in the Clouds*
2. *The Murder in the Links*
3. *The Murder of Roger Ackroyd*

Figure 1

draining the life from literature with the scalpel of analysis. The novelist creates: the critic merely dissects. As with all things, criticism and its milieu can become a *reductio ad absurdum*. Daniel Stern wrote that 'suicides were God's graduate students. . . . Their act was at its best, superb literary criticism.' How can this statement help us to better appreciate *Jude the Obscure*, *Anna Karenina*, *Madame Bovary*, *Another Country*, *Sophie's Choice*, *The Heart of the Matter* or *The Judge*? A friend recently told me that after reading a large number of academic journals, he had proudly mastered the use of the semi-colon. Presumably, this means that there is a Procrustean ideal of punctuation. What's more, he had mastered it in order to get his work published, not because he had experienced an epiphany. All the same, he may know something that I don't because Mary Gordon revealed to me that when she was writing *Final Payments*, she stole Virginia Woolf's use of the colon, and she is a good writer.

You can understand the negative attitudes toward criticism when someone like Jacob Glatstein declares: 'A good critic is armed for war. And criticism is a war, against a work of art – either the critic defeats the work or the work defeats the critic.' The most common view of the relationship between fiction writer and critic is that expressed by Coleridge. Critics are 'usually people who would have been poets . . . if they could; they have tried their talents . . . and have failed; therefore they turn critics'. Northrop Frye wrote sketches of novels and attempted short stories but he realized that he would have nothing to say as a fiction writer that others hadn't already said better, whereas he felt that as a critic he might have. As one of the foremost critics of our time, he was right. The writer's antipathy for the critic can be vituperative, despairing and humorous. Brendan Behan once fumed that critics are like 'eunuchs in a harem. They know how it's done, they've seen it done every day, but they're unable to do it themselves.' The Nigerian playwright, novelist, and poet, Wole Soyinka, has charged certain critics with 'neo-Tarzanism' – that breast-beating, drum-beating, desire to simplify the African reality. Robertson Davies calls some critics 'Thanatossers', a view somewhat similar to Dr Erwin Chargaff's 'sapientivores', his term for the predators of scholarship. V. S. Pritchett loathes the present academic habit of turning literary criticism into technology. 'Literary criticism', he says, 'does not add to its status by opening an intellectual hardware store.' Margaret Drabble resents the insistence on 'marking books as though for an examination'. Graham Greene has written of the writer's middle-aged fear that he no longer controls his method:

He is more afraid to read his favourable critics than his unfavourable, for with terrible patience they unroll before his eyes the unchanging pattern of the carpet. If he has depended a great deal on his unconscious, on his ability to forget even his own books when they are once on the public shelves, the critics remind him – this theme originated ten years ago, that simile which came so unthinkingly to his pen a few weeks back was used nearly twenty years ago in a passage where . . . [18]

The painter Barnett Newman has delivered this final shot: 'Aesthetics is for the artist as ornithology is for the birds.' Enough of this! It's like shooting fish in a barrel.

Might it not be possible to apply Lytton Strachey's comment about biography to criticism? He said that 'uninterpreted truth is as useless as buried gold'. My literary experience has been better for having read fine critics who at their best do not sterilize creation because they raise themselves to the level of the work or the subject at hand – Eudora Welty on Ross Macdonald, George Steiner's *The Death of Tragedy*, Northrop Frye on Blake, Simone Weil on *The Iliad*, and most recently, Annie Dillard's excellent *Living by Fiction*. Criticism does not have to be like jogging with a nail in your shoe as Hugh Kenner said of post-Structuralist prose. The eminent Northrop Frye believes that lucidity is a prime value in criticism. Although he respects structural critics such as Derrida, Lacan and Foucault, he objects to the 'cat's chorus in the background'. He thinks that 'if you're talking about language, you ought to turn up with a prose style that doesn't sound like a horse drinking water'. Frye's call for lucidity speaks to the fear that many people have that writers may begin producing books that will appeal mainly to university teachers and critics seeking something to explain. This writing of 'systematically ambiguous' works may be the next literary development as writers try to provide grist to the academic mill.

It is important to acknowledge that while criticism may have its detractors, it has its champions too. In 1921 in *The New Republic*, H. L. Mencken wrote: 'The motive of the critic who is really worth reading . . . is not the motive of the pedagogue, but the motive of the artist. It is no more and no less than the simple desire to function freely and beautifully, to give outward and objective form to ideas that bubble inwardly and have a fascinating lure in them, to get rid of them dramatically, and make an articulate noise in the world.' Other critics have argued for the possibilities of 'creative' criticism. Harold Bloom has reintroduced the idea of the critic as a creator: 'As literary history lengthens, all poetry necessarily becomes verse–criticism, just as all criticism becomes prose–poetry.' Anatole Broyard has written that an enthusiastic critic's response to a novel is almost like another novel written in counterpoint to it. The Canadian poet and critic Eli Mandel agrees that criticism is a novel; they are both imaginative constructs. The Tunisian poet and critic Hédi Bouraoui takes these ideas even further. He says that 'every critical act incorporates a poetic dimension, and every poem implies some critical thought'. In his book *Haïtuvois* (Montreal, 1980), he has merged the two approaches into a new genre, the poem–essay. The dichotomy in Haiti between the tropical paradise experienced by tourists and the grinding poverty of the people suggested to him that the traditional forms would be inappropriate. In the book's introduction, Jacqueline Leiner writes: 'The baroque architecture of the work, sometimes in verse, sometimes in prose, this style here compressed, there freed, this hieroglyphic or transparent message, is in the image of the cultural anarchy which characterizes the Haitian situation.' Bouraoui's experimentation with genres allows him to express poetic thoughts, literary analysis and art criticism.

In the beginning was the word, recalled Isaac Bashevis Singer, and in the end is garbage. Singer is talking about the flagellation of the word 'masterpiece'. He believes that there are a very few literary talents in every generation. Bryan F. Griffin has also charged that ours is a time of 'desperate superlative'. Let me conclude without committing any of these sins and simply say that the writers in this book are worth reading.

NOTES

1. Hans Habe, *All My Sins: An Autobiography* (London: George G. Harrap, 1957) p. 285.
2. Mark Harris, 'Saul Bellow at Purdue', *The Georgia Review*, Winter 1978, pp. 715–54.
3. Carolyn Heilbrun, *Reinventing Womenhood* (New York: W. W. Norton, 1979) p. 22.
4. Eudora Welty, 'Place in Fiction', *South Atlantic Quarterly*, vol. 55 (1956) p. 62.
5. John Fowles, 'Notes on an Unfinished Novel', in *Afterwords: Novelists on their Novels*, ed. Thomas McCormack (New York: Harper & Row, 1969) p. 175.
6. Gustave Flaubert, 'Style as Absolute', in *The Modern Tradition: Backgrounds of Modern Literature*, ed. Richard Ellmann and Charles Feidelson Jr (New York: Oxford University Press, 1965) p. 126.
7. Annie Dillard, *Living by Fiction* (New York: Harper & Row, 1982) pp. 47–8.
8. John Fowles, 'Notes on an Unfinished Novel', p. 165.
9. Gore Vidal, 'French Letters: the Theory of the New Novel', *Encounter*, Dec. 1967, p. 14.
10. Harry James Cargas, 'Elie Wiesel and the Holocaust', *Commonweal*, 10 Sept. 1976, pp. 594–6.
11. Harry Levin, *The Gates of Horn: A Study of Five French Realists* (New York: Oxford University Press, 1963) p. 468.
12. Sidra Dekoven Ezrahi, *By Words Alone: The Holocaust in Literature* (Chicago: University of Chicago Press, 1980) pp. 2–3.

13. Carlo Levi, *The Watch* (New York: Farrar, Strauss & Young, 1951) pp. 70–1.
14. Mary Gordon, 'The Parable of the Cave or: In Praise of Watercolors', in *The Writer on Her Work*, ed. Janet Sternburg (New York: W. W. Norton, 1980) p. 28.
15. Robert Jay Lifton, *Death in Life: Survivors of Hiroshima* (New York: Vintage Books, 1967) p. 474.
16. Dena Justin, 'From Mother Goddess to Dishwasher', *Natural History*, vol. 82 (1973) p. 44.
17. I. I. Revzin, 'Notes on the Semiotic Analysis of Detective Novels: With Examples from the Novels of Agatha Christie', *New Literary History*, vol. 9 (1978) p. 386.
18. Graham Greene, *Ways of Escape* (Penguin, 1981) p. 105.

1 Carlos Fuentes

DCC: In your novel *The Good Conscience*, Lorenzo tries to unite the lessons of his reading with the conditions of the life he had known. Have you done this in your life?

CF: Naturally, I think that if you come from a bourgeois, middle-class milieu as I do and you set out to be a writer and particularly in a developing country, you are forced to do battle with the actual conditions of your life, of your society, of your family existence. Most writers in Latin America that come from this milieu have faced the options that Jaime faces in *The Good Conscience*. Lorenzo is something different; he's an idealized proletarian. All novelists are Don Quixote in a way. We all try to live what we read.

DCC: Could you give me some specific examples of lessons that you have learned?

CF: If you part from the evidence that books are more than the children of life, the children of other books, you insert yourself into a current. In a way you have to become fictionalized yourself in order to participate in the world of books. Don Quixote, whom I have just mentioned, has many offspring. He has two mad, intemperate daughters: the heroine of *Northanger Abbey* and Madame Bovary. They are daughters of Don Quixote as they also believe what they read and go out into the world to apply the precepts of the literature and fall on their faces. Myshkin, Dostoevsky's Idiot, is a grandson of Don Quixote, a man who wishes to be good, who personifies good, one of the most difficult things to do in literature. Evil is rather easier. So you insert yourself into a world which has its own reality. I believe much more in imagination than in experience for writing books. I think there is an element of experience, but I don't bet on it as much as many American writers do. They feel

Carlos Fuentes (*photograph: Trevor Clark*)

they must play the piano in a whore house, then steal the doors, be race car drivers, boxers, in order to be able to write. I don't think so.

DCC: You have written that literary men are cannibalistic, each persuaded, way down deep, that he alone is right, his fellow writers fools, and the world a stage on which each struts, mouthing his own version of the Gospel, hiding his own hollowness with the persona-mask, the image that he fondly holds, to deceive himself even more than his fellow-man. Is this really your experience, as it seems contrary to the man who freely acknowledges his admiration for other writers?

CF: It is really a caricature of the extraordinary thing Rimbaud said and which defines so much the attitude of the modern writer, 'the poet is a little god'. There is the creative attitude, which can lead to enormous hubris and petulance, and even the fall from a molehill is a fall, nevertheless. These little dramas are re-enacted by writers. There is a relationship between writing and creation and therefore a relation between being a writer and the idea of God. Of course, if man hadn't fallen to begin with, he would have had nothing to write about. Since God is invisible and silent, man decides to write; an artist decides to occupy in a way the place of God. You do feel that you have this incredible power at times to create things out of nothing, to put words into the mouths of people, to invent kingdoms, geographies, obsessions, everything you wish. There's a price to be paid; as always when you exceed yourself, you find you pay the price.

DCC: Perhaps that is why Isaac Bashevis Singer has said: 'Writers were not born to change the world. We cannot even make it worse.'

CF: [*laughs*] He's right. You can do very little through literature. You cannot change the world in the exterior manner in which the world likes to think of itself as being changed. I think the novelist does something better than changing the world. He adds something to the world, he enriches the world. Oh, probably a Dickens novel improved the working conditions of children. But generally, when you try to change the world, you do not change the world because you write bad literature. There are so many novels in Latin America about the plight of the Bolivian tin miner that do not change the life of the tin miner and do not add anything to literature. So Singer is right in this essential sense that a writer and a book must be true to themselves, to what they are essentially. How they affect the world is something else. The novelist provides an accretion of the reality of the world and an increase of reality in the world, an enrichment of the world through writing.

DCC: I suppose that you are still plagued with questions about your political affiliations, your Marxism. Some people have suggested that you betrayed the voice of the Revolution. Are you impatient with these questions?

CF: There is a confusion between what I say and what I do as a citizen. I am a Mexican citizen. I have my rights. I'm interested in communicating politically, in employing rostrums to address myself to issues of the day, but this should not be confused with my literary work. I first published a book of short stories in 1954, and the same critic hit me on two grounds: 'This man is full of social preoccupations which debase the religion of "art for art's sake".' At the same time he said, 'this man is a contemptible, decadent bourgeois'. So where is the truth? Well, thank God that first critic said these things because he only reaffirmed my certitude that I do not own the truth, that I am searching for truth continually as I write. I am not in possession of any dogmas. I am investigating the nature of men and women through fiction, with a constant yearning to widen the experience, to widen the possibility of the experience of literature which is called imagination. There is this great confusion because people are accustomed in the everyday world to believe that knowledge is acquired through science, ethics, philosophy, and politics. This all reverts to what Wittgenstein would call 'propositional language' and to a knowledge which is based on the principle of causality, on logic, etc. However, literature has a particular knowledge of its own which is called imagination, which is not given to us by science, or by politics, or by ethics, but which makes ethics and politics and science possible because literature takes place in the origin of language constantly. There is a source of language in literature that is always there, drinking from this source and speaking from this source. This is where poets and novelists are. There is a confusion because in this origin of language, in this imagination, you can deal with many subjects. You are not damned to deal with them and to deal with them always within the purlieu of the logic and causality principle.

DCC: Many would agree with you. You must be familiar with Tom Stoppard's statement in *Travesties* that: 'If you are a revolutionary, you have no more business being an artist. If you are not an artist, you might as well be a revolutionary.' Octavio Paz has also written, in *Labyrinth of Solitude*, that in Mexico: 'The revolution has been unable to relate its redeeming and explosive force to a world vision, nor has the Mexican mind resolved the conflict between the insufficiency of our own tradition and our need for universality'.

CF: Octavio Paz, and with him many other writers and artists in contemporary Spanish America, have discovered that we have a past. You see the great problem for Latin America has always been to forget it has a past and to go towards a future, a modernity, generally designed abroad. In the early nineteenth century we decided that we should refuse our Spanish and Indian past, which we consider a burden, in order to become as quickly as possible modern, capitalistic, democracies based on the model of Britain, France, or the United States. This failed miserably because the legal country created had nothing to do with the real country which was still colonial and underdeveloped, with a culture that had nothing to do with a culture that created the conditions for a parliamentary democracy in Great Britain. When this model of modernity failed, we embarked on the search for the socialist model, and, as we know, the socialist model had been proposed ecumenically from Moscow and it had nothing to do whatsoever with our past, with our traditions, with what we are. It is a façade once more. So the problem as Paz points it out and as he has insisted in his writings, is that of creating our own model of progress, with our own traditions, with the knowledge of our own past. This is why I've delved into the past of Mexicans, into the past of Latin America, into the past of Spain and tried to find our roots even into the Mediterranean and as far as Palestine in my novel *Terra Nostra*, because I think that we are very poor politically, but that culturally we have a great continuous tradition. It is from this richness that we can perhaps bring out this model of progress which is authentically ours, but which also proves that Mexico and Latin America are poly-cultural civilizations, that we cannot depend on only one little model imported from Washington or from Moscow, that we have to elaborate this model with all the strains of our culture which are, as I say, varied. Sometimes the traditions go way back to the Indian civilizations which are alive in countries like Mexico, or

Peru, or Bolivia. How can you achieve universality? This is the problem. I think no artist can really propose for himself as a recipe, 'how can you make a best seller, how can you become universal?' Who knows? Who would think that a crazy Spanish squire, accompanied by a fat, stoddy little peasant, riding around the Plains of Castile, La Mancha, should become a universal couple? Why? But they are.

DCC: History is important in your writing. How does the novel, for example, go beyond history, as you have said, in order to see history from outside history and not be condemned to history, and not be the prisoner of history?

CF: The novel does this by understanding first that it is a product of history, by not refusing this reality, by accepting the historical forces that fashion it. The novel becomes a freer way of appropriating time. We are all condemned to time, to the time of the calendars or to the philosophical sense of time we have in different civilizations. The novel is an appropriation of time at the level of imagination. Therefore, it is a response to history. And, the novel has a right to do this because a novel is by definition, the artistic form that has best dealt with the problem of time at a critical level. The novel is a literary form, an artistic form, that constantly criticizes society and history because first it has criticized itself; it is a form under continual demand to criticize itself. I've read so many novels where I feel that one of the basic thrusts is to criticize not the form of the novel in abstract, but the form of *this* novel I'm writing; in my work this is seen most notably in *The Change of Skin* or *Distant Relations*. The writer is criticizing the novel and therefore gaining in a way a right to criticize history, to affect history.

DCC: In *Terra Nostra*, we see that history can also be rewritten: 'nothing changes completely. Everything is tranformed. What we believe to be dead has but changed place. What is, is thought. What is thought, is.' Could you explain that?

CF: I think that the great humanistic revolution really comes at the beginning of the eighteenth century when Giambattista Vico says for the first time that men create their own history, that the individual can only know what he creates. He cannot know nature really because it was created by God, but he can know history because he created it. There is this great moment where man becomes independent from God and assumes the charge of his history, the charge of his experience. That is what marks the creation of the modern age, that you do take charge of your history. But then, we have no right to complain and say, 'oh, where is God', when we are in trouble, because whatever has been done in the world we realize is done by us, it is only ours. I think that the past has a future and one of the things the writer must do continually is to give the past its future. So we are not condemned to carrying around a dead weight which is not assimilated or not understood and which will come back through the door and avenge itself as a ghost. This is a way of rewriting history.

DCC: I'm intrigued by your ideas about the nature of the novel. Your novels are a criticism of the novel, of its assumptions, of its hypotheses, of the way it is done. How do you do this in your novels?

CF: Good. I have come to an extreme case in my novel, *Distant Relations*. This is really my own treatise about what you have just asked me so pertinently. This is a novel where an old man in Paris is telling me, Fuentes, a story, although this is not known by the reader until the very last pages. He's telling me a story about a Mexican family he's met and the strange relations he had with them. As he tells the story, and I intervene and ask him questions, the story grows in effect more and more distant. Elements that seemingly had nothing to do with the story appear contiguously to the story but never as a cause and effect relationship until I, Fuentes, am immersed in the story to such a degree that I will do anything to find out what the story is really all about, and what the end of the story is in order not to be left with an unconcluded story in my hands. This, I fear, is like a gift from the Devil, to have an unfinished story in your hands which will burn your hands and which will force you to be the narrator of the story, to continue the narration and to find another person to whom you will tell the same novel without fully understanding it. So I go to violent extremes, I, Fuentes, in the novel, in order to wring the secret out of this old man. It is the same story that

Pushkin tells in *The Queen of Spades*, to wrest the secret from the old dying lady. And the fact is that this man does not know the whole story, the man I am talking to, which is sheer desperation for me, since I will not be left – I know he is dying – I will not be left with an unfinished story. I would like to have the finished story so that I can quickly pass it on to someone else who will then have the burden of carrying the narrative, of carrying the story, because what I was convinced of as I wrote this novel, and at the end of the novel, is that no story ever ends. No story ever begins and no story ever ends, and what is but a transitional figure that takes the story and tries to take its burning substance out of your hands and pass it on to someone else, the reader, is a devil's gift.

DCC: You were talking about Don Quixote before. He's a double victim of reading, the first hero to read about himself. Could you expand on your interpretation of Cervantes' aesthetic: 'I shall create an open book where the reader will know he is read and the author will know he is written.'

CF: Yes, he's the fountainhead of everything for me. I think that Cervantes creates the modern novel. Ian Watt has written a marvellous book about the origins of the modern novel, and he places it securely in the appearance of a wealthy, book buying and reading middle class in England in the seventeenth and eighteenth centuries. But here we have the case of a penurious writer called Cervantes, living in the Spain of Phillip II, who was capable of imagining this extraordinary book, which really, for me, marks the beginning of the modern world. Sometimes I'm asked, 'where does the modern world begin?' I say it begins when this gentleman goes out of his house to wander the fields of La Mancha in order to prove that what he has read is true, and falls on his face because he represents the medieval world of homology, where everything resembles everything, and you have an explanation for everything. Everything was related. In the modern world, there is no more analogy, everything is different, everything is individualized. Don Quixote is this man of homology, of analogy, who goes out into the world of differentiation and this, for me, creates a marvellous tension immediately in the world of fiction, because it establishes the modern novel as an enterprise that is yearning for its lost analogy, while maintaining its richness of differentiation constantly. This is the great gift of Cervantes who incidentally makes us conscious also of the fact that he is writing a book. Curiously enough, he creates realism in the novel by throwing the most intense light of doubt on that same reality. Don Quixote's mad, he goes around thinking that windmills are giants and he takes inns for castles, he confuses reality all the time, but it so happens that *this* reality becomes more powerful.

DCC: Norman Mailer and yourself have said that you are created by your novels. Does this relate to what you were saying before?

CF: Yes. Cervantes casts so much doubt on the reality he's describing because he says, 'remember that this is a book where the protagonist in the book knows he is being written about', and this goes on indefinitely in the hall of mirrors of literature. The result of this openness we're mentioning, and I'm now quoting Mailer, is, of course, that you are caught in a web of this added reality whereby the novel ends by creating you, its author. You have no existence before you write the book, you are what your book is, you are written by the book. You are hopeful that the book will also create the readers, that the readers will be written or write the book and that this total circuit will be created as the great connection between the book, its author and its readers, its possible readers and its possible authors. Listen, when I take up *Little Dorrit* or *Great Expectations* and read them again, I am recreating the books obviously. I'm becoming Charles Dickens in a way, and I'm sure that Charles Dickens comes to life through my reading.

DCC: I agree with that myself. Certain themes occur in your novels over and over. One is the exploration of values born of failure, defeat and pain, such as in *Where the Air is Clear* and *The Death of Artemio Cruz*. I'm reminded of William Faulkner's statement that 'we shall be known by the splendour of our failures'.

CF: This reflects my concern with liberty, with utopia, with tragedy. Freedom is always something to be conquered. If you think you have freedom, if you secure your freedom, you are just about to lose it. In the act of looking for freedom you are free. Now this is particularly important to know in the continent of Utopia which is the American continent. I think the greatest value in literature is the tragic value and therefore no literature has been greater than the literature of the Greeks. The tragic value is the only one that is capable of reconciling and not of condemning, of avoiding the notion of guilt in favour of the notion of a shared responsibility and a shared recreation after the Fall. I think this is something we sorely lack in the New World because we're founded on the idea of the Utopia. The vision of the New World was to be the Golden Age once more, this is what the Europe of the sixteenth century wished to have. A Utopia over the seas. Well, Latin America has certainly not lived up to its Utopia. Utopias have failed constantly and they've failed because we have been looking for Utopian things instead of looking for more modest things. It has also made the tragic experience impossible amongst us. We must keep alive the promise of the New World, and so instead of tragedy we have melodrama which is what many of my novels have had to deal with. Most people in Latin America live soap operas all day long. Utopia fails, and tragedy is not there. The United States is the only nation in the world that has thought that it is its own Utopia. So when that Utopia fails and cracks, all sorts of very strange things happen as we are seeing today after the failures in Vietnam and Watergate. Of course, the United States has the great privilege of having the only tragic writer in the New World, William Faulkner. He is the only man who understood the nature of tragedy. This came from a sense of defeat because he was a man of the South who felt the defeat. He did not feel it in military or political terms because the South was defeated by the North. He felt it because he knew that the South was defeated by itself before it was ever defeated by the North, that it was defeated by its own division, by its own sense of alienation, by slavery. We, in Latin America, haven't been capable of creating a Faulkner. If the novel is literature and a great region of the human spirit is to have any future at all, it will be thanks to the great tragic novelists who are Dostoevsky, Kafka, Faulkner, Hermann Broch and Samuel Beckett. It's a very pertinent question. It is very important for what I'm trying to do now. The sense of tragedy is that you do not judge good and evil, you refuse to consider that good and evil are values.

DCC: Hegel said that tragedy is not between right and wrong, but between right and right.

CF: That is exactly what I mean.

DCC: In an article, you wrote that myth unites nostalgia for the past to desire for the permanent present, and that all myth is external and communicable. But some would suggest that we live in a de-mythologized world. Is it the artist's job to reawaken our mythic sensibility? To create new icons that reflect the contemporary world? Many of my students do not know what I mean when I say the word 'Madonna'.

CF: Myths keep on repeating themselves; the great archetypes keep on recurring. Nobody understands the word Madonna, but probably if you said Dolly Parton, everyone would understand and get the picture of a Madonna figure, a Madonna figure of the neon age of course [*both laugh*]. James Dean is a Prometheus of the American fifties, he's the great rebel against the Establishment. All the great myths are repeated. I agree with the Jungian idea that myths are what keep the tribe together, in the subconscious of the tribe. They are not, he says, an interpretation and expression of the psychic life of the tribe, they *are* the psychic life of the tribe itself. If you don't have them, there is no psychic life and the tribe has no soul. Roland Barthes wrote this beautiful book called *Mythologies* where he deals with avatars of the modern myth. We're simply investigating the deeper structures, the constants of the myth, but we must also realize that these structures which are resonances of the past, unconsciously keep the past alive. Yet they always present the past in the present as it were. The past is never the past. Myths come alive today through many figures of pop culture, of modern civiliazation. They are there in an unconscious way. I feel a book should be written about the mythical content of popular culture, popular culture as proposed by the United States, which is the most popular, most powerful, popular culture in the world today.

DCC: Mircea Eliade seems to agree. He wrote that modern man longs for a total and definite renewal and I think that contemporary fiction certainly reflects the search for psychic rebirth, as you do in *A Change of Skin* and other stories.

CF: Yes, I think this is being done constantly. We're hungry for a redefinition of our mythical soul. There are too many energies, too many images, too much knowledge. I think of Erasmus having only two hundred books in his study. That was all the knowledge the world needed for the most brilliant man in the year 1505.

DCC: Perhaps this plethora of knowledge is too much for our conscious mind. The road to rebirth in your work is often through the subconscious. But both the conscious and the subconscious seem to be fraught with agony for modern man. Camus said that if a story is tragic, it is because the hero is conscious. Yet, you have said that it is the subconscious that is a sort of Virgil who guides you through the twelve circles of his own inferno.

CF: We're living in very unharmonious societies. This is why people are cracking up, because this sense of harmony, of being one, is lost. It is good to know that it is lost and therefore we must fight for it. We're being overfed with images, with ideas of publicity, with gadgets, with technology of all sorts, and this creates anguish and fear of losing touch with your own soul. I made a crack recently against computers in a toast I gave at a dinner, and Jules Feiffer was there and said, 'Don't knock computers, Carlos, for all you know you may be one yourself.' I'm probably R2D2 talking to you [*laughs*].

DCC: A number of artists are portrayed in your novels, such as in *A Change of Skin* and *Where the Air is Clear*; artists who fail under the pressures of an apathetic and ignorant society, and who fail to keep their original idealism, integrity and creative energy. Are these real dangers in your own artistic life?

CF: Well, I think in everybody's life. The whole problem of energy, which you've just mentioned, is so important that you often feel the whole society's conspiring against you to take your time away, your energy away, to suck your energy from you. But if we were totally free and totally the masters of our time, of our energy, I wonder if we would finally do anything at all. This great divorce between the artist and his society, which I think Thomas Mann described better than any other twentieth-century writer, has to do a lot with the way we envision death. Our society believed it had conquered death. Paul Valéry said that civilizations too are mortal. Civilizations did not want to believe it, even after the terrible experiences of the two world wars. There was a refusal, a constant beatific belief in progress. This is what has broken up, this is what has cracked open, and, maybe as I say, it is good that we are facing these challenges. Societies can die, just as men and women can die. Even worse, nature can die. Nature by definition was immortal. We are seeing that we can even murder nature. This is a big change from the artist that Thomas Mann wrote about, whose drama was that the society gave no value to death, wanted to cast a shawl over death, to put death into oblivion. Therefore, the artist, whose traditional function has been to warn man about death and to offer a way to overcome death through art, had no place any more. Suddenly death is there again, and what a death; a death worse than the death the Middle Ages could have imagined. This death is into suicide, a death which is full of vengeance and hatred against nature because we know nature will outlive us. It's always outlived us, and now it seems that we've come to this final horrible conclusion that nature must die along with us. It is terrifying because it has never happened before in history and we have the instruments to kill nature this time. We can now say, 'If I'm going to die, you're going to die with me', which is terrifying. Then the function of the artist as a herald of death, as a humanizer of death, as a man who says that death is a part of life, that death and life are not separated, again becomes very, very important. One sees a renewal of the arts, and of writing in particular, in the coming decades because the faith in progress has been lost and the faith in progress rendered death useless.

DCC: It has been suggested that women are a form of death in your writing. Linda B. Hall has criticized your depiction of women. She feels that woman is shown as destroyer and love is a kind of death, whereby the usually older woman takes the man's innocence. Another critic, Lanin Gyurko, also feels that most of your female characters are compelled to play a dehumanized role, such as in *The Death of Artemio Cruz*. Is this a fair evaluation of your depiction of women?

CF: I'm very concerned with women as I see them or imagine them in Mexico. There is a social reality here, an historical reality which is obviously changing, and what I'm writing about is one of the most terrible traditions in the world with respect to feminity. In the Mexican traditions three terrible things come together: Aztec, Arab and Spanish. The Aztecs considered that women were the goddesses of the Aztec Pantheon which are always terribly ambivalent figures that spell life or death, purity or impurity. Tlazolteotl, who was the goddess of dawn and night, was also the goddess of purity and impurity. She hears the confessions of the warriors before they go out to battle, in order to purify their souls, but she is also the scavenger, the vulture that cleans the fields. You know a civilization that could take young women and give them to the warriors and then kill the young women at the pyramid because they had become whores, is the greatest Catch-22 I have ever heard in my life [*laughs*]. How do you get out of that quandary? You're going to have to give yourself to the warrior or he will kill you. Now you've given yourself to the warrior, he would kill you because you're a whore. Imagine a society built on this imagination. Imagine the Arab strain on our civilization, the idea of the harem, the supremacy of the male. Imagine the spanish tradition. There's a proverb in Spain which says, 'women should be in the kitchen with a broken leg so they can't move'. Buñuel made a movie out of this proverb, which is *Tristana*, where Catherine Deneuve actually lost her leg. Look at this figure of Tristana and look at my feminine figures; they are defending themselves. I think that it is a perverted thing to think that I depict women who are castrators, figures of destruction; they are women who are concentrating their forces to defend themselves against the onslaught of the 'macho'. If their methods are not always as pure as people would like them, then do they want a Polyanna figure, do they want me to give them Lillian Gish in a bonnet? My women are what they are because they must survive. They have no other way of surviving. Maybe this is changing. I think it is, because women in Mexico are much more independent, they own their bodies now, much more than ever. When I was a young man of sixteen, seventeen in Mexico, you had no solution but masturbation or the whorehouse; there were no women available. I'm writing of a situation that is charged with history. Women are not out to castrate men. I think they are out to survive and to use sometimes very ruthless arms to survive, like Claudia Nervo in *Holy Place*. She's a rather ruthless character, but that's the way she maintains her independence. She's a fully independent woman because she's been very nasty. Why do we accept that Artemio Cruz can do all these things, and not a woman like Claudia Nervo? They are twin figures in a way.

DCC: In *Terra Nostra*, the new world is ushered in by an androgynous Pollo Phoibe.

CF: *Terra Nostra* is a novel that finally implies two births; one is a terrible birth because it is the birth from death, it is a cadaver who comes from death, this cadaver made by the Queen of Spain from bits and pieces of all the kings and queens and princes. She takes the shin bone from one, a tooth from another and an ear from a third and makes up this androgynous, bisexual monster made from men and women. It is an entity born from death, which for me, is the ultimate definition of the Baroque. The other possibility is the androgynous experience by which a man and a woman making love at the end of *Terra Nostra* become only one, and therefore a being who can copulate with himself and fertilize himself and give birth to another being. What this other being would be I don't know, but still I prefer androgyny to death, to the other possibility. I prefer the mystery of life to the mystery of death.

DCC: You assail many of the systems by which we have tried to order our lives. One of them is language. Was Ludwig Wittgenstein right when he said that language disguises thought?

CF: I agree very much with Wittgenstein where he talks generally about the limits of propositional language, the language we associate with thought. The sciences, logic and philosophy, do not take care of the mythical, ethical level of imagination. The language of thought cannot propose poetry, cannot propose enigmas really. He says we must keep silent about that other language which is probably the language of literature. You can't say anything about it, it talks for itself. There's a poem by the French poet René Char, and he says the time is arriving when only that which is unexplainable will convoke us. I think he's right. This is the essence of modern literature, that there are no solutions, and this is extremely shocking to the propositional mind. You don't have to prove anything in literature; the mathematician, the engineer, the lawyer, the Indian chief, want you to prove what you're saying, but the writer doesn't have to prove anything. The painter doesn't have to prove anything. Picasso doesn't have to prove a damn thing. So this creates two realms which Wittgenstein has distinguished more brilliantly than anyone ever.

DCC: How would you describe your technique since so many others have tried to do so?

CF: I'm not really sure of this, I don't think it's very conscious. I feel I'm very much immersed in a sort of continuum when I write and what I write comes from so many, many factors I could never enumerate all of them here. There's so much genetic information in the nine months I spent in my mother's womb. It started there. This dictates the technique. I don't think that much about technical problems.

DCC: Your novels are often structual and thematic paradoxes, and you define *Terra Nostra* as 'an aspiration to simultaneity', through which you, as the master of the text, would overcome the determination of the acts of reading and writing. Just for a moment, could you step outside your role as the master of the text, and tell me what kind of response you hope for in the *reader* first of all?

CF: I'm convinced that a novel has its own destiny, whatever it may be, and it now creates its readers as we've said before. It cannot conceive them beforehand. I hope the novel finds readers, I don't hope it has readers already before I write it or when I publish it. Hopefully it will create readers. Therefore, if what I do is really right, very much what I want to write, under the conviction that this is what eventually I can give to the reader, I will find the readers for that book, and anything else is a waste of time. If I were to fabricate a beautiful formula, then it is preconceived and prepackaged for the reader. This takes the whole sense of adventure and of truth and of greatness out of literature. I hope my readers will find the book and the book will find them. *Terra Nostra* is a book that has gained in readership in Mexico. Everybody made jokes and said, 'you need a fellowship, you need a sabbatical year to read the book' [*laughs*]. But it has gained readers and I'm sure it will continue to have readers.

DCC: How about the critics and book reviewers?

CF: I have mentioned my first experience with a critic. He demanded everything from me, demanded what I was not, and demanded that I be all the things to all men, which is impossible. Something terrible happened with that critic. I wrote this book in order to impress a girlfriend of mine whom I wanted either to lay or to marry, and when this man finally called me a blasphemous bugger –

DCC: Perfect critical language, of course [*both laugh*].

CF: – she turned away from me forever. I lost this girl because of the review, so I hated this man, I hate him enormously to this very day. I lost any possibility with that particular girl, so that irritated me very much, but then I came to the conclusion that book reviewing is really a branch of the literature of the fantastic, of the supernatural, so I read book reviewers as I would read Edgar Allan Poe or Ray Bradbury, and say yes, magnificent, I never thought of that. Super! What imagination!

DCC: If you could find the ideal critic, what would you hope for?

CF: It's more than I hope for. I've had it on many, many occasions, thankfully. This has been a century of great critical writing; Walter Benjamin, Simone Weil and others. God almighty, these are super critics! What do these critics offer? Why are they critics? Because they offer an equivalent at the critical level of the work they are referring to. It doesn't matter if the critique is twenty pages long and the book is five hundred pages long; that is of no consequence. When you read Simone

Weil on *The Iliad*, there is the same level, one being the great epic poem, the other a magnificent piece of criticism. She is at the level of the work. She's not sniping at it or demanding from the work that it be what it is not; she is literally correspondent with the work, she is recognizing the work and the work is recognizing her. This is what you expect. I've had very good experiences in that sense.

DCC: C. S. Lewis once said that 'the truth is not that we need the critics in order to enjoy the authors, but that we need the authors in order to enjoy the critics' [*both laugh*]. Are you aware of the different critical methodologies that are applied to an interpretation of your work? For example, Floyd Merrell did a semiotic analysis of *The Death of Artemio Cruz*.

CF: Well, you know we were at a very interesting symposium called 'The Spanish Novel Today', at the University of Indiana, organized by a very good critic, a Peruvian critic, by the name of Oviedo. I refused to go to all the seminars where they talked about me. I said no, I'm not a masochist; I prefer to go and see John Dillinger's museum, which is more interesting than hearing people talk about *Terra Nostra*. Juan Goytisolo did go to all of *them* and then the next day he made a public declaration, saying, 'I went to all these meetings and I heard a lot about semiotics and diachronic and synchronic. The only thing I did not find was myself. I was totally absent. I think the best service I could do for critics would be to shoot myself and disappear completely, and they would be in full possession of the semiotic structure and I would not be there bothering them, it would get me out of the picture completely.' I would agree with Goytisolo.

DCC: I've heard that you like to mystify and mislead 'pedants', critics and interviewers, by giving them erroneous data, such as biographical details. I assume it's because you dislike the invasion of your privacy. Do you also do this with questions about your work?

CF: No, no, it also depends on who's asking.

DCC: Some years ago in an interview you said that you write with the nerves of your stomach, and pay for it with a duodenal ulcer and a chronic colic. Is this still true?

CF: No, no, the main thing is I have a very good personal life now with Sylvia and my children, so that's one thing. With time, you learn so many things of course, and amongst other things I have found that I have learned how to write without the anguish of the white page; something that has anguished every single writer in the world. Hemingway had a formula for it; he said never end a sentence, always leave it in a colon, semi-colon, comma, and then go off and come back the next day. I've finally been able to learn how to write in my head what I'm going to write the next day. Here in Princeton, there is quite a literary geography, intellectual geography around. I make a little walk, a one mile walk around more or less, every afternoon. I go first to the house of Einstein, then I go to the house of Hermann Broch and to the house of Thomas Mann, thinking all the time what I'm going to write the next day. Then I come back and I read and see my children and I see television, I go to a movie, I get up next day and everything is in my head. I just go to my typewriter and tick, tick, tick, it all comes out. It has all germinated over night. I found out how to do this, because before, I arose, saying, 'Almighty, what am I going to say?' I saw this white page and the ulcer started acting up.

DCC: I certainly understand that. Like the painter, Julian, in *Terra Nostra*, who does not sign his art because it is an act of creation, not stupid individualism, you also freely thank friends, other artists and thinkers. *Aura*, for example, shares an affinity with Faulkner's 'A Rose for Emily' and James's *The Aspern Papers*. To what extent does the collective sharing among creative people affect your work?

CF: I'm trying to introduce a bit of medievalism in the sense that Chartres Cathedral is not signed by anybody, or the pyramids in Yucatán which have no signature. I think literature is a great collective work. It's an unending wheel; no literature is created from nothing. It is always very minor critics who are harping on the problem of influences, who do not understand the problem of tradition and creation. Delacroix said something which is quite truthful; he said, there are children who are not baptized, that is true, but what there has never been is a child without a father and a mother. There is this constant relation, I think, with the past. Many people say *Aura* is a derivation of *The Aspern Papers*. I say no, there is a central figure, the figure of the white witch, of the white goddess Robert Graves talks about. When I was writing *Aura*, what triggered me first was really the vision of a marvellous Japanese movie called *The Tales of the Pale Moon After the Storm*. This is a wonderful story of a young woman who comes back through an old crone. This old crone appears and talks with the voice of the young woman to the man who recognizes the voice, but is repelled by the hag he is seeing. This is a great figure, the figure of the white goddess, the figure of the old woman who is capable of recreating life, of giving and taking life that is in Henry James, in Charles Dickens with Miss Havisham, in Pushkin's Countess. Listen, you go right back to Homer and Circe and the power of changing men and to the Witches of Thessaly in *The Golden Ass*. It is one of the longest running figures in literature. You simply have the conscience that you belong to a tradition, that you add something to tradition, that you could not write without the tradition in your bones. As Virginia Woolf said, you have to have the whole of Western literature, and if possible, of Asian and African literature in your bones when you write. You can't pretend to originality; I think that it's a ridiculous attempt. I come from many places and I'm related to many things, and the elements of originality are not so important, it is the element of tradition that is important. All of these elements come into focus through you, that is true, but let us recognize the vastness and generosity of the world.

2 Margaret Drabble

DCC: Many critics feel that the ambivalence of womanhood, a growing feminist consciousness, a search for alternatives, and a struggle for female self-awareness are major themes in your novels. Yet you have pointed out more than once that your books are not 'about' feminism. Also, these same themes are treated in the work of traditional novelists – Richardson, Hawthorne, Henry James. What is your feeling about the particular kind of labelling that goes on in the critical world, especially the feminist critical world? Are female novelists a special breed and do they therefore demand a new way of seeing, a new methodology for responding to their work?

MD: No, I don't think so. I very much admire some of the feminist critics, such as Ellen Moers and Mary Ellmann. They're very perceptive and they have read very widely, not only in twentieth-century literature but in the past. Therefore, I think they do shed a new light on the past, which is always interesting and it's also relevant to life. I like criticism to relate literature to life and how life is lived or should be lived. But it's not the only thing that needs to be said. When I'm writing I don't think of myself wholly as a woman but partly as a writer. And indeed in some of my books I've tried to avoid writing as a woman because it does create its own narrowness.

DCC: Are you tired of being referred to as a 'cautious feminist'?

MD: No, because I think that's true. I am a 'cautious feminist' in that I think that there is no way of producing revolutions overnight. Overnight revolutions usually end in disaster and backlash. Any change of consciousness, which I think has been taking place over the last fifty years, not the last ten years as some people seem to think, is a slower process. In order for the

This interview first appeared in *The Atlantic Monthly*, November 1980.

Margaret Drabble (*photograph: Trevor Clark*)

change to work, it has to be slow. This is a very English attitude as opposed to the attitude in America where people think that the revolution can change things much more rapidly. I think you have to educate your menfolk. In order for it to be a true change, it has to be slow. And, by 'cautious', I mean a slow revolution rather than a rapid one.

DCC: Are categories, such as the 'female novel', limiting rather than revealing?

MD: There are some very fine female novels. There are some subjects in which women are naturally and clearly more interested than men, children, childbirth and so on. I don't think there is such a thing as a female novelist but one can usually tell from the work, even if one didn't already know, what sex the writer was. It is perhaps a mistake to try to write in a too neutral or masculine way.

DCC: Virginia Woolf said that the best novelists – writers such as Thomas Hardy and D. H. Lawrence — had androgynous minds. She felt that the poor writers had exclusively masculine mentalities and she listed Kipling, Galsworthy and Arnold Bennett. Now I don't think you would agree with her on Arnold Bennett?

MD: I certainly don't agree on Arnold Bennett because he's a very androgynous writer and he writes superbly about women and women's preoccupations, domestic life, worrying about furniture and peeling potatoes. I don't think he's a masculine writer. And I think there are masculine writers who are harmed by being masculine; they're the writers who go in for machismo like Hemingway. Hemingway is extraordinarily dated; his was a machismo period, which was in a way I suppose a backlash against Virginia Woolf and Bloomsbury. Androgyny can be rather dissatisfying. I think E. M. Forster is dissatisfying. I admire him immensely and enjoy him very much but there's something slightly too unaligned about Forster.

DCC: It has also been suggested that your female characters seek female self-definition. But I have always felt in reading your novels that the search for self-knowledge relies much less on their gender than on a life that is absurd and chaotic, shifting and contradictory; a life that contains great gaps between what one wants and what one gets, the ideal and the real.

MD: Yes, this is true of both sexes. I find it easier to write about my own sex for fairly obvious reasons. It's easier to know what the details of women's lives consist of. I think exactly the same problems confront men. We're all looking for spiritual satisfaction or fulfilment and the gap between what you're seeking and what you find is very great. But you're nevertheless driven on to seek. And that's true of both sexes.

DCC: You have said that you were separating from your husband when you wrote *The Needle's Eye*, and you suggested that you might possibly have changed the ending if you were in another situation. Yet I felt that the ending that you did write worked perfectly in terms of the character that you had created. Would you have really changed the ending if you were not separating or in a different position?

MD: No, because it was entirely proper for her. This is one of the curious things about fiction and life; when I was writing that novel I did create an impossible situation for her. I created this deliberately. I created a husband who wanted the children as much as she did and therefore she had to stick with him, but that's a very rare situation. I had exactly the same problem in *The Millstone*. I think that probably in *The Millstone*, the woman would eventually have told the father that the child was his child. But artistically this didn't seem satisfactory. Maybe ten years after the book was written she would have told him, I don't know. But in terms of the shape of the book and the shape of the character at that moment in time when you're writing about the character, this is the proper thing for them to do. It's perfectly possible, that if you look at *The Needle's Eye* not as a novel but as a slice of life, in five years' time she might have left her husband after all or he might have left her. But at that point in time, they had to stick together because that was the whole direction of the book.

DCC: I did not agree with Monica Mannheimer that *The Needle's Eye* was a defeatist novel. I agreed with you that it was a novel about people in a state of continual effort, rather than in a state of despair; that happiness is not the point.

MD: Yes, happiness is a by-product and it's a momentary by-product. In *The Needle's Eye* they do have moments of profound happiness during the book. But they don't see that that's what they ought to be seeking. I think the idea that you're here in order to enjoy yourself is very wrong. You're here in order to do the right thing and to seek the depths in yourself which aren't necessarily very happy. It's more important to be in touch with the depths than to be happy. And you can be happy on a superficial level while you're estranging yourself from the most important things in life. And that presumably makes you unhappy in the long run. So, in a way, if you seek and persevere, then you're more likely to be happy, but that's not why you're doing it.

DCC: Many people quarrelled with the ending of *The Needle's Eye*, and I tend to feel that feminist critics insist on a particular kind of ending: the super-woman who can live alone happily, who sees life's choices logically and clearly, who can transcend life's vicissitudes, who never makes a mistake. Do you see that tendency in feminist critics?

MD: Yes, they like positive, strong endings. I like fairly optimistic endings. I thought the ending of *The Needle's Eye* was fairly optimistic, in that here were two people in an impossible situation, determined not to give in to it but to continue living as best they could in the intolerable situation that they'd been given. This is one of the reasons that in my novel *The Ice Age*, which was criticized on the same grounds, I presented the female character with a truly intolerable situation. Life isn't fair, life isn't easy, and not everybody can be happy. If you have a defective child or if you are crushed by an appalling illness, then you just say, 'Well, life is supposed to be happy, so I've got to turn this into happiness.' That's a very simplistic view, I think. But I agree with the feminists in that I don't like people to give in. I believe in continued effort. I think that my characters go in for continued effort. Sometimes they're defeated, but all one can do is be honourably defeated. I haven't read as much feminist criticism as perhaps I should have done. I don't read it because it rather confuses the mind when you're writing. You do stop to think in terms of how this will be regarded. If I end with a marriage, it's going to be seen as a mistake; if I end with a woman alone, it's going to be regarded as a triumph. All you can do is write about how it seems to you to happen at the time. How it seems to you to be true to the characters at the time. In my novel *The Middle Ground*, the woman does end up entirely alone, which may be regarded as a true feminist tract and may be regarded as a complete failure. I don't know and I don't care.

All I know is that that is what happened to this woman during the course of this book, and that it was true to her situation in life. The truth is more important than ideology. On the other hand, I have to say that in a way, fiction is a search for an alternative life. It is a search for a new model. Doris Lessing says in *The Golden Notebook* that we're all looking for the beautiful and impossible blueprint and it's the search that's important. In fiction, you can create things that you can't necessarily create in life. She also says that it is worth the act of imagination, that you're imagining a better life. But that's not solely in terms of the woman's life. It's in terms of society as a whole. One could also say that as the men in my novels are inadequate for the women, so are the women inadequate for the men. I'm not at all keen on the feminist view that there's a male conspiracy to put women down. I don't think that's true. Society is organized so that these collisions and disasters take place, which they have noteably. There's no use pretending that marriage is in a good state or that the relations between the sexes are happy at the moment. It's no good blaming patriarchy or men for this. Both sexes are at fault. And the institution of marriage itself is at fault. This is one of the things that novels can explore without any preconceived ideas as to what the answer should be.

DCC: A common criticism about female novelists is that they do not handle their male characters well, whereas many male novelists have created strong, fully drawn female characters. Mary Gordon has told me that she agrees that her male characters are not well done. John Updike has said that your male characters are vague. I couldn't agree less. Your men, for me, are most memorable when I think of Simon Camish and Anthony Keating, and Karel Schmidt and a host of minor characters in your books. And, Michael Ratcliffe, in *The Novel Today*, states that the men in your books are not needed, except for making babies; they are not even treacherous, but simply absurd. How do you respond to that?

MD: Well, I don't think it's true. A lot of my male characters are rather admirable men and perfectly real. He must have been thinking of *The Millstone*, in which, indeed, there is a very shadowy man. But it's a man whom I found very interesting. Because it's a first person narration, there was no possibility of telling his side of the story. If I were to write that novel now, or to write a sequel to it, I would be in a much better position to write his side of the story. I was conscious in my early novels of the fact that the men were shadowy characters. This was partly through a reluctance on my part to blame men, which I still feel. I think that it's not proper to blame people for the bad situations in which women themselves have put their men. Certainly Rosamund in *The Millstone* is guilty of putting Geoge in a very false situation. She behaves much worse than he does. He is vague only in that she can't see him clearly.

DCC: Exactly. The reader sees George only through Rosamund's eyes.

MD: Yes. It's her fault that he is vague. If the novel had been written in the third person or written from a different point of view altogether, he could have been a completely different character, which I, at that stage, was probably not capable of doing. Now, I think Michael Ratcliffe's view is possibly a traditional sexist view that the women seem to dispose of the men. I suppose this could be said of Jane in my novel *The Waterfall*, who disposes of her husband in a rather high-handed way. And she doesn't seem to miss him. But then, that is what the book was about. It's a real situation, not an ideology. It's what I have observed happening.

DCC: In Doris Lessing's novel *A Proper Marriage*, Martha Quest seeks clarification of her problems through reading books. And she asks of novels, 'What does this really say about my life?' Martha's conclusion is that they say very little about life, although I'm sure Lessing would disagree. Alternatively, you have said that you find out about living and about the values of living from reading novels, and your characters often use literature as a means of 'guidance or help or illumination'.

MD: Yes, I think literature is one of the ways of mapping out territories and problems. Doris Lessing does see literature as an exploration, as a guideline. I certainly do. Sometimes it can be very dangerous. I read Henry James at a very dangerous age, eighteen or nineteen. I was too conscious of the kind of moral problems that he was posing, and his stress on renunciation.

Lessing said, in *the Golden Notebook*, that women are leading the kind of lives that women have never led before. There's a very interesting passage where Anna's talking to her psychiatrist, Mother Sugar. Mother Sugar says that, of course, there have been women who have sought sexual freedom, and who have insisted on their own identity. Anna responds by saying, 'I know that I'm leading the kind of life that women have never led before.' I agree entirely with both of the characters. Mother Sugar was right; there were women in the past who insisted on identity and freedom. But I also think that the actual social form and the predicament that women are in today is different in kind and in quality. It is very much an unchartered ground. One of the reasons that women's novels are particularly interesting at the moment is that women are charting this ground where the rules have changed, the balance of power has shifted, and women are writing about what happens next. Often with a very vague vision of the future. But I'm trying to find out where we are going.

DCC: As an extension to what you said about the meaning of 'literature', your novels clearly echo with the literary heritage of England. And like Sarah in *A Summer Bird-Cage*, you think in quotations. But these references are not superfluous and they're not 'showing off' as T. E. Apter has said in her article. Emma comments in *The Garrick Year* that the poems of Wordsworth are 'uninflated truth'. Could you further expand on your use of other literary works in your novels?

MD: It's certainly not 'showing off'. On the contrary, I have to suppress a great deal of what I know, because it's incommunicable and creates a barrier rather than furthering communication. I don't like books that are simply literary games, and I don't think that my own books are literary games. Naturally, what I've read is as much a part of what I think as the people that I meet and the problems that I encounter. And when I find myself in what seems to me to be an unprecedented situation, I often say to myself, 'Now, what would so-and-so have written about this? What would their characters have felt in this situation?' I'm certainly not the only person who thinks in those terms. There's a marvellous bit in H. G. Well's *Ann Veronica* where Ann Veronica is assaulted. And she says to herself, 'Now what would Jane Austen have thought of this?' And of course it is absolutely true that Jane Austen's characters could never have been in that position. So, women today are finding themselves in situations, physical and emotional situations, for which there are no literary guidelines. But it's very interesting to compare how characters in the past would have reacted. Indeed, one can find fictional models written not only by women but also by men, by Henry James for example, of women who have transgressed or stepped out of the circumscribed roles and have made discoveries. So, I don't see it as decorating one's books with literature. I think that literature is a part of life. I read Bunyan at a very early age. And he profoundly affected my moral thinking, but I'm not alone in that. He profoundly affected the moral thinking of the whole of the seventeenth, eighteenth and nineteenth centuries. Everybody read *Pilgrim's Progress*. It was a way of looking at the world. It's like saying, 'Is the Bible irrelevant?' No, it's not. You may not believe it, you may not even read it, but it's in your consciousness.

DCC: Could you give me some examples of writers who have or still do play 'literary games'?

MD: I think Muriel Spark plays 'literary games'. People who are more interested in form than in content play 'literary games'. I'm really only interested in life and how it should be lived. I see literature as part of that.

DCC: What about writers like Pynchon and Barth?

MD: Oh, yes, I can't bring myself to read their books. I've read Barth. But I don't like Pynchon. It is very literary and, to me, arid.

DCC: Why are you pleased when people call you the George Eliot of your age and not pleased when compared to Charlotte Brontë?

MD: Oh. I don't know if that's true. I think Charlotte Brontë is wonderful. I admire them both immensely. If I ever did say anything to that effect, it could only be that I suspect that I'm a very emotional person, and therefore like the ballast that George Eliot has. She has a little wider range than Charlotte Brontë. You know, Charlotte Brontë's range is very limited and also there's something very distressing and painful about her work. George Eliot does achieve a greater harmony, so I suppose she's a better model in that way. It would be nice to think that one had a fairer mind than Charlotte Brontë. But I think that Charlotte Brontë is a marvellous writer.

DCC: In *The Waterfall*, Jane Gray says that she doesn't like Jane Austen. Do you admire Austen?

MD: Yes, I reread her constantly. I think she's truly great but a rather mystifying writer. She misses out an enormous amount. I admire George Eliot so much because she's so inclusive. She does tackle a very large range of subject matter. And Jane Austen doesn't. She didn't care what was going on round the edges of the society that she lived in. But her distinctions between morals and manners are ever fascinating.

DCC: I agree. But isn't that one of the problems with the criteria by which we judge literature? The idea that the great novel is *War and Peace*, the one with the larger societal scope. Women have often been criticized on the basis that they write about the house and the room, the small and narrow. And it has been pointed out that perhaps one doesn't need that larger, synthetic sense of society. The great novel traditionally has encompassed the philosophical perception, the historical overview, the synthetic social analysis, and books that look at one portion of life in other terms, tend to be seen as inferior in some way, less clever.

MD: Yes. But there's some validity in that; the greatest works do tackle a great range. *Mansfield Park* is a great work. I don't think there's anything diminishing in writing about home and rooms and domestic life and birth and sex and death. I don't think these are small themes. I don't think writing about battles is a necessary thing. One of the books I've never managed to read is *The Charterhouse of Parma*, which I know I ought to read, but I simply can't. But my anxiety about Jane Austen is not so much the smallness of the range as the class problem that it presents; she ought to have had a slightly greater awareness of what was going on in the rest of England. It's got nothing to do with range, it has to do with social conscience, which George Eliot had and which gave her books a greater breadth. Now Mrs Gaskell had a very great social conscience, and although her books are narrow in a way and they're women's books in a way (she wrote about motherhood extremely well), she had this passionate concern for the unfortunate, which is something that I'm very much drawn to in fiction and in life. I think that novels that concentrate on a very small section of society, however brilliantly, like Evelyn Waugh's for example, are missing out too much to be truly great. I would qualify that by saying that *Mansfield Park* does seem to me to be truly great but possibly only because it does have a working class family. In that book, Austen does venture further outside her territory than in any of her other books. She almost raises the question of the slave trade but not quite.

DCC: And this question of social consciousness is part of the reason that you like Arnold Bennett?

MD: Yes.

DCC: And you have said that he has influenced your attitudes, especially in your novel *Jerusalem the Golden*?

MD: Yes. He has a great respect for ordinary life and ordinary people who don't necessarily achieve much or lead glamorous lives, although they may aspire to. He came from a very poor background himself, as did my family, and he never forgot it. And because of this grounding in knowledge of ordinary people, which Virginia Woolf, for example, did not have, Arnold Bennett tells you things that Virginia Woolf simply didn't know. Although I suppose Virginia Woolf is a greater writer.

DCC: A long time ago, I was reading something that Woolf had written. She said that paradise for one of Arnold Bennett's characters was the best hotel room in Brighton. I thought two things. First, how perceptive of her. But on the other hand, it bothered me because she meant it as a negative criticism. It seemed to deny a whole world of people who, in fact, are not conscious in the way that we think of consciousness perhaps; who are not educated; who are not tuned into the subtle nuances of the mind; and for whom the best room in Brighton is heaven. They can perhaps get genuine pleasure from this experience. However, pleasure is such a debatable term because the pleasure that some may derive from Wordsworth's poetry is not comparable to the pleasure that some would have in the best hotel room in Brighton. Very often criticism seems to be distinction more so than definition.

MD: Virginia Woolf's comment about the best hotel room in Brighton seems to be the remark of a snob. She was a snob and she was malicious. And she was not very imaginative about the lives of people that she couldn't imagine. Arnold Bennett was much more imaginative about other people's lives; he could imagine Virginia Woolf's life but she couldn't imagine his. And he had a wider range. If one is thinking of distinctions, I would say that Bennett's novel *The Old Wives' Tale* is a much better book than *The Waves*. But *To the Lighthouse* is another matter. She's a very interesting case, Virginia Woolf, because in some of her polemical writing, she did articulate very sound principles about caring for the helpless, and bettering the lot of every woman. But she couldn't do it in fiction. And I think she was aware of that. She was absolutely right to choose Mrs Dalloway because that suited her talent. But I think that she felt there was something a bit worrying about her fictional range, and that, in a way, there's something much more nourishing in Bennett's fictional range.

DCC: There is a relationship that exists between your work and Wordsworth's, particularly *The Needle's Eye* and *The Millstone*. What is his influence on your work?

MD: He believed in plain living and high thinking, something that always haunted me. This is what Rose tries to go in for in *The Needle's Eye*. He also believed in living in the depths. He believed in those spots of time in one's life when one is in touch with something slightly beyond the immediate. Arnold Bennett also does in a curious way. It's the transfiguration of the everyday, which Wordsworth was so good at. And of course, Virginia Woolf is good at it too. It's something that can be done in fiction as well as in poetry. In a way, Wordsworth's *The Prelude* is a great psychological novel; it's the most marvellous poem. Yeats does that too. He has this quality of writing about an everyday incident and making it profoundly emblematic.

DCC: When I'm reading your novels, I am reminded very often of Pascal's, 'The heart has its reasons which reason cannot know.' And I know you admire Hume, particularly the statement: 'I might as well rely on the instincts of my heart.' Do you trust emotion and instinct over reason, even though the world of the mind is important to you?

MD: Yes, I think that if your heart is dried up, your spirit is dried up; then, you can sink yourself into your grave and it will profit you not at all. You have to be in touch with your own emotional centre, your spiritual centre.

DCC: The pain and confusion of your characters often comes out of the fact that life registers consciously with them. Feelings are filtered through a recognition of the mind.

MD: That's a very difficult one. I think that consciousness can be a saving comic grace rather than the tragic element. Perhaps emotion is tragic and consciousness is comic.

DCC: That's Horace Walpole's distinction. He said that this world is a comedy to those who think, a tragedy to those who feel.

MD: Yes.

DCC: Hermann Hesse also picks up that theme of the tragedy of consciousness in *Siddhartha*. So does Milton in *Samson Agonistes*. I find that often in your novels, intelligence is an isolating force. Many of your characters are lonely. Very often it is connected to their intelligence. Sarah, for example, in *A Summer Bird-Cage* says that she's 'so bloody brilliant that every one else inevitably seems to be at half pressure'; and Rosamund in *The Millstone* feels that she is lonely and isolated 'through superiority of intellect'. Socrates said that the unexamined Life is not worth living. Do you think the examined life is any better?

MD: Proust, I suppose, was a great example of the examined life. But he wasn't very happy. No, the emotional life, even though it might be more tragic, is more satisfying than the conscious intellectual life. The conscious intellectual life is very dry. This is one of the things that Rosamund suffers from. She suffers from dryness of the spirit because she's so clever. She doesn't allow herself to feel. That is a tragedy for her. And that's a tragic novel. But she does find happiness in the very basic human emotion, a redeeming emotion, love for her children. I see emotion as both redeeming and tragic. I'm not terribly interested in consciousness anymore. I used to be very worried about consciousness and self-consciousness, but it seems to be less of a problem when one gets older. Or it may be that when I first started writing, I was aware of certain barriers that intellect raised. But they've become irrelevant simply because as one grows older one seeks one's own society and finds people who are much more intelligent than oneself. So you don't feel cut off. You feel stimulated. I think it's a young person's problem, the problem of acute consciousness. Unless, of course, like Proust, you're so neurasthenic that nobody's at your own neurotic pitch. This is one of the reasons I admire Wordsworth and Arnold Bennett, because they do hold on to the ordinary human emotions, the ordinary human duties, the ordinary common human experiences that everybody can share in. *The Prelude* is the growth of consciousness. But, it isn't the growth of an isolated cut-off consciousness. On the contrary, the moments of which Wordsworth is joyful and knows that he is working well, are the moments when he is in touch with his sister, with Coleridge, with the community, with the people that he meets. I think that this is a problem for the artist; that you want to be part of the community, but you're cut off by the fact that you feel yourself separate. The writers that I most admire are the people who strive to retain their links with the community and not indulge in their own consciousness to such a degree that they become very rarified, like Henry James.

DCC: The idea of consciousness in the West is linked to the notion of imposing order on chaos, reason on the unreasonable, structure on the unstructurable, and boundaries on the infinite. And like Thomas Hardy, your novels often reveal a life governed by accidents where people are at the mercy of fate.

Frances Wingate feels that she owes her good luck 'to fate, and to chance'. In that novel, *The Realms of Gold*, there is the parallel device of the mislaid postcard that we also find in Hardy's *Tess of the d'Urbervilles*. In *The Ice Age*, Callendar says 'something has gone wrong with the laws of chance'; and of course, that novel is full of accidents of birth, reversals of fortune, random assassinations. If we live in a world of chance and accident, what responsibility does the human 'will' bear?

MD: Well, we certainly do live in a world of chance, there's no disputing that. The duty of the human will is to seek to make sense of it and to resist being swamped by the arbitrary and saying because it's arbitrary there's nothing you can do. You have to endeavour in the face of the impossible. That's what we were put on this earth to do: to endeavour in the face of the impossible.

DCC: To continue with the idea of accident, you have said that life is unfair. People are not born with the same hand of cards. Several characters in your novels want everything but learn that they must settle for much less. Rosamund sees 'the facts of inequality, of limitation, of separation, of the impossible, heart-breaking uneven hardship of the human lot'. Emma sees that the enormity of her hope is the measure of the enormity of her failure and disappointment. But human beings do not accept this philosophical view of life. They do not go gently into the night. Are there perhaps only a few who ever could achieve the 'state of grace', given your definition of it as not fighting one's fate, even if the 'state of grace' came? Or were made possible?

MD: Yes, I think there are very few people who make the moral effort. I think everybody could make it, because everybody is given the spirit to try, but a lot of people give up. They don't continue to strive. They make wrong choices and then they don't fight back when they've made the wrong choices. It's quite obvious that we're all going to grow old and die. And that seems to me to be such an important and interesting fact that there's no point in fighting it. You have to accept the possibility of tragedy. You have to have dignity in the face of the possibility of death and the death of your loved ones and so on. It's more honourable to accept the possibility of disaster than to be a facile optimist or to shut your mind to the possibility of 'grace'.

DCC: I've read so many contradictory interpretations and evaluations of your work. Do you read the critical responses to your novels?

MD: I don't read much of it. I find it confusing and I start worrying about what I really meant. The trouble with critical explanation is that in a novel one is saying so many contradictory things. This is one of the reasons the novel is a form that appeals to me a great deal. But it is not an answer to anything. It's an exploration of a lot of contradictory impulses. There is no correct interpretation of the novel. There is no answer to a novel. A novel is like a person's life. It's full of complexities and therefore any explanation is unsatisfactory. It's the constant flux, the going to and fro between various emotions, that makes fiction interesting to me.

DCC: Criticism does tend to be Procrustean.

MD: Yes, it makes things clear that aren't clear. Life isn't clear. Fiction isn't clear. I mean, it's slightly clearer than life. You mentioned just now the idea of imposing order on chaos. Fiction is not wholly that. To me, it's revealing a pattern in the chaos, seeking for a pattern. There isn't necessarily a pattern. It's one's duty, it's one's nature to look for the pattern. But there may not be one. And if at the end of the day or at the end of the novel you see there is no pattern, or that it really is just bad luck for all the characters, then you have to face it.

DCC: Critics often discuss the use of images and symbols in a writer's work as though they were the product of a deliberate, conscious, and coherent effort. Yet several novelists, yourself and Robertson Davies for example, have said that they write from the unconscious, and you have gone so far as to say, 'I don't know what my images mean. . . . I use them because I don't know what I mean in words.' Are criticism and art essentially at odds with each other?

MD: They are different activities of the brain. Criticism can quite validly illuminate the meaning of symbols that the writer perhaps wasn't conscious of. Somebody will say to you, 'Well, you use such an image because it suggested so-and-so', and you look back and you think, 'Yes, that's absolutely right.' But it doesn't arrive out of the part of the brain that makes the comment. It arises out of another part of one's being. I can look back at a book after ten years and see what the symbols are meant to be doing. But when I'm writing it, I don't coldly construct a symbol. Mary McCarthy has written the most brilliant thing on symbolism. She says that all the leaves on a tree are naturally all the same, and of course they are. And that's the way symbols grow. It's not that you're thinking, 'I'll make that symbol fit with that symbol.' It's just that your preoccupations are a certain area of subject matter or feeling, and therefore the symbols grow out of that. But sometimes, people's comments are very revealing. It's a very dangerous game, criticism, because you're seeing things that were not necessarily in the writer's mind, and could not have been in the writer's mind. Now, a very interesting essay about *The Realms of Gold* pointed out that I clearly was quoting from Darwin, and that the bank that Frances Wingate sits on as she looks at the newts is the bank in the last paragraph of *The Origin of Species*. I happened not to have read *The Origin of Species*, so it couldn't have been. But then I read the Darwin and she was absolutely right. I mean, there was the very bank, and of course the book is about evolution. I hadn't thought of connecting the octopus and newts and these strange forms of life. But, from the critics point of view, the comments she was making were valid. She thought I had read *The Origin of Species*. But, for me, the connection was in the unconscious. They weren't symbols, they were just things I'd observed and found interesting. I knew that Frances Wingate was the kind of person who'd have found it interesting.

DCC: Various critics have perceived a formidable range of 'isms' in your work – Calvinism, existentialism, empiricism, determinism, and nihilism. How useful do you find these terms in response to your work?

MD: I try not to think about them. No, I never sit down and think, 'Well, now I'll write about Calvinism or now I'll write about empiricism.' It's perfectly valid to spot bits of Calvinism in my work. But we could spot bits of Calvinism in almost anybody who'd ever read the mainstream books in English literature. I mean, you're bound to be affected by it. I find the existentialist writers very arid. I'm quite interested in the people who write to me about free will and determinism. I find that such a fascinating problem. But then I'm not the first person who found that interesting; it just is an interesting question.

DCC: I was fascinated in *The Ice Age* by your use of Boethius. *The Consolation of Philosophy* seems to be important to the meaning of *The Ice Age*. Anthony asks many of the same questions as Boethius – the nature of chance, the disintegration of empires, the logic and illogic of history, and to use Edith Milton's words, the place of private enterprise and private happiness in a system which seems governed by the iron laws of chaos. There are parallels between Anthony's life and Boethius' life. Both of them were former successes; they were both convicted for political ideas they in fact never really held; they both have a transcendent delight in music and birds; and they both search for meaning in the midst of events which defy it. Could you comment on your use of Boethius?

MD: What a very difficult question. I only thought of Boethius rather late in the day. I was thinking of the difference between philosophy and religion, and which of them was truly more consoling. I find it extremely difficult to say why I used him, except to say that he was living through hard times, as Anthony was, and worrying about the fate of civilization. That's why I used him. It's as simple as that.

DCC: Simple as that [*laughs*]. I feel as though I'm doing a parody of myself as critic [*both laugh*].

MD: I also thought, to be honest, that there was something quite funny about the fact that Anthony was reading *The Consolation of Philosophy*. It had a comic aspect to it. He's got *The Consolation of Philosophy* in prison. In the airport he's reading *Antigone* who died for a lost cause, and John Le Carré which he can't make head or tail of. And then he comes across *The Consolation of Philosophy*. Well, that was partly just a joke. It was partly a joke, but it was a serious joke.

DCC. Scholars and critics invariably have a yardstick of superiority and inferiority. You have said in your book on Arnold Bennett that you dislike those who insist on marking books as though for an examination. What is the appropriate critical response? How do you respond critically to literature? Or is critically a word you would even use?

MD: It's not a word I use. I read to find out what's going on in the world and I read to find out what's going on in me. I don't think in terms of critical evaluation very much. I know that some books mean a great deal to me that wouldn't necessarily be described as 'good' or 'great' books. They've taught me something that I didn't know.

DCC: I agree for the most part. So often the 'seriousness' of your novels is stressed. Yet I find your books full of humour; for example, Karel's false teeth hanging around Frances' neck. In *A Summer Bird-Cage*, Sarah says, 'I dislike a book without jokes' and Frances enjoys the idea that God had created everything 'for fun' in *The Realms of Gold*. Would you sometimes like to insert a note to the reader, 'Laugh here'?

MD: Yes, I suppose I would. I mean I think my books are quite funny. The people who read me properly also think they're funny. For me, a book should also be entertaining.

DCC: 'Entertainment' seems to be a dirty word in the literary world. It is a word that has haunted Graham Greene's reputation.

MD: There are some books one wants to read. There are some writers that one respects immensely and just never wants to read again. And I would like to think that life itself is an interesting mixture of the serious and the amusing.

DCC: I know what you mean about reading a book and knowing it's important, yet something is missing. I felt that way as well when I read Stendhal's *The Red and the Black*. I was aware that I was in the presence of greatness but I did not like the book.

MD: Yes. But I think that may just be you and me. It's not for us. There are other people who consider it a passionately moving work. We simply don't see it that way. Whereas, Flaubert's *Madame Bovary* or *Sentimental Education* are absolutely wonderful. And I can't quite see why. Why should I like one so much and not the other?

DCC: I have always wondered that myself. I think that we are wrongly led to feel that at any point in our life we should recognize the greatness of a book. I think we come to different books at different times in our life.

MD: Yes. Doris Lessing says that 'you find what you need and it isn't necessarily great literature at all'. It's just what you need for your mind to work on, or your spirit to be moved by at the time. And there it is. I mean, it doesn't matter whether it's good or bad. It's in some ways furthering your own being. On the other hand, on the academic critical side, I think it is possible, to do the critics and the academic world justice, to make oneself, by education, like things that one hasn't a natural feeling for. I'm reading Spenser's *The Faerie Queene* at the moment. And frankly, it's not the kind of thing that one picks up lightly. But you can get your ear in by forcing yourself to read it. You can get your ear in and then you can like it. You can gain a certain pleasure from it. But I shall never get the pleasure from it that I get from Shakespeare. I was having an argument with a friend of mine about Christopher Marlowe. He was saying what a frightfully bad playwright Marlowe was and how overrated he was these days, and how he wasn't a patch on Shakespeare. I agreed. He's not as good as Shakespeare. But nevertheless, it seems to me that if you can't hear Marlowe's verse, there's something wrong with you. I said to him, 'You mean you can't hear these lines.' He said, 'Well, they're very monotonous.' And I thought, 'Well, why should I bother with him. There's plenty of things he does enjoy, why should I try and make him like Marlowe.' On the other hand, I do like Marlowe and because I like him, I feel that everybody ought to see it.

DCC: Well, you want to share your enthusiasm.

MD: Yes, you want to share it. This is good teaching.

DCC: I've often been surprised that novelists that I've talked to are unfamiliar with various critical methodologies and debates. Are you familiar with current literary aesthetics? Are you influenced? Or do you care?

MD: I try to keep very, very far away from it. It's extremely dangerous for a writer if you become self-conscious in a way that is not good for you. Linguistic analysis is terribly dangerous because your style is like the shape of your face. You have grown it that way. It expresses you. It's much better to unconsciously develop than to start imposing something on yourself from outside.

DCC: I take it you haven't developed a particular aesthetic theory?

MD: No. I think images grow in the dark. If you bring them out into the light, they shrivel up.

DCC: I like that. You have described Doris Lessing as 'one of the very few novelists who have refused to believe that the world is too complicated to understand'. When Frances in *The Realms of Gold* visits her cousin's apartment, she sees a translucent block of quartz and it moves her to observe that, 'Human nature is truly impenetrable.' However, the welter of contradictions that is humanity is not a source of despair for you as it is for some other writers. Suicide or survivor, weak or strong, fragile or resilient, tormented or secure, we all seem to reflect for you, without judgement, aspects of life.

MD: Yes.

DCC: Does it never plunge you into despair?

MD: Occasionally it does, but not most of the time. If it comes to me as a real despair, I stop writing altogether and shut off. But, no, I keep on trying to make sense of the incomprehensible. Frances had been so bloody pleased with herself all through the book and she decided that she couldn't really understand after all. It doesn't matter that one can't understand, it's still very interesting. Life is very interesting.

DCC: The contradictions in your novels remind me of the medieval understanding of conflict. Life's contradictions were unified by a system of parallels in contrast. René Guénon has talked about the universal whirlwind which brings opposites together and engenders perpetual motion, metamorphosis and continuity, in situations characterized by contradictions. In your novels, you very often have contradictions that are part of a whole; the millstone is both a burden and a salvation; love is both destructive and nourishing; freedom and bondage go together; hardship and sorrow can be in themselves a source of great joy; our possibilities and our limitation both trap us. Is it fair to say that these contradictions are not in opposition so much as a part of the whole?

MD: Yes, as part of the whole. Yes. Life is a constant shifting from one extreme to the other. This is the dynamic movement of D. H. Lawrence; the fact that everything turns into its opposite or is both at once.

DCC: One contradiction that is seemingly whole is motherhood. On the one hand, it is destructive; it perverts character. On the other hand, it is fulfilling; it gives great joy. Rosamund is both destroyed and created by having her baby. You have said that your own children have given your life reassurance and regularity. Do you see motherhood still in those terms?

MD: I see motherhood in such positive terms that I feel almost embarrassed to state it. I think it's the greatest joy in the world. But it is also a very personal thing. I just happen to like it. And it's a relationship that, in fact, avoids the problems of sex. It's a very pure form of loving, which sex rarely is. The accepted view today is that sex is a power struggle of some sort or other; or else it's fragile and about to go wrong. Whereas, maternal or paternal love is permanently good. I see parental love as an image of God's love. There's a wonderful bit in *Ulysses* where Stephen Daedelus looks at a little boy, and thinks that his mother loves him and God loves him, although he's so ghastly. I think this is true, that you love your children in a way that has nothing to do with reason or with justice. It has a great deal to do with goodness and love and lack of self-interest.

DCC: Yet most of your characters are not close to their families. Families are very often paralysing in your novels.

MD: Well the older generation are, but my mothers usually get on well with their babies. The younger women do. I think, paradoxically, being a daughter is not much fun. But being a mother is wonderful [*laughs*]. Was it E. M. Forster who said that we can never love our parents as they have loved us? And that's true. So you're redeemed by your love for your children. But they never love you back quite as much. I also do think, seriously, that it's much easier to be a good parent now than it used to be. In England, family life was frigid and rigid and difficult. Nowadays, certainly among the people that I know, it's much more flexible.

DCC: You feel that environment directly influences personality. In your essay on Thomas Hardy, you stated that 'landscape is seen to determine character' in both the novels of Thomas Hardy and Emily Brontë. You have also said that people in the north of England have something wrong with them; they are sour and it is something either in the water or in the chemicals or in the environment that is hostile to human happiness. Frances in *The Realms of Gold* agrees and adds that it is also the flatness of the landscape. But this 'sourness' helped to give creative shape to some of Arnold Bennett's novels. Also landscape feeds our dreams, lost or realized. It also feeds our arts, as I think you have so beautifully shown in *A Writer's Britain*. Again, this contradiction...

MD: Yes. In *The Realms of Gold* when I discussed the Midlands as 'bad for you', it was partly a joke. I wasn't entirely serious. This is something I think about quite a lot, that living in an urban landscape probably isn't very good for the spirit. This is what *The Middle Ground* is about. It is the paradox that living in an urban landscape is difficult and that it's one's duty to confront the difficulty rather than going off like Wordsworth and living with lakes and trees. Certainly his writing is nourished by lakes and trees.

DCC: Both Arnold Bennett and yourself saw your childhood environment in a better light when you returned as adults. Was it simply the sentiments of the returning conquerors?

MD: No. I always loved the part of the world that I was brought up in. I always thought it was extremely beautiful. I think that's something to do with age. Living in London gets more and more tiring. And there's a lot to be said for living somewhere more peaceful. I don't think I'd like to live in a provincial town again, but I wouldn't mind living in Yorkshire, the countryside.

DCC: When you wrote the introduction to *The Millstone* in 1970, you said that you admired the way some writers can show characters undergoing a process of change – developing, growing, softening, hardening. At the time, you felt that *The Millstone* was the only one of your novels that showed this process. Do you feel that you've shown this change in any of your later novels?

MD: Not very much. No. I tend to use rather a short time span; the characters haven't got time to change very much really. I'm never quite sure if people do change. Somebody pointed out to me that I tend to work the time span of my novels to be almost exactly the time span I take to write the book, which is nine months to a year, sometimes even shorter than that. Also the changes are usually in the past. What I usually do is take characters who are reassessing how they've got to be what they are, rather than showing, as in a Bennett novel, the time span viewing how they become it. I admire people who can do the longer time span. But I tend to look back rather than carry them through the course of the book. I find it more interesting for some reason.

DCC: Your particular narrative style has opened up the form of fiction. You shift effortlessly between the third- and first-person narrators. In your later novels, you use a multiple narrative viewpoint also very well. Your third-person narrator never intrudes, isn't necessarily omniscient. I find myself having consciously to register that now I'm back in the 'third' person or the 'first' person, because it all seems to float so beautifully together, yet still observing.

MD: I'm never quite sure who the third person narrator is. It's not quite me. But I do have a sense, sometimes in the middle of a novel, that there are things happening in the novel that the narrator doesn't know about, and the narrator sometimes comments on that. And they really don't know what's going on. That's what I feel about life. There are some people that I understand very well, there are some people that I don't understand, but they're there alright, and they just have to act in the novel and be in the novel without being fully understood. This is very different from the kind of novelist, like Muriel Spark, who manipulates the characters entirely, and knows exactly what everybody is doing. She makes them do it. My narrator, not I, is more of an observer, who is sometimes astonished by what is going on. As indeed one is in real life. One is very surprised to hear that so-and-so suddenly left so-and-so; or suddenly married so-and-so; or decided to have another baby at the age of forty-three. You think, 'Good God!' And yet you know that that is how life is and your characters behave in this peculiar way as well. And I think my narrator has this slightly bewildered attitude toward some of the events of the book.

DCC: Yes. And that's unique. I haven't ever seen anybody else do it quite that way. You also often talk to the reader, which is a device we see in nineteenth-century novels and more recently in the work of John Fowles. For instance, in *The Realms of Gold* you invite the reader to 'invent a more suitable ending if you can'. What are your reasons for this technique?

MD: I've got lots of reasons for it. The reason I say 'invent a more suitable ending if you can' is that I was perfectly aware that my feminist critics weren't going to like my ending the book with a marriage. It seemed to me a perfectly good ending. But, I said, 'If they really think there's a happier way of living for this particular woman and this particular man, then let them, indeed, (and I didn't mean it ironically) let them indeed create their own lives in which they do something different rather than telling me that I should have done it differently myself.' It's asserting one's own right to do what one wants with one's own characters, but conceding that not everybody's going to agree with you. I also intrude at times just to remind people that it's a story, a mixture of life and reality. There's a bit towards the end of *The Waterfall* where Jane says, 'Goredale Scar is a real place. It exists, unlike James and myself.' This was meant to be, I suppose, a reflection on the fact that Goredale Scar is a real place. And if anybody wants to go and look at it, they can. But, in a sense, it's less real than the passions of the characters, who, although fictitious, are emblematic in some way, or true beyond truth. True beyond the material representation. They're not real people, but they're true.

DCC: Could you describe *The Middle Ground* in your own words?

MD: I can't find the words to describe it. Writing the blurb was a nightmare because nothing really happens in it at all. It's about a woman journalist who has written about women's matters. And she's reached a stage where she's rather fed-up with the narrow little ditch that she's got herself stuck in, which could be an analogy for the novelist who is fed up with the feminist critics. She can't get out of this particular position because she's got absolutely nowhere to go. She's an uneducated girl who has been very lucky to have had a flair. She could never write a book because she hasn't got the staying power. And so she's really wondering what the hell to do next. Where do you go from there? Do you just repeat your life? Or do you break out and do something else? There is not a very satisfactory answer to this in the book. The book, in fact, ends up with a literary joke, a Mrs Dalloway-type party, and ends on a note of total ambiguity. I call it 'guarded optimism' in the blurb, in that it's a pretty miserable book. I got a friend of mine to proof-read it for me. And she looked pretty bleak at the end of it. She said, 'Oh dear, that was depressing.' However, some of it is quite funny. *The Middle Ground* is about living in London. It's not quite as gloomy as *The Ice Age* because the things that happen aren't as bad. But it's partly a feeling of discontent and malaise and middle-of-the-road. I wanted to call it *The Middle Years* but Henry James had got the title. Or I wanted to call it *The Light of Common Day*. I was very keen on that idea, which is Wordsworth again. *The Middle Ground* is about one's children growing up. My children are all teenagers now, and it's hilarious but ghastly. I've dedicated it to my daughter, because I use quite a lot of copy from her. It's about being a mother to teenage children and knowing that the children are going to be gone any minute now. And you've done all the things in your life you meant to do – what next? She knows there's something next and she doesn't know what it is. And it's about whether or not she's still a proper feminist. She had always thought she was a proper feminist. But she's getting very, very sulky with all the people who go on at her about what a feminist she is. (It is in a way a response to, not so much feminist criticism, but feminist journalism. The novel is about the change of tone and consciousness. And whether feminism is still a good cause.) Do you just go on reiterating the old platitudes that you think everyone else ought to bloody well know by now? And she's bored with herself. That's what it's about.

3 Nadine Gordimer

DCC: You have stayed in South Africa when other writers have left because, as you have said, 'the roots of other countries, however desirable, were not possible for a plant conditioned by the flimsy dust that lies along the Witwatersrand'. You have also talked about the way white culture superimposed foreign literary forms upon the rich oral tradition of the blacks, without any attempt to incorporate those forms. Blacks suffered the suppression of black culture; whites, in turn, now suffer the deprivation of never having had the good sense to appropriate anything from those traditions. Have you ever benefited from that tradition in your writing?

NG: Not in the style because you must remember that there was no written literature in South Africa...

DCC: I thought in hearing...

NG: Yes, of course, I benefited enormously from the human contact, from coming in contact with different attitudes to life which arise out of the African tradition. I do believe that we are all basically exactly the same in our *needs*. But these needs have been formulated and dealt with differently by different societies and it is always extremely enriching to make this contact. This is the charm, for instance, of being in an Italian village, of seeing how people deal with their children, of the way young people behave when they are in love, the different patterns of life. All express the same thing and all, when it comes to art, seek to explain the inexplicable in life, seek to find a form that transcends the business of being born, living through life, procreating, dying.

DCC: The political nature of your work is often stressed. Yet, in 1965, you said that: 'I am not a politically minded person by

This interview first appeared in *London Magazine*, February 1983.

Nadine Gordimer (*photograph: Trevor Clark*)

nature. I don't suppose, if I had lived elsewhere, my writing would have reflected politics much. If at all.' Do you still hold to that view now?

NG: Yes, I wonder! I think I would cross out the final phrase, 'if at all'. Obviously if I had lived elsewhere, even in apparently 'happy' countries, like Sweden and Canada, shall we say, there are always particular trends in society, particular problems, that would again affect people's lives, that would have come into my work, so that there would have been perhaps directly or indirectly some kind of political concern. But I certainly think it would have impinged much less upon my imagination.

DCC: Grigory Svirsky, the author of *Hostages: The Personal Testimony of a Soviet Jew*, said to me that unpolitical writers have been invented by American literary scholars. I got a feeling from you that you would agree with Svirsky that writers are political.

NG: Yes. Novelists and short story writers provide implicitly a critique of their society. The proof of that is the importance given to Balzac's *Human Comedy* by critics in the Eastern European countries, critics who stem from the extreme left. Balzac himself was an extremely conservative person politically, very reactionary, but in his *Comedie Humaine* he gave such a truthful, marvellous picture of that very society of which he was part, that in the eyes of the leftist critics, socialist critics, he gives an unbeatable picture of what was wrong with the bourgeoisie at that time, of the seeds of its own destruction that were within it. A good writer can't help revealing the truth that is in his society and by that token there is a political implication and he is politically committed.

DCC: In your writing the life of the imagination is often a public creation. You have commented that: 'in a certain sense a writer is "selected" by his subject – his subject being the consciousness of his own era. How he deals with this is, to me, the fundament of commitment.' How do you differ from writers whose subject is not their own era but rather themselves?

NG: It all depends upon the range of the writer. There are some people who may be wonderful writers but they are their own principal subject. There is a whole school of writing like that. Names immediately spring to mind, people like Céline and Gênet. There are many writers like this. In a sense, one can say that such work is narrow, that the writers apparently cannot go beyond themselves, but on the other hand there is often so much *within them* that perhaps in the end to know one human being fully is enough, even yourself… Other writers with a different approach and a different kind of scope often choose to write about people very, very different from themselves and I have been that kind of writer. The main character in *The Conservationist* is somebody who is extremely unlike me and lives a life totally unlike the life that I live. There are other characters in my books who do live the kind of life that I live and would approximate somehow to my opinions and my convictions. I would dismiss any suggestion that my fiction is spun entirely out of my own life. That it is spun out of my own society is another matter. Goethe once said: 'wherever you live, if you thrust your hand deep into the life around you, what you bring up will be something of the truth'. I think the key phrase there is to stick your hand into the muck or into the rose petals or whatever there is *there*.

DCC: Your work has evolved from a literary tradition that was South African to one that is defined as African or what you have called an 'African-centred consciousness'. Your later novels, *The Conservationist*, *Burger's Daughter* and *July's People*, reflect this change. Because there are so many different cultures on the continent of Africa, what are the links between such varied societies, over and above the experience of colonialism?

NG: Oh, I think there are very deep links and they are in the African peoples. There are strong threads that run from country to country that characterize African life. There is, as you know, a Tower of Babel of languages and there are many different religions and many different ideas in African societies but there is a greater similarity, a greater instinctive understanding between people of different countries within the African continent than between the people in Spanish countries and the people of Europe or of North America or the Far East. There is some kind of basic cultural link. I distrust people – writers, too! – who lean upon a mysticism of the land and the earth but the fact is that there is something that comes through from the earth itself in each continent. And I think that even if you are white, if you were born in Africa and you have rejected both consciously and subconsciously the colonial consciousness, if you are not just floating on the surface of the society in which you live and ignoring its true entities which are the overwhelming presence of black people, if you don't ignore this then you too share in the real sense of Africa, the human sense of Africa and the physical sense of the land. It enters into your work through your perceptions. Where do writers get their earliest perceptions? They come from the quality of the light, the kind of mud you play with, the kind of trees you climb. Well, I am white, but those trees and that mud were Africa, so they are inside me and they come out, I suppose, in one's work.

DCC: In most of your novels and some of your short stories, you seem to ask what kind of white commitment and participation are morally and realistically possible for white men and women during and after black revolutionary struggles. Elie Wiesel has written that 'some words are deeds'. Do you think that the act of writing is a physical act in a political sense?

NG: It is. In a country like South Africa, as in Eastern European countries and the Soviet Union, writing is an act. It is an act in the way that a novel by Saul Bellow is *not* an act in America. It may be a revelation, but it is not an act. But the revelatory function of literature becomes an act in a country where much is suppressed or where much is called by the wrong name or much is concealed; where so much is double talk. However, I would still draw the distinction between that and the kind of other direct act that I was talking about, in a sense the non-verbal act, though it may also involve words – joining a political party, appearing on a platform, being active in an underground organization, even being a fellow traveller with an underground organization. In countries like Czechoslovakia, like South Africa, like Argentina, guilt by association is a fact and therefore the friendships you form can be a political act. This circumstance, this way of life, is very complex. People think that a political act is signing a declaration or planting a bomb, but there are all kinds of political acts in countries where there is a great political struggle going on.

DCC: In his Nobel prize address, Solzhenitsyn said: 'It is within the power of world literature in these troubled times to help mankind truly to comprehend its own nature and to transfer concentrated experiences from some of its parts to others.' In *July's People*, Maureen discovers that 'no fiction could compete with what she was finding she did not know, could not have imagined or discovered through imagination'. That character seems to be contradicting Solzhenitsyn.

NG: Yes, there is a contradiction there but that contradiction is indeed the very challenge of literature, the very challenge that your work gives you as a writer. It comes back to something you quoted from me before: to find the right form and the right words to contain what you discovered, what you *know*, what you are in the process of discovering. Now, Maureen tests a writer or writers and finds them wanting. Perhaps that is a message even to myself in that book because *I* am writing that book. I am writing her story. Have I written her story in a way that she would find meaningful, that would relate to the experience itself or would it fall far below it?

DCC: The personal life of many of your characters is often drained by their political life, recently explored in *Burger's Daughter*. Is it inevitable that one obliterates the other or are they one and the same?

NG: I don't think it is inevitable but I think, from life-long observation and involvement with people affected by politics by one way or another in South Africa, that radical political involvement imposes an enormous strain on personal life. Let us take an extreme example. I know a couple who were both highly involved in politics, active in the most active sense of the word and the husband received a long sentence. This is a white man and he went into jail. It was apparently a good marriage, they were young, they had a small child, they were in love, they appeared to be happy. Naturally, I am sure (here is a gap that the writer fills) that she must have assured him – 'seven years – you know I will be here, it is all right, this is part of our life, of being politically active here'. But the fact is that while the seven years were passing, she was young, she met somebody else and indeed she divorced that man while he was serving that long sentence. Now how are we to judge her, how do we know how he feels about it? He was shut up in prison, he couldn't fall in love with somebody else. She was outside, young, good looking, in exile, struggling to look after their child and still taking part in political action in exile, and she met somebody else and fell in love with him. Perhaps she lived with him and felt, 'it will be an affair, and when my husband comes out it will end'. Maybe the affair became stronger than the memory of the marriage, and they married. Well indeed, there is a novel I am giving you there [*both laugh*]. But this shows you the kind of strain, the kind of complication that a dedication to politics (this is an extreme level) brings into people's lives. And then again there is the question of how different people deal with it. She divorced and married someone else and when her husband came out he had to start his personal life all over again. There was a political case a few years ago involving a black man and the man got twelve years. It isn't easy for people to go and see their relatives when they are in jail. And his wife, a simple woman, as we say, a country woman with a blanket around her, jumped up in court and shouted, 'twelve years, my husband, it's nothing!' I am still moved when I think of it. It was such an extraordinary thing. Now I wonder what happened to her. Did she stick by that cry, 'it's nothing!'? I don't know because I did not know them. These are some of the strains imposed by the political or the personal life. In *Burger's Daughter* I have looked into what happens to the children, what effect does the political faith and involvement of their parents have upon them.

DCC: The children of radical parents sometimes do not want the legacy. They have a desire to distance themselves from the tradition of radical political commitment they are born to. Bobo in your novel *The Late Bourgeois World* wishes his family were like other people; that they didn't care. Rosa Burger understands that 'even animals have the instinct to turn away from suffering. The sense to run away.' Is the legacy of radicalism sometimes as oppressive as the legacy of conservatism?

NG: I am proposing something there. I am asking, I'm not stating, whether or not they want the legacy. I am asking whether there isn't sometimes resentment at that legacy and whether there isn't a point where a young person wonders why this legacy should have been imposed, why other people can live more easily. That, of course, is the point for taking off with Rosa Burger in *Burger's Daughter*.

DCC: That novel illustrates the way in which black activists have been ignored while white South African activists attract world attention. Whites articulate black grievances – they become their voices. Lionel Burger is memorialized on television and in the papers, whereas no one seems to remember that Baasie's father, too, had died in prison for fighting apartheid. Is it changing now?

MG: Yes. Apart from the prominence of black political martyrs, such as the great Steve Biko, there is a whole new generation of black writers coming up to speak for blacks. I welcome this as absolutely right and necessary. But I think that if terrible things are happening in a country, let whoever has the talent and the knowledge bear them forth. Black or white, painter, writer or musician. White and black live separated and there are areas of life lived by blacks that I don't think a white writer is qualified to write about. And the same applies to blacks writing about whites, though it's mostly academic because few blacks attempt to do this. Perhaps they feel they have enough subject matter among their own people. But, at the same time, for three hundred and fifty years and more, we have been not merely rubbing shoulders but truly in contact with one another, despite the laws, despite everything that has kept us apart; there is a whole area of life where we know each other. And I really say the word *know*. Yes, we know each other in ways that are not expressed. We know the different hypocrisies that come out of our actions and our speeches; indeed we know each other in the sense that we can read between the lines. Sometimes if I am with a black friend or an acquaintance, there are two sets of conversations going on. There is what is being said and what is unspoken. But each understands what the other has not said and this is truly *knowing*. Now there is so much of that *knowing* that it is a subject in itself. I talked recently to a young black playwright called Moise Maponye, and he was very bitter. He had got up at a writers' meeting. His remarks were directed against white writers generally. He said, 'whites take our lives and make their books out of them, and these books are published and everybody reads them and nobody wants to publish my play'. It was a typical statement born of confusion, literary and ideological standards and all sorts of strains and undercurrents. So after this gathering I went up to him, because I know him well, and said, 'look, do you really think that you cannot write about somebody like me and other whites that you know? You have lived among us so long, we talk together, we have rows, and moments of empathy... There are other areas in which, obviously, you have mixed with whites and there are other relationships in your life; you can't tell me that you are not fit to write about us. Of course you are.'

DCC: Toni Morrison has said that you write about black people in a way that few white writers have ever been able to write. It is not patronizing, nor romanticizing, it is the way they should be written about.

NG: I would say the answer is that I don't romanticize because I don't feel patronizing. The relationship that I have with blacks I am prepared to deal with honestly, and indeed I am having to question myself all the time because I have been brought up like every other white South African – I would say everybody else of my generation. I think of my children who have been brought up with a very different attitude toward people who may have a different colour. I feel I have gone through the whole bit, you know. I have gone through the bit of falling over backwards and apologizing because I am white. I have thought about it all, worked my way through it all, and achieved a position which as a human being is unsatisfactory, but at least I hope is honest. I feel inadequate as a human being in my situation as a white South African but as a writer I think I have arrived at a stage through my work where if I write about blacks or I create black characters, I feel I have the right to do so. I know enough to do so. I accept the limitations of what I know.

DCC: You have written that 'the human condition is understood dynamically, in an historical perspective'; that these themes are statements or questions arising from the nature of the society in which the writer finds herself immersed and the kind and quality of the life around her. What are the aesthetic requirements of 'the novel as history'?

NG: I think the aesthetic requirements are the requirement of the novel *per se*. It is the attitude of the novel as history that sits the novel on a particular grid, so to speak, on a particular framework. Again this slippery element of the truth comes into it. We come back to Balzac. What he wrote was history, a remarkable social history of part of nineteenth-century France. The requirements there are not just truth to events, you could check dates in any history, but an attempt to discover what people think and feel and most important, the most important requirement to my mind, would be to make a connection between their personal attitudes and actions and the pressures of the historical period that shapes such actions. So that if you are living during a time when one portion of the population is extremely affluent and the other is very poor, the historical importance of that work of fiction would be in how it would show that that extremely affluent group managed to justify their existence to themselves, never mind the world, while round the corner they knew there was a starving mob, in their houses they had the daughters of a starving family scrubbing floors. I think that is where the novelist goes much further than the historian. The historian can tell you the events and can trace how the events came about through the power shifts in the world. But the novelist is concerned with the power shifts within the history of individuals who make up history.

DCC: The details of life.

NG: Yes.

DCC: Georg Lukacs defined critical realism as a work in which 'everything is linked up with everything else. Each phenomenon shows the polyphony of many components, the intertwinement of the individual and social, of the physical and the psychical, of private interest and public affairs.' In *A Guest of Honour*, you quoted Turgenev as a central motif to the novel: 'an honourable man will end by not knowing where to live'. In *Occasion for Loving*, Jessie turns to the novels of Joseph Conrad and Thomas Mann. One of the epigraphs is a quote from Mann: 'in our time the destiny of man presents its meaning in political terms.' Do you see your work in relation to the European critical realists, particularly Balzac, Stendhal, Conrad, Turgenev and Mann?

NG: Not really, not in relation to *the* critical realist, Balzac. As time has gone by, certainly, I have sought more and more to find the one form to fit each particular novel and it is always a different form, so the nineteenth-century novel of Balzac can't contain what I want to say. The last novel that I wrote in that way was *A Guest of Honour* and even then it had elements obviously influenced by my great mentor Marcel Proust, and many others whose work I read when I was young. But they go unacknowledged because, as someone said, they taught you something and then you forget that they taught it to you and you carry on from there. Indeed, people are rather amazed when I say that I had and continue to have this feeling that I was tremendously influenced, like so many writers, by Proust. My view of the world was changed by him; a film was peeled off my eyes and I understood my life and my own emotions in a way profoundly influenced by him. People would think that the Proustian view of life, when one is looking at and living in a country like South Africa, would seem unsuitable. Proust does not deal with that kind of event, really, at all, except perhaps the Dreyfus case and that was drawing-room politics, wasn't it? But influences are part of the whole business of finding your own style as a writer. You experiment on the basis of all sorts of things you have learned, to find a way to express your particular vision. For me, style and content must be married completely or the approach to a piece of writing does not work. I couldn't write *The Conservationist* the way I wrote *A Guest of Honour*. The style for *The Conservationist* essentially had to express the kind of disruption, the disjointed consciousness of the central character. And there I had a big problem. I was writing about an unfamiliar country whose laws bring about certain morbid forms of behaviour. Can one leave out entirely an explanation of these laws? Well I did it; I decided that I must find some way of assuming the reader will make the jumps from the consciousness of one person to another to achieve understanding of the effects of the colour-bar laws if not the *letter* of the law itself. So indeed I used (if you want to look for models out of the past) a Proustian, Joycean, Woolfian approach and mode; one just can't say how one evolves these things but I hammered out what was to me the only voice in which to make this book find its particular tone and tell its stories. When I came to *Burger's Daughter*, once again I evolved something for myself. I have moved on stylistically in challenge to new themes that couldn't be expressed in the way the earlier books were. In *Burger's Daughter*, I could not ignore direct information, the way that I chose to do in *The Conservationist*. The theme *would not* allow it. Well, if you want to be very technical about it – and I didn't think about it in a very direct way at the time – it came to me as I was writing the book.

The early life of Lionel Burger, his history – how would this reoccur naturally in Rose's life when she is at that stage when she is concentrating on the past? And then it came to me, well, her father is dead, probably some people or several people are wanting to write about him and they will come to her for the hard facts. Here was a natural, inevitable way of imparting this information, and also of showing how inadequate bald information is. When the future biographer of her father comes to talk to her and he presents her with dates and factual accounts of a political trial in which her father was one of the accused, she relates this to the man she knew, to little incidents at home and references that were inexplicable to her as a child; and now they fit together ... The personal history and the documentation mesh. So these are the ways in which, for me, the form and style of a book come about, through the demands of the content.

DCC: Graham Greene has written that the revision of an author's novel seems endless because 'the author is trying in vain to adapt the story to his changed personality – as though it were something he had begun in childhood and was finishing now in old age'. John Fowles rewrote *The Magus* and Toni Morrison said she would love to go back and rewrite all of her novels.

NG: Something I don't understand!

DCC: If you could go back to *A Guest of Honour*, it would have to be written the way it was originally?

NG Yes. There is an inevitability when I write the last word of the story of a book. Unless there is an inevitability about the way it has come out, then I have failed. I do believe that there is always only one way to write a book. I can't understand people who rewrite. If there is something in a book that I fail to see in the theme at the time that I wrote it, that is indeed part of the book.

DCC: This is in part what you were saying before about searching for a new way of saying something – a search for a new vocabulary. In *July's People*, the irrelevance and inadequacy of our present vocabulary is emphasized. Bam Smales uses formulas like 'counter-revolutionary pockets' and 'rural backwardness' when confronted with an old village chief who wants to help the white government kill the revolutionary blacks. Words like this obscure rather than illuminate. Does the use of symbolism, memory, fantasy and many voices in *The Conservationist* partly eliminate this?

NG: Of course, *The Conservationist* is a book that people make tremendous mistakes about. And I don't mind, really, because life is open to countless interpretations. I like books to be open-ended, so to speak.

DCC: Some have criticized your use of narrative point of view in *The Late Bourgeois World* as mismanagement. I don't agree. Elizabeth's limitation reflects precisely the problems of self and the society she lives in. She doesn't have Max's courage to fail at trying to change the world. She is inclined to play safe. The narrative viewpoint reflects that search for the self, her pseudo-liberalism, her inconsistency as a rebel. Do you feel that critics and scholars react best to narrators who are coherent, rather than to those who are less well-defined voices. Voices that are searching, fumbling, failing, finding and then losing again.

NG: I have never thought about it and of course you are using the term 'react to' pretty broadly. There is the real critic, somebody who has spent his life reading and evaluating literature, and when he looks at a piece of writing, he comes to it with a whole body of literature with which to compare it and evaluate it. Oppose this approach to that of some cub reporter on the Hicksville *Enquirer* who reads a book like a school primer, an isolated taste without reference to the purpose of literature, which is to make experience transcendent. I know that there are some real critics indeed who do welcome any writer's attempt to trap human consciousness in a new way or to take from traditions and recombine them in a way that perhaps somebody else hasn't done because somebody else doesn't *need* to do it. Critics find different things in the same work and that is satisfying too. For instance, Conor Cruise O'Brien reviewed *Burger's Daughter* at length and he reviewed it as a profoundly religious book. This aspect of the novel never occurred to me; I am an atheist. But in a way I think that he is right, if we take the doctrine of suffering and redemption which is explored in that book. In that sense an unbeliever may write a profoundly religious book. Perhaps, indeed, that was what Rosa was struggling against: a doctrine of suffering as a revolutionary for the redemption of a classless freedom. The imposition of faith coming from a profoundly religious background since the kind of Marxism that her parents accepted so uncritically was indeed a religion; it was a demand for faith. So I don't think that one can say that critics worthy of the name respond more to a simple straightforward narrative than to the other one.

DCC: You have said that a writer should write as though she was already dead. What do you mean?

NG: It is something I first said long ago and I keep repeating particularly to myself, because it becomes more and more true to me as my life goes on and as things happen in the world, to me and to other writers. I really think that this is the one freedom that the writer must hang on to desperately. Whether writers are in the Soviet Union, declared mad and put in asylums, whether they are in prisons, whether they are forced into exile, whether they are censored in countries like South Africa and the Latin American States, the writer must claim that freedom. The writer shouldn't be pressed into any kind of orthodoxy – a critics' orthodoxy, a political orthodoxy, a regime's orthodoxy, even the orthodoxy of friendship and loyalty imposed upon him/her by family and friends. The taking of this freedom is both the bravest and the most monstrous side of what a writer *is*. You must give yourself the freedom to write as if you were dead. It is very difficult, and nobody can carry it out to the hundredth degree because you are still alive; you care about your relationships with other people and there are some insights you have but cannot use because you would hurt and destroy, and you would end up by being totally isolated as a human being. But given those extreme cases, I really think that you have in the end to ignore what people say about your writing. I do read reviews, though certainly not all of them. There are a few critics whose opinions I value, whose praise elates me and whose criticism, although it might hurt, although it might annoy me, helps me to stay self-critical. Learning to write comes from your own recognition of what is wrong in your own work. But I think you must claim freedom to do it; that is the way you discover for yourself. Graham Greene has put the claim best: 'To a novelist his novel is the only reality and his only responsibility.' Not everyone will understand that this reality is a transformation of the substance of reality into its essence, and the responsibility is nothing less than an attempt to take on the truth. Kafka said of writing that 'the more independent it becomes, the more incalculable, the more joyful, the more ascendant its course'.

4   Robertson Davies

DCC: In the past, dust-jackets of novels might have summarized the author's life this way: 'Bill Robertson has been a sailor in the merchant marine, a professional magician, a newspaper reporter, an insurance salesman and a concert pianist.' Today the dust-jacket tends to look more like this: 'William Robertson is the recipient of several Canada Council grants, and a fellowship from the Guggenheim Foundation. He has taught Creative Writing at several universities and has a Ph.D. in English.' Your background is more like the former. Both yourself and William Faulkner did not agree with writers applying for grants. How important is diversity and eclecticism to a writer?

RD: It's entirely an individual matter. Some writers have lived restricted, quiet and almost hermit-like lives and that has served them well. Others have done all kinds of extraordinary things and some of them have almost made a professional mannerism of it, like Hemingway who made a great display of expertise in sports and being a he-man and a great drinker and all that sort of thing. It depends entirely on temperament. Writers may be all kinds of people. There have been some academic writers who were very fine indeed but I don't think you can say just what is going to suit a writer.

DCC: Do you weary of being challenged for your élitism, even though like Samuel Marchbanks your writings and statements indicate that you are a 'Concertina Brow', that is to say, neither highbrow nor lowbrow?

RD: People who talk about élitism generally have a motive which is not very much concealed; they are afraid that any application of severe standards is going to exclude them. They take that very personally because they are driven by the North

Robertson Davies (*photograph: Peter Paterson*)

American notion that somehow or other they must succeed on every conceivable level and that anything which stands in the way of their success is necessarily bad. I personally don't care about these standards, and any kind of élitist distinctions which exclude me I am quite prepared to accept and respect, in a reasonable way. For instance, I do not regard myself as being a particularly original thinker or philosopher or even a very highly educated or a coherently educated person, and when people say so, it doesn't grieve me. I know it is true. But I am some other things which enable me to get on, and do what I wish to do. People who become excitable about talk of élitism are ridden by a sense of inferiority. We all are inferior in a great many ways; why make such a big fuss about it? I do irritate people sometimes, I know, by taking attitudes which they resent, and I do it mischievously to irritate them. For example, I'm amused by people who are passionate for what they call innovation and freedom from structured ways of behaviour and who don't want any kind of social pattern in their lives. It seems to me to be much more exhausting to be perpetually inventing a way of living than it is to take a well-understood code of manners or behaviour and live inside it, and think what you like inside it but use it as a means of greasing the wheels of life.

DCC: I assume that you are like your character, Humphrey Cobbler in that you are an advocate of Ornamental Knowledge rather than Useful Knowledge. You have said that you like to rummage in the rubbish heaps of literature.

RD: That is another thing that I say to irritate people who have categories of knowledge that they think are important and others which they discard. I don't believe that there is any such thing as useless knowledge. Now I was a journalist for twenty years (rather more than that, about twenty-two years) and I never found that there was anything I knew or had learned that was not useful to me in some way in my work as a journalist. The more you know, the better you can do almost anything that you set to work to do. So I think that this business of pretending that certain categories of information are absolutely obligatory for everybody is nonsensical. I think that I have seen the 'inclusive' plan work out in the lives of a great many people I know. They know all kinds of curious things that somehow or other come in useful. Everything is useful.

DCC: That's really what you're saying in your writing. You've written two wonderful trilogies. What is there about that form that appeals to you?

RD: Well, nothing; nothing at all. You see, neither of them was intended to be a trilogy. The first one about Salterton is held together only because it's about a particular place, and the people who live in it, and the manner in which they live there. That's the cement that holds it together. The second one is much more a trilogy in that it is three versions of virtually the same story; the same incident gives rise to all three books but they are seen from three different points of view. So that makes it a trilogy. But when I set out to write those books about the Deptford people, I never intended to write a trilogy, I meant to write one book and it just grew into three, without conscious intention.

DCC: The world of dreams, the marvellous, the impossible, the mysterious, all intrigue you. In your novel *Fifth Business*, Father Blazon says that 'mythical elements . . . underlie our apparently ordinary lives'. Is art, literature, the theatre, music, in a sense more real than life in that it orders and makes conscious the poetry and wonder of the dunghill?

RD: Yes, I think it does that and also it keeps reminding us of something which a great many people are perpetually trying to avoid: that is that what we call our minds and our consciousness is an extraordinary jumble of fleeting ideas, half-perceived impressions, intrusions from the unconscious, and all kinds of things which certainly don't make what 'serious' people think of as coherent thought. But, you know, if any of us could have a tape recording of what actually runs through our minds for half an hour, some of us would be shocked: scraps of music, obscenities, irrelevancies, stupidities, apparently quite irrational impressions, as well as a good deal of coherent thinking about what's happening or what we are doing, or something of that kind. The mind is an extraordinary heap of odds and ends.

DCC: Very few people really use the mind in motion. For instance, in some essays or lectures I want to start off by saying 'I am confused.' And then show the mind in motion and confusion because I think so often the questions and confusions are just as important a learning experience as ...

RD: Yes, but they are very difficult for students to seize upon and use, because what they want very often is something which is almost a sermon. They want the Milk of the Word; they want the Truth; they want something from which they need never deviate. And that in the study of things like history and poetry and literature is generally quite out of the question. There is always doubt. And there are always not two, but twenty-two points of view.

DCC: In your novel *Tempest-Tost*, Solly remarks that in Canada 'we have very little ceremonial sense'. All of your work reflects a concern for rituals and a framework. What is their importance?

RD: If they are fine ceremonials and frameworks, they give beauty and a processional charm to life. Now, we are impelled to have ceremonial by just the fact of our humanity and to provide a plan for things that can't exist without a plan; if we don't have good ceremonial, we shall certainly have very bad ceremonial. You observe this all too frequently here in Canada. For instance, when you go to something like a public dinner you observe ceremonial immediately; you see something which I think you ought to resent as intensely élitist – that is that everybody remains standing until the Head Table comes in and sits down. Then immediately you get a ceremonial that follows it; you're asked to drink health to the Queen and you're asked to drink it in cold water. Why? Not because anybody gives a damn about drinking to the health of the Queen (and nobody has any consciousness that it is an age-old idea that if you drink somebody's health in water, you're wishing that they would drown) but simply in order that people may smoke if they want to. Then, when that has been done and some of the meal has been eaten, you have another ceremonial; the chairman gets up and says, 'And now I'm going to present to you your Head Table; please reserve your applause until everyone has been introduced.' Then he introduces the people in ascending order of importance, finishing off with the Big Cheese, whomever it may be. That is another ceremonial, and they all stink. They are all poor, ill-considered, shabby little things instead of doing the thing in a high style. If you don't have good ceremonial, you'll sure as hell get bad ceremonial and it will be the kind of thing I've just been describing, which I find chillingly crude and jejune and hickish [*both laugh*].

DCC: I'm interested in your religious sensibility. You have said that you are religious because you are conscious of unfathomable powers. Benedict Domdaniel in your novel, *A Mixture of Frailties* says that you don't have to be religious to feel the religion in Bach's music. And I'm thinking that Paul Tillich, Carl Jung and yourself have all made a distinction between sign and symbol. For Tillich, a rock by Cézanne was more religious than Christ on the Cross by the sentimental German painter Uhde because Cézanne's rocks had permanence, ultimate concern, honesty in a way that Uhde's did not. In other words, numinosity.

RD: As you say, a nobler feeling had gone into the rock than had gone into the sickly painting. This again, you see, is where I get into trouble. Nobody wants to face the fact that art is remorselessly élitist and that Cézanne, as compared with Uhde, immediately imposes a category: one is a great artist; the other is a commonplace artist. And this is the kind of élitism which seems to me to be inevitable in life. Some people just do things better than others.

DCC: What is the religious sensibility in art for you?

RD: Well, the religious sensibility in art reveals itself, as people like Bernard Berenson say in such a variety of ways, in that it arouses in the beholder and the appreciator, great things which lie beyond what can merely be observed. And you see this particularly in religious painting. You look at a picture of the Madonna and Child and it may be a disgusting chocolate-box picture of a pretty woman with a fat baby, or it may be something which superficially looks like a rather ugly or plain woman with a strange-looking child. But the one arouses a sense of the miracle of the Miraculous Child and of the eternal recreation of life, which the pretty picture does not. The 'pretty' is so frequently the enemy of the great.

DCC: Why are religion and the *Arabian Nights* true in the same way?

RD: Because they are fables which are designed to arouse a deeper sense of meaning inside you. I think, you see, that only very naïve people accept Bible stories as literal truth; I don't think that their meaning becomes apparent if you do simply look at them purely as literal truth. They are stories which have come down to us through an Oriental sensibility – an Oriental concept of storytelling – which has nothing to do with what people think of as truth if you regard truth simply as police court evidence. It seems to me perfectly reasonable that the impact of Christ upon His disciples was so powerful that they said that when they lost touch with Him, He had vanished as though He had risen bodily into the air – the Transfiguration – and disappeared forever. That would be their way of describing a great and transcendent experience, to make it apparent to people to whom they were talking. It's not literal truth; it is something which is intended to convey an emotion and religious sensation. So, too, the *Arabian Nights* is also a kind of teaching book. It's full of fables and moral tales, and so on and so forth. It is intended to arouse in you a sense of the splendour and variety and richness of life rather than to tell you something that really happened. When people try to tell you what really happened, so often it is boiled down to a mere record of incidents which in themselves don't say very much at all. You may be able to describe a traffic accident in that way but you can't describe a very great experience in that way.

DCC: Several contemporary novelists, such as Mary Gordon, Leonard Cohen, Robin Jenkins, and Graham Greene, have explored the relationship of saints to humanity, but I'm fascinated by your exploration. Your notion that saints are not outside humanity but rather that they extend our humanity is intriguing. Dunstan Ramsay in *Fifth Business* must learn that saints are not merely subjects for scholarly knowledge but also for self-knowledge, the saint within oneself. Who or what is that saint?

RD: Hard to answer: it is an extension of your sensibility and your understanding and your personality at what you might call the upper end of the keyboard. If you think of your totality of being as a piano keyboard, there's no use muddling around in the middle octave and always rushing back to middle 'C' as if that was the only place you felt safe. There is the evil which is, let us say, down in the bass end of the keyboard which you should explore for the three-and-a-half octaves in that direction, and there is what is noble and fine which you should explore at the treble end of the keyboard; and you want to have your full seven octaves tuned, rather than just perhaps twelve notes somewhere in the middle. People nowadays are ready and interested to explore the bass end of the keyboard, but what they don't understand is that you can't do it that way; you have to explore both ends if you're going to understand either one. It's like learning to sing, you know. When you're learning to sing, your teacher doesn't say to you, 'I think I'm going to train you to be a very high soprano.' You can't do that. Very high sopranos, have, usually, a not very good, but very substantial deep register. You have to train the voice at both ends, or it isn't effective at either end. This is where the saints fit in, you see. They are the people who are very strong in the treble end of things.

DCC: There are several archetypes in your Deptford Trilogy – *Fifth Business*, *The Manticore* and *World of Wonders*. Since archetypes must be felt in our consciousness and experienced, not just known, have you experienced these archetypes in your own life?

RD: I think everybody experiences them at some time or other. It is simply an occasion when you are seized by feelings which are beyond your rational control, and everybody knows this; people have it when they become very angry. They are frequently seized by feelings which make them do things which they afterwards regret, and which they would never do if they were in full control of themselves, like hitting somebody in the eye or occasionally, in the worst instances, killing somebody. And there is falling in love, which is an archetypal situation, and which is almost inexplicable, and comes to everybody freshly. This is the thing about an archetype; everybody experiences it in their personal way and they think it is new; they think that nobody's ever felt that way before, but of course people have; it's just that the archetype perpetually renews itself in each person who experiences it, and anger and falling in love are two archetypes. Another archetype is the one of what they sometimes call 'the crossroads', where you have to make a very difficult decision which you know is going to influence, if not the whole of your life, at least a considerable amount of the foreseeable part of it. This archetype of being drawn in two different directions is one which most people experience at some time or other, and it's very strong. The thing about an archetype is that you have emotions and a strength of feeling which goes beyond what you can explain simply in terms of the situation. Sometimes people say, 'I don't know why I am making such a fuss about this thing; it really isn't worth all that bother, is it?' Then you know they're in the grip of an archetype; very frequently they're being dragged somewhere by a pattern of feeling which is stronger than merely the surface of their emotion. The patterns are universal but they come freshly to our individual experience.

DCC: You said that you think intuitively, through your fingertips, not through your brain, and you believe in omens, such as the fact that yourself and St Augustine, Tolstoy and Goethe were born on 28th August –

RD: [*laughs*]

DCC: – and the fact that you divined that the Bollandists wrote in 'purple' ink. Barry Callaghan feels that he's a 'diviner'; he feels that he can find water wherever it is hidden with a forked willow branch, and this is an important part of the meaning in his *Hogg Poems*. How important is this intuitive, subconscious force to the art of creation?

RD: Oh it's very important indeed, but I would not want to exaggerate it absurdly or pretend that it's mysterious. I say a great many of these things in order to irritate people who think quite differently and who are very impatient with me when I talk in this way; I make it sound a great deal more mysterious than it is. But I am simply the kind of person who gets his impressions by snap judgements and intuitions, and I am not going to complain about that, because on the whole it serves me very well. It's awfully irritating to people who argue their way through everything, and reason their way through everything. Such people are generally very solemn, and it's fun to tease them.

DCC: Is that what you were doing when you said that the writer really doesn't know what he's doing when he's expressing myths, but he does consciously when he's creating the patterns?

RD: Yes, I feel that's a fair comment.

DCC: I notice that in your novels especially, even though you scorn characters like Hector Mackilwraith who tend to reduce life to mathematical equations and to pros and cons, you also respect the strength and positiveness of those people who believe in this lifestyle. I think that at one level, Dunstan is stronger and more whole simply because he has participated in both the utilitarian world of Deptford and the mystic world of the marvellous. Would you agree with that?

RD: Oh yes. Absolutely. I would agree with that. And you see, although I have a lot of fun with Hector Mackilwraith, he comes out of things very well. He's true to himself, and although he has undergone a miserable adventure and been seized by an archetype, and has been rather roughly used by it, he comes out of it successfully; you know what he's going to do. He's going to get a good civil service job, and that is his idea of heaven. He gets his reward. Oh yes, the world cannot do without such people, but it's unwise to take them too much at their own valuation. I've known people like Hector, and if you give them half a chance, they'll try to make you like themselves. And that's intolerable.

DCC: On the other hand, though, people who are into the mystic world of the marvellous are just as often dogmatic, I find.

RD: That is perfectly true. They are sometimes stupidly and absurdly dogmatic in an area where dogmatism is dangerous and misleading. But you see, one of the things about me which all my life I've had to cope with, and which gets me into an awful lot of trouble, is that I have a strong spirit of mischief inside me which makes me want to see what people will do under certain stimulus, and this leads me to say things which they take perfectly seriously, and then later on they say, 'But you said so and so' and there's no saying to them, 'Oh well, I said that *yesterday*', because they don't understand it. Now I don't particularly know why this is so; there are explanations I can put forward to irritate serious people. One is, that I was told by an astrologer that when I was born the planet Mercury was in the ascendant at the highest point it ever reaches, and this makes me mischievous. That's a conceivable explanation; another is that I have predominately Celtic blood and Celts are sometimes inclined to be mischievous people, and that's why they've been given their dreadful reputation as liars by people who don't understand creative imagination [*laughs*]. That is a possible explanation, I suppose, and also I think I have a rather active sense of humour, which leads me to want to upset people who are very solemn, and the world's full of them. They're awful pests, because they're always certain that their solemnity provides the real explanation of everything, and often they're as stupid as can be [*laughs*].

DCC: I'm very interested in synaesthesia, particularly converting music and its form into langauge. Several great writers, James Joyce, Hermann Hesse, George Moore, Ralph Ellison, Thomas Mann, and yourself are among those who have done this successfully in your writing. What are some of the musical devices that you have transferred to the novel, particularly the Salterton novels?

RD: That's hard to say. I think it is very difficult to do much about music in a novel because music is a language of its own and music is a language of emotion. To try to transfer real feeling from one mode of creation to another is frightfully difficult and never completely successful. Some people have had a try at it because they are fascinated, as I am, with the musical concept of form. I try to give my novels musical form, which I find effective in holding them together. When you don't do that, they are likely to fly apart into pieces. If you have a sense of form which is essentially musical – that there must be introduction, development, coda and so on – you are much less likely to get off at a foolish tangent and make a mess of your book than if you neglect it. You know, Shaw said that he wrote his plays in musical terms and I think that I might claim to write novels in musical terms; they are full of duets, passages of rhapsodic development and concerted passages and also the sort of 'stretti' which come at the end of a novel when everything is quickly pulled together and whisked into a froth; and then you bring the thing to a conclusion, perhaps with a few thumping chords, or perhaps with what musicians call 'a disappointed climax'. That kind of musical form fascinates me.

DCC: What music do you like best?

RD: Oh, I'm fond of a wide variety of music. I used to disturb my musical friends by the breadth of my taste. I'm very fond, of course, of the accepted classical music, Bach, Baroque music, the Romantic composers, extremely fond of the literature of song, particularly German lieder; I'm very interested in a rather neglected area of music, which is the music of England; I'm interested in folk music because when I was a young man I was very interested in the folk songs of the British Isles, and especially Wales which is where a lot of my ancestors came from. And another area that I'm very keenly interested in is what some of my very puritanical musical friends call 'junky opera'. I love opera below the level of the best. I love the best opera, but I also like opera which is way below the best, like Flotow's *Martha* and Benedict's *The Lily of Killarney* and things of that kind. I find them fascinating and I'm comforted that so did James Joyce. You read Joyce carefully and you're perpetually finding echoes of lyrics from things like *The Lily of Killarney* and *Martha* and this is fascinating because it ties in with a theory which I've long had, that you can't know what the best is if you don't know what is other than the best. And if you know what is other than the best in both literature and music, you can find an enormous amount of enjoyment in stuff which is not top-notch but is awfully good. You just try to write an opera as good as *The Lily of Killarney* and you'll find out how good it is. These things did not become enormously popular because they were trash. I'm very fond, for instance, of the operas of Offenbach, which I think are superb; they are now being recognized as masterpieces of the kind of music that they are. But I remember when I was a young man studying music, my teachers were very down on him because he wasn't serious. They thought Brahms was the stuff. My lifelong problem – and also I think one of the things which has made me on the whole a very happy fellow – is that I'm interested in almost everything. I love a good, meaty movie which is just made to entertain. I'm very strong on the concept of entertainment and it seems to me to be one which is frequently neglected by very serious artists in literature and everything else. Entertainment and, of course, narrative.

DCC: As an extension of that, what was there about Jessie Fothergill's novel *The First Violin* that made you use it in *A Mixture of Frailties*?

RD: Because when I was a small boy, it was a book which was to be found in the houses of innumerable people who were intelligent without being immensely cultivated or professionally aesthetic. They read it and they took it seriously. There was a copy in my house which I read when I was a boy, read more than once. It was given to my mother by her boss because he thought that it would be a delicate compliment to her to give her this fine-feathered novel, and it is fine-feathered indeed. But you know, it is also archetypal; the archetypal story of the innocent girl who goes to another country and is aroused from her innocence by the demonic musician von Francius and then finds her true lover in Courvoisier, the violinist. It's an archetypal story and it was a kind of counterpoint to the story I was telling of the innocent girl who went to another country and met the demonic musician and eventually found a better kind of musician, not quite like Courvoisier; it was a counterpoint to Monica's life. And that interested me because I see a lot of truth in *The First Violin*, corny though much of the expression is.

DCC: In your novels, you often consider the relation between the artist and his or her life. What is that relationship essentially?

RD: You see, it is a relationship rather like the coming of religion. You know what Christ said to his followers: You must leave parents, family and all that if you are going to follow Me; that is what the artistic vocation says and that is what is hard for Monica in *A Mixture of Frailties*. She has to do a thing which is frightfully difficult for everyone, and particularly difficult for a Canadian girl of her kind, which is to realize that she is different from, and cannot be held down by, the ideas of her family and her friends. She's got to be something other than they are.

DCC: Another thing that I find interesting in your writing is the Faust legend. Many great writers have been drawn to this legend and you use it in *Fifth Business*, *The Manticore* and *World of Wonders*. It is a central myth in our culture and we find it in music and painting as well – Gounod's opera, Liszt's symphonic poem, Wagner's overture, Busoni's opera, Mendelssohn, Schumann. In painting, we find it in Delacroix, Rembrandt, Kollwitz, Redon, Nolde. But the interpretations differ in focus and very often the legend is changed to suit the artist's vision. What aspect of the Faust legend is most important to you?

RD: I think it is the fact that Dr Faust learned an awful lot from the Devil. Perhaps he didn't learn quite enough from the Devil, and that is something I've tried to explore in some of the things that I've written. Faust was a great scholar but he was a singularly naïve man when he first made his pact with the Devil. He hadn't even come to terms with his sexuality, for instance, and what happens to him in the legend? The first thing that he does is to fall for a simple village girl who is delightful and charming but not the kind of person that you would think would immediately appeal to a man of great breadth of knowledge and cultivation. But this is what happens. If you watch scholars who get into middle age and who have never had any contact with women, they always fall for some simple pretty girl. Now what happens in Goethe's *Faust* is that Faust progresses in Part Two beyond simple Gretchen and he gets to people like Helen of Troy in his sexual relationships, and that is immensely educative. There is much to be learned from contact with what we sometimes think of as the evil or inadmissible in ourselves but which isn't that when examined; it is just what has been rejected.

DCC: Which do you personally prefer in the artist: the mountain torrent or the fountain, the potent enchantress or the bardic singer, the sprinter or the miler?

RD: Oh, I like them all. there's something fascinating about the whole thing.

DCC: Yes, that was the feeling I got. Your work explores the balance between the Dionysian and the Apollonian world. Art is that balance. Whereas D. H. Lawrence, for instance, clearly leans towards the Dionysian. Why is that equilibrium so important to you?

RD: Because it seems to me to be an equilibrium which has its origin in the creative impulse itself. I think that creation is the arising of matter from the Dionysian unconscious of the artist, which is then refined, undergoes a selective process, and is prepared for the world by the Apollonian spirit. There must be a nice balance between these two in that both are sons of Zeus, and you mustn't give yourself over totally to one or the other, or you're going to end up with some very queer stuff. It's balance, you know, that matters.

DCC: Where would we find balance in the notion of pushing the limits of human experience? A number of characters in your novels are always trying to prove to other characters that they are capable of powers that they don't know are within themselves, and they push the boundaries of human experience. Now some people fear what might be called the 'more life school' because very often it leads to murder, sado-masochism and death. The push towards truth and revelation very often is involved with physical violence. What are the limits, and should there be any limits, and how far do we push?

RD: It's a matter of courage, and it's a matter of faith, and when you get to that, of course you get into quite another group of values. A favourite writer of mine is François Rabelais, and his great abbey at Thélème which he set up as a place for people of high quality, is an élitist establishment. The only rule is 'Do what thou wilt.' Now this turns a lot of people off because they think 'Oh, that is terrible advice to give to anybody.' Actually, Rabelais, who was a great scholar and cleric, was quoting St Augustine, whose words are 'Dilige, et quod vis fac': 'Love God and you may do as you please.' That is what I very, very firmly believe. If you try to attach yourself to the love of God, the great overwhelming, dominating power of life, you're not in danger, if you go to the Dionysian side, of killing somebody, or if you go the other side of going off the rails and losing your mind because you've become too enlightened. Of course, you may get into messes, but you must *trust*. Courage! The adventure is much more important than fear of what might happen. Courage in spiritual things is of the uttermost importance.

DCC: You have talked about the writer's conscience. It is self-judgement and self-recognition. The novelist, John Gardner also wrote extensively about moral fiction, about the immorality of modern fiction. He saw himself as a modern-day Tolstoy. Do you see a disparity between his ideas and the fact that he plagiarized his book on Chaucer?

RD: [*great snort*] Tolstoy is a truly great artist, you know, but when he began to be a moralist, he was just a tedious old bore. I'm frivolous about Tolstoy. It seems to me that a man who can't see that Shakespeare's a great writer shouldn't be talking. Tolstoy was himself a great writer, a great sort of natural genius, but he didn't know beans about morality or literature [*great laugh*]. The notion that people who write books – even great books – are necessarily great experts on literature is a lot of hokum. An artist need not be a critic.

DCC: Now I have a rather long and roundabout question. You've written about Shakespeare's boy actors who played girls' roles and you've written two masques for the boys at Upper Canada College where the boys also played girls' roles. Valentine Rich in *Tempest-Tost* plays the male role of Gonzalo just as Sybil Thorndike played King Lear. In addition, the Deptford trilogy has several androgynous figures. Opera is full of travesti or 'trouser' roles: Adriano in Wagner's *Rienzi*, Cherubino in Mozart's *Marriage of Figaro*, Octavian in Strauss's *Der Rosenkavalier*, Leonore in Beethoven's *Fidelio*. Drama is also full of women characters who pretend that they are men, most notably Shakespeare. Many male roles are played by women. Peter Pan is always played by a woman. Both Sarah Bernhardt and Judith Anderson played Hamlet. Bernhardt played Pelléas to Mrs Patrick Campbell's Melisande. Now all of this is by way of asking you what are your thoughts on androgyny?

RD: I don't know that I have any very coherent ideas about it but it does seem to me – and has seemed to me all my life, I think

– that the division between male and female is much less rigid than a great many people like to pretend. This came to my attention earliest when I was a boy here in Canada where it was the accepted idea in the kind of society in which I moved that the line between boys and girls was utterly rigid; yet it was obvious to anybody who would take a look that it wasn't. You saw exhibitions of emotions that were thought to be the property of one sex in the other at all times. I encountered this very vividly, when I was quite a small boy; there was in the country school I went to an awful bully, a terrible tough, and he was always punching people around (me included), but there came to this rather remote Ontario town, a company playing *Uncle Tom's Cabin*. The school-children were let out of school in order that they might go to a matinée of this great, improving drama. I was much moved by it but I remember that I saw this fellow, whose name was Murray, at the death of Little Eva, sobbing and weeping and snuffling and wiping his nose on his sleeve and I thought that 'this fellow is a cream-puff'. And he was a cream-puff; underneath all the toughness, there was a strong strain of sentimentality, and I suppose you could almost call it in crude terms 'feminine' feeling, in him. I have noticed this sort of thing all my life. The tougher they were, the sappier they were when they were touched on a certain emotion; it is so also with women. Women can be absolutely frightening when they are angry. It is the maenad strain, very alarming to the male. Their anger and physical violence is horrifying, and two women fighting is a dreadful sight because there is a kind of archetypal fury which arises which I don't find nearly so strong when men are fighting. So I think the division is a much more artificial one than we pretend, and that the notion that we are all split up in terms of our physical sex is just sheer nonsense. But that is now widely being recognized, because of the increased attention being given to homosexuality, though I don't think it has anything to do with androgyny. Homosexuals are not necessarily effeminate men; the whole range of feeling is much more widely spread about over the whole of human kind than a great many people are prepared to admit. There are still people who will tell you that certain things are for men and that certain things are for women, and there are some cases in which this is true. There are kinds of physical activity which men can endure in a way that women cannot and vice versa.

DCC: What about the androgynous figures in *Fifth Business*, and the rest of the trilogy?

RD: They bear out what I've been talking about. A figure like Liesl is enormously feminine but her appearance is hideous and superficially, perhaps, it might seem to be masculine. Some of her attitudes of mind would be described as masculine by a man who hadn't met very many women; but that kind of strong-minded, mischief-making spirit which is apparent in Liesl, I think is very feminine indeed. Also it exerts itself in men.

DCC: Consistently in your novels various characters feel that the death, suicide, or attempted suicide of other characters is malice, an effort to cause them harm. Dunstan Ramsay suggests that Boy Staunton swallowed the snowball stone as a final act of malice, 'having the last word'; Ramsay is angry with Leola's attempted suicide for she leaves a tactless suicide note that would have put him in an intolerable position; Monica Gall feels that Giles Revelstoke clutches her letter in his hand when he commits suicide in order to implicate her and cause her harm; Mrs Bridgetower's malicious will is like a Dead Hand on the Living. The title of one of your novels is *Leaven of Malice*. Why is malice so often at the centre of your novels?

RD: Because I think it is an unrecognized element in daily life. People don't like to think of it as having any part in their own living or thinking, but I think that it does, and I emphasize it. Another feeling that I have which I have allowed to find its way into a lot of the things that I have written is that the dead are not really dead. That is not to say that they creep around in white sheets and haunt us, but their ideas and influence do not die the minute they are put in the grave. Anybody who has been associated with a very strong influence, parental or in any other kind of association, knows that those people never really die; they come back and they talk to you and they tell you their opinions. You have to be very careful about that sort of thing and I think that is what haunting really is. A lot of it goes on in my books. You know, Monica, when her mother died, was always hearing her mother make unsuitable remarks.

DCC: The idea of malice often extends itself to the question of

'Who kills?' in many of your novels. It is connected to the question of guilt. Who killed Boy Staunton? Who killed Giles Revelstoke? Who mentally or spiritually killed Gloster Ridley's wife? Who makes Hector Mackilwraith try to kill himself? Why does this question fascinate you?

RD: In the end we all die of being ourselves. Whether somebody knocks us over the head with an axe or whether we die in a very long, agonizing illness or whether we die of a sudden stroke, it is a kind of outcome of what we have been, rather than an inexplicable natural disaster. Of course this runs into difficulties when you think of deaths for which we cannot conceive of any explanation, like the sudden death of a child or something of that sort.

DCC: In your novels you continually look at parent–child relationships, especially the possessive, domineering parent, usually a mother, and the too-compliant child. Often the relationships have erotic overtones. Why do you consistently look at the parent–child relationship in your work?

RD: Because I have been intensely interested in it as it has evinced itself in my own family for several generations on both sides. I have been aware of what happened to my parents and indeed to my grandparents because of their relationship to their parents. It seems to me that this is a somewhat neglected field. We are the children of a vast number of ancestors and it all seems to me to be very interesting that family trees, when you look at them drawn out beautifully in family Bibles, are full of branches with people on them, but they never have any roots. The roots are the things that make all the difference, and you cannot escape the experience that you take in very early in life which comes right from the roots of your family and may come from a very long way back. As you see, I'm a believer in the supposedly exploded notion of heredity, but I do feel that it shows itself strongly.

DCC: You are hard on critics, the schematizers, the symbol-sniffers, perhaps even the thanatossers. What did you think of the critical response to your work?

RD: Well, it has varied enormously, you see. When I make harsh remarks about critics, I do it among other things to irritate them because they are usually very sensitive; they are quite unaccustomed to criticism of themselves. They're great at dishing it out but they never think it's going to come back. Also I've been subjected to some kinds of criticism which I find hilariously funny; like criticisms by means of computer. Criticism is a very delicate, human process; it's not a machine. The critical reception of my novels has been pretty much what you would expect. I was writing novels which were not typically Canadian (if there is such a thing) and they seemed to many Canadian critics to be untypical in a way they didn't like. Now they've grown more used to what I do, and as I won't go away and I won't stop writing they have to take account of what I say and give it some sort of serious consideration. One of the things that has been very important in the critical reception of my books was the warm reception they have had in the United States. It's rather sad, but that influences Canadian critics heavily. When *Fifth Business* appeared, the Toronto *Star* was very critical of it. But then, you know, the man from the *Star* came back after it had been well received in the States and sat in that chair and said to me, 'I don't understand this at all. We knocked it, but down in the States they like it. How do you explain that?' And all I could say was, 'Well, I think it's for you to explain.'

DCC: There are many critical methodologies floating around now; it is a Tower of Babel; the 'Death of the Novel' debate, semiotics, structuralism, surfiction, all these very forbidding and foreboding words. What do you make of all that?

RD: Of course, there has to be fashion because critics have to keep the mill turning. These people keep going by writing critical articles, usually for academic publications, which tend to have a circulation of between two and three thousand copies. Now that is not what you'd call a very big circulation, and I sometimes wonder who reads them. They take in one another's washing in this way and they get some kind of mark in the Dean's office for having got an article published in this, that or the other thing. And that's all very well; it's a game they play. But you've got to be perpetually refreshing it, renewing it, or you've run out of steam. So they're always finding new methods for criticism. But it doesn't really matter a damn, because the real criticism is whether a substantial public (and I don't really mean a gigantic public, but a public that is perceptive and critical in the ordinary sense of the word) likes the work, and whether it lasts or not. Because junk tends to drop out of sight fairly quickly. If things continue to attract readers, they must have some quality. I depend for my public on what I call 'the clerisy' – the intelligent public that reads for pleasure – not necessarily easily obtained pleasure.

DCC: A major stereotype of the Canadian people is one of 'common-sense'. Thoreau asked why do we use our dullest perceptions and call them common-sense. Peggy Stamper in *A Mixture of Frailties* says that art begins where common-sense leaves off. Do you agree with Peggy Stamper?

RD: Yes I do. I also agree with Thoreau. What people call common-sense is generally what you could achieve without any intellectual effort at all. In Canada we talk about common-sense, but then look at the way we behave, politically, and in every other way! It's not very common-sensical if common-sense means careful and cool decision.

DCC: Also, Canada clearly suffocates your creative characters; it tries to stifle the eccentrics and they all seem to find transformation and regeneration outside the country, somewhere else. You have remarked before that society hates exceptional people because it makes them feel inferior. Is there anything else involved in that?

RD: No, I think the fact that a lot of my Canadian characters go elsewhere to recognize themselves and to realize themselves, is not so much meant as a suggestion that they can't do it in Canada, as it is an archetype of the journey which is very important in the kind of novels that I write; you travel, you leave somewhere and go somewhere else, and in the course of getting there, you find out things about yourself. But you could do it just as well going from Toronto to Vancouver, I expect. You've got to go somewhere where you're not known, where people haven't got two or three strikes on you by having known you as a child, or having known your uncle who went crazy.

DCC: It has been suggested that your work contains the myth of 'Paradise Lost' and that your characters yearn and slowly move toward this 'Lost Age'. Is that just symbol-sniffing or do you agree?

RD: I think that's symbol-sniffing and I don't think it's 'Paradise Lost'. I think that they are looking not for paradise but for self-recognition, and self-knowledge in some measure, and a lot of them find it.

DCC: There is much speculation about the metaphor of *Fifth Business*; that it is Father Blazon, not Ramsay, that it is misused and not developed. Do you feel as William Faulkner did that he said what he had to say in the novel, so an analysis or confirmation by yourself isn't necessary?

RD: Exactly. That's the way it is. This perpetual picking and pestering doesn't reveal very much. As for the *Fifth Business* thing, there are a lot of people who think they know a lot more about what *Fifth Business* is than I do. Have you ever read that epigraph at the beginning of *Fifth Business* from *Den Danske Skueplads* by Tho. Overskou?

DCC: No, I haven't read it except in *Fifth Business*.

RD: I'll tell you how it came about. I first heard the term 'Fifth Business' from my wife, who had heard it from an old European opera singer. It captured my imagination because it fitted something I wanted to write about – the central importance of some people who are often overlooked. The book was going to be published in Canada, and Macmillan in England was considering it. The head of the English Macmillan – a well-known publisher called Maclean – was visiting Canada, and he liked the book but the title worried him. Couldn't I supply something easily quotable, that people could read, that would explain the strange title? Something out of a book of reference, for instance. That was a facer, because I had never seen it in a book of reference, or in print of any kind. But I turned up the next day with a quotation translated from Tho. Overskou (who has never been translated into English) and Maclean thought it would do splendidly. Of course I have never even seen Overskou's book *Den Danske Skueplads*, which is a history of the Danish stage, but I knew of its existence. I *invented* the quotation. In a scholarly piece of writing I would not for the world invent or fake a reference, but I thought, 'Well, if they simply *must* have a reference – this is a work of fiction, after all?' When the book appeared people began to pester me for the exact situation of the piece, because Overskou runs to something like ten volumes. I knew what would happen; they would print the exact attribution, having got it from me, making themselves look very clever. I only knew one person who checked Overskou, and he got lost before he found Fifth Business. The only people who tumbled to the joke were two Danish colleagues of mine who said, 'We knew it wasn't Overskou, because he never wrote anything as unequivocal as that.'

DCC: [*laughs*] That's wonderful. I was one of the people who didn't tumble to it.

RD: I made it up because I thought it was useful. But the expression Fifth Business is a genuine opera term.

DCC: But people have written articles and books on the subject!

RD: This gives me great delight.

DCC: Your work is humorous and witty but always with a bite. You have defined humour as a result of tension in the mind. Could you expand on that?

RD: Well, it is a tension between deep disillusion and irritation, and a sense of the hilarious unimportance of a great number of things. I have wondered within the last year or so, whether humour is not possibly even an archetypal thing. It is a sense of the baselessness of so much that appears to be absolutely serious and solid. And so humour is always an explosion. Freud says it is an explosion to relieve tension, and when you are aware of the folly and the stupidity of something that is going on, you have an explosion which sends it up in a joke. But a great many people haven't any of this quality, this sense of incongruity, this sense that things are not exactly what they seem – and [*laughs*] there it is!

DCC: I have been led to many writers in the past by you through your writing, to know and to enjoy. Which contemporary writers do you read and enjoy?

RD: Oh, well ... That's a little difficult to answer, because for the last few years I've been reading mostly writers who are not actually contemporaries, though there are certain contemporary writers with whose work I do attempt to keep up, like Graham Greene for example. And Angus Wilson, whose work I admire. And while she was living I thought Sylvia Townsend Warner was one of the most extraordinarily underrated writers. She has written superbly. Her books are really magnificent. But you know, people talk about great women writers, and they hardly ever mention her. She's one of the really great modern writers, both of short stories and novels. And it's fascinating; you'll find quite a few of them in any good library, and you'll find them delightful because she has not just wit, but humour, exquisite style, perception of a superb kind, a most enviable writer's equipment. I had a brief correspondence with her just before she died, which she did when she was at a very advanced age. She was over eighty. And she was just a delight. A really wonderful person. And this is what I always think of when people talk about a really liberated woman. She was not chained down by anything, but neither was she a rabble-rouser and a sign-carrier [*laughs*]. She had a magnificent career, you know; she was a fine musician, and it shows in her writing. For a long time she was the chief assistant to E. H. Followes, the editor of that superb musical compilation, *English Tudor Church Music*. She was a great musical editor. And she's just a wonderful writer; I enjoyed her work tremendously. Margaret Drabble – I admire her work very much indeed. I find it intensely interesting. And I'm a great admirer of Isaac Bashevis Singer, as you might suspect. A great writer. A really great writer. I rather plume myself on the fact that I think I spotted him for a writer of top-notch importance ages ago.

DCC: Do you like the South Americans? People like Gabriel García Márquez?

RD: Oh, yes. I think he's stunning. Sometimes I get crabby when people say I'm an old-fashioned novelist. I say 'old-fashioned, to hell. Look at Márquez.' He writes in the nineteenth-century vein and he's as fresh as tomorrow.

DCC: What evolution do you see in your work?

RD: I don't know. It's very difficult to tell. I think that it has deepened in feeling and range but it's very difficult for me to comment on that because I'm inside it. I can't see what's happening.

DCC: You should because if you don't, other people do [*laughs*].

RD: Other people are always telling me about myself and they tell me the funniest things. I remember one Canadian woman critic complaining about my books because she said that all the attractive women in them were not Canadians. And yet when I think of Monica Gall, she's absolutely delightful. Pearl Vambrace is charming and intelligent. But they say 'Well, what about Liesl?' Well, what about Liesl? Liesl is extraordinary; she'd be extraordinary anywhere. But I think that pitiful girl Leola in *Fifth Business* is a nice person. There's nothing wrong with her except that she got into the wrong league.

DCC: I simply must ask this. Considering your passion for teasing, may I inquire if I have been the recipient of any mischief-making during this interview?

RD: How could you suspect me of such grossness when you are a guest in my own house? No, I have tried to be honest with you. But it is difficult to be honest about oneself because one does not wholly know oneself, one has modesty about talking of oneself, and some reticence must be retained even with the most sympathetic interviewer. I am tempted to be mischievous with interviewers and critics who talk to me as if I were not a fellow-creature: they ask such probing questions which they would not dream of putting to even an intimate friend. I recall an interviewer who was convinced that I must have been on bad terms with my mother, because there are some disagreeable mothers in my books. She asked me, bolt outright, 'What was the cause of disagreement between you and your mother?' As if I would tell her! Even supposing I had been at odds with my mother, would I tell her all about it so she could make copy of it? It did not occur to her that family loyalty would make any answer to such a question impossible. One does not become public property because one has written a few books ... But as to yourself, no, I have not made any mischief with you, because you have a sense of humour and would know it immediately ... But people with no sense of humour present a terrible temptation, and sometimes I have yielded to the temptation to pull their legs. Being born so much under the influence of Mercury, you see.

5   Erica Jong

DCC: What do you like best and what do you like least about your work?

EJ: That's a very tough question. I think what I like best about my work is that it has authentic energy and passion, and I try to preserve the energy and passion even at the risk of technique. As a college student and as a graduate student, I was very literary, and the work I loved best was highly structured verse, Nabokov's novels, things that were puzzles and literary games. As I got older and as I began to write myself I began to hate that graduate-student quality in contemporary literature. I came to distrust that writing of fashionably obscure books to be unravelled by literature students. And I discovered that what was most important to me in literature was the quality that makes the work of Whitman so great and makes the work of Mark Twain so great – energy, life, perhaps even vulgarity. To me, *that* is the important strain in American literature. I find the crabbed, cerebral strain in American literature to be the antithesis of what our spirit has brought to the world. I mean if we are going to write that way, we might as well be English.

DCC: Or French.

EJ: Well, French literature is another problem, although certainly many French writers are terribly cerebral at the expense of the heart. What I like best in my own work is its naturalness, its closeness to life. At times I've become upset when I've reread *Fear of Flying* and thought, 'what a damn shame to have become famous for a book that is so full of wisecracks, and so full of itself'. And yet I know that that kind of book was important for a woman to have written at that period in history. Also, it has undeniable exuberance – not a usual thing, especially for women. Women writers are always so

Erica Jong (*photograph:* © *1985 Thomas Victor*)

terribly constrained by 'What will people think of me? What will Daddy think? What will Mommy think?' Historically, they often silenced themselves. The curse of the woman writer is the need for social approval. It was absolutely necessary that somebody come along and break down those barriers. And I was the one whose fate it was to do that. I was speaking not only for myself but for something that was brewing in the atmosphere at that time. And by God, there are still so many women writers who are afraid to question authority. Ultimately, I think that, as with all writers, my strengths and my weaknesses are so intertwined that I myself cannot separate them. If I load myself with self-consciousness and I say, 'Don't be vulgar, don't be this, don't be that', I won't write at all. So I have to write to my strengths, although I certainly see the weaknesses in my work as well as anyone; perhaps better.

DCC: Do you ever fear the silences of Hardy, Melville, Hopkins, that Tillie Olson talks about in *Silences*?

EJ: I fear being silenced by critics. I fear my own depression when I'm attacked. I fear the retribution that falls on a woman who writes about sex. I fear the retribution which falls from the literary establishment. I fear the Bible-thumping puritans who all want to silence women who write about passion. I don't think I write so prolifically. My output has not been so large. On the contrary, most writers spend most of their life in various kinds of neurotic rituals. They spend a lot of time drinking, they spend a lot of time in bad relationships. I write about two-and-a-half pages a day when I'm working on a novel. I work about six or eight hours a day, four to five hours of which is really creatively productive. I don't think that's a lot. I don't think two-and-a-half pages a day is much for someone who's a full-time writer. I do think that the output of most writers is so pathetically small because they make fetishes out of their weaknesses and they don't work most of the time. That's the truth, and it's very sad. People work to a fraction of their creative ability. I think that even I don't work to a fraction of my creative ability. I hope that someday I will.

DCC: You've said: 'Learning is good for a poet as long as she doesn't become a professional scholar.' What do you mean by that?

EJ: Read everything you possibly can. If you are going to be a writer, the chief way you learn your craft is by reading and writing. And read everything. Read Smollett and Defoe and Dickens and all the poetry you can. Read archeology and the history of religions and the Bible and everything that will give you a sense of language and everything that will give you a richness of knowledge and self-knowledge. One of the writers I admire is Robert Graves – and it's partly for these qualities of expansiveness. He's somebody who's written novels to make a living, and poetry because the Muse inspired him; but he's written about the history of poetry, archeology, religion, myth, and the White Goddess. I think he's an inveterate sexist but I can still learn from him. He doesn't write the kind of poetry I write, his concerns are not the same as mine, but I love his kind of Renaissance spirit. That's the kind of writer I really want to be. The trouble with being a professional scholar (as I found when I was doing my never-completed Ph.D. in eighteenth-century English lit. at Columbia) is that scholars are asked to write books *about* books *about* books, rather than books. I don't want to spend my time arguing with some scholar who says that *Tom Jones* is really a Marxist parable. I don't think that what's interesting about Swift, let's say, is whether we decide he's an ameliorist or a pessimist; what's interesting about Swift is not what scholars decide about his themes but that he's an incredibly energetic and vigorous writer who has the gift of life in his writing. That's why his books are read today. The Marxist or the Freudian or the structuralist debate doesn't interest me much anymore. I think such debates are artifacts and, as such, they're bullshit.

DCC: Do you think the 'Death of the Novel' debate is artifact?

EJ: Yes.

DCC: Do you think that people like Anaïs Nin who write books about the future of the novel are doing something useful? Do you see any need to prophesize about the future of any art form, the future of the novel, the future of poetry, giving death chants for either form?

EJ: I think it's wishful thinking on the part of blocked, self-hating writers. The critics and the academics in this country have managed successfully to kill poetry as a popular art by demanding that poetry be crabbed and difficult and impossible to understand. They have so put over the notion that poetry be impossible to understand, that they have, in fact, killed the chances for poetry to ever be a popular art form again. They would like to do the same to the novel by exalting Thomas Pynchon over anybody who writes intelligible prose, and I think that if given their own way, they would be a greater danger to literature than the people who pay Judith Krantz three million dollars! Because I don't see the pop-novel as a danger to literature. There'll always be publishers eager to make a buck out of what they think will be the new profitable trash. And that frightens me far less than the desire to force upon the public work that is unreadable. So I'm not bothered by the huckster aspect of the paperback scene. It's unfortunate that those book deals get so much publicity because it gives the impression to young writers that there's just money, money, money; whereas most writers in this country make an average of two thousand dollars a year from their work. Most of the members of the Authors' Guild of America average 2.5 thousand a year from their writing and work at teaching or advertising or something to make a living. There are perhaps a hundred writers in America who make a living from writing fiction. I am one. Vonnegut, John Updike, and Philip Roth are a few of the others. You can count them, really, on just a few people's hands. This, by the way, also accounts for the viciousness of the criticism that commercially successful writers receive. It accounts for it almost better than anything because the only word to explain it is 'envy', really.

DCC: There seems to be a rage for order in criticism. But new art forms are always evolving. Would you agree with Archibald MacLeish or Dylan Thomas that it is almost impossible to define art or to create categories for art?

EJ: If you study the history of literature, you see that certain art forms decline and others arise. In the seventeenth century, the novel was considered a trashy, low, literary form, suitable for serving-maids who wanted to pervert their minds. In the early eighteenth century, before Richardson and Fielding, the novel was also considered trashy. Who would have dreamed then, that in the twentieth century the novel would have become *the* great art form and the modern successor to the epic? Eighteenth-century writers were always apologizing for writing novels at all. Fielding apologized for writing anything so low as a novel, and he called *Tom Jones* an epic to elevate it. That's why I think we should be very wary of making these predictions about high and low art, because we really don't know. The novel is alive and well as long as people buy it and read it. The fact that Judith Krantz can make three million dollars is proof that the novel is alive and well. Maybe her novel isn't one of the enduring ones, but the novel is a lively form, and let's say it's read by lots of people. What the successor to the novel may be, I'm not sure. For a time in the sixties, wishful journalists asserted that the novel was dead and journalism was the coming form. Indeed a lot of novels were influenced by this, including my own first two, *Fear of Flying* and *How to Save Your Own Life* (which I wrote as sort of mock-memoirs). I tried to make those first two novels seem not like novels but like autobiographical projections. I succeeded so well in fact that nobody believes they *are* novels [*laughs*].

DCC: Do the literary and academic efforts to create structural responses to art really in fact create a Tower of Babel? An excluding language of semiotics, phenomenology, structural fabulation, and on and on ...

EJ: Those things have nothing to do with the creative process except to impede it. If a novelist is stupid enough to listen, they create self-consciousness which is the enemy of art, the enemy of creation. I cannot see that that does anything to help the writing of books. Maybe it's good at some point in your life to help organize your view of literature. When you're a student of literature in college and you're confronted with this mass of material for the first time in your life, and you can't understand it, it may then be useful to have certain constructs to help you absorb it. It is important to understand why the novel rose to dominance in England in the eighteenth century (based upon the rise of the new reading class and so on). I think it's helpful to look at the nineteenth century and try to understand why a novel of interior psychological exploration should have arisen in that particular century. That's interesting. But the other more arcane kinds of constructs that literary critics think up, are useless self-indulgences. I think they help academics get promoted and that's about all. They have a certain limited utility as teaching tools but I don't think they have any use artistically at all.

DCC: 'Open form' aesthetics, which became increasingly popular in this century with the influence of the East in particular, created a new sense that art is anti-Aristotelian, anti-teleological, anti-beginning, middle and end. Literature in this century, perhaps starting with D. H. Lawrence or Joyce, and continuing with Susan Sontag in her book *Against Interpretation*, is calling for a literature that is more transparent, and a critical structure that is what Sontag calls, 'Descriptive rather than prescriptive', the here and now, the organic. What do you make of all those ideas?

EJ: It's shocking that there's been so little experimentalism in contemporary literature. I think it's shocking that here we are, fifty years or sixty years after *The Waste Land*, after *The Waves*, after *Ulysses*, and almost nobody is publishing novels using the kind of freedom from narrative structure that those early modernists tried to teach us. I find it rather amazing that so many of us are still writing novels in a nineteenth-century literary tradition. I'm all for experimentation. I am not anti-Dada or anti-open form or anti-non-linear narration (if you can make it *interesting* and *readable*). I hate the idea that everybody's going to go back to writing sestinas for a new generation of new critics. I see a whole reactionary trend in the arts right now, and I think we should stay open to experimentation. But we should not use experimentation faddishly. We should use it to develop our own styles. I don't believe that there must be a beginning, a middle, and an end in a novel absolutely, and I'm sympathetic to open form, but a novel has a reader, and you can't make things so hard for the reader that the reader won't finish the book. I mean if you want the reader to read your fucking book, make it readable! I want to be read. I don't want to turn off my reader on page one. And the purpose of a story, a plot, a beginning, middle and end, is not to fulfil some crazy formalistic Aristotelian rule, but to get the fucking reader to read the fucking book. The reason for having suspense, for having sympathetic characters, for having a readable story, for doing some work for the reader so that the reader can enjoy the book, is to get people to read your work so that you can communicate with them! Therefore you *must* create some principles of organization to lure the reader from page to page. Why talk about it from an abstract intellectual point of view? Let's talk about it pragmatically. When you read

Great Expectations, you want to know what's going to happen. When you read *David Copperfield*, you wade through a lot of stuff that's boring because you want to find how it turns out. When you read *Anna Karenina* you go through all that information about farming in Russia because you want to know: will Anna and Vronsky get together? Those are very simple practical reasons for having a plot and a story, a beginning, a middle, and an end.

DCC: That makes sense [*both laugh*]. Is the best criticism empathetic? Doris Lessing speaks of a critic who is the alter ego of the writer. She says: 'Writers are looking for the other self, more intelligent than oneself, who has seen what one is reaching for.' Have you ever encountered any critics like this?

EJ: I have never encountered such a critic. The problem with most critics is that they have never actually written a novel, nor published one, nor do they know the problems a novelist faces; they are in a different world. They seem not to know that the novelist is dealing with certain things, such as, 'How can I get the reader to turn the page?', and they seem to think that this is irrelevant, whereas to me that is the most relevant of all.

DCC: So are the best critics other writers?

EJ: Well they would be, ideally, except that the economic and literary rewards of writing are so capriciously distributed, that other writers are likely to be jealous. Other writers who have had less success than oneself, tend to be eaten up with envy. If they are teachers whom one has superseded, they may also have their own jealousies. If they are other women and they feel there is only room for one token woman in our male-dominated literary scene, they may be jealous. So, ideally other writers are the best critics, but in practical reality they often attack one simply because they feel so threatened themselves.

DCC: I have often seen two types of book reviewing and criticism. One practises a kind of 'kill–tear–maim–rip' of which I think Lance Morrow in his review of *How to Save Your Own Life* is one type of piranha –

EJ: I didn't read it –

DCC: Just as well. The other kind of critic is a sort of 'protect–baby–suckle–pamper'. Canadian critics writing about Canadian literature are often a type of 'help the cripple' criticism [*both laugh*].

EJ: We don't have that type in the States. In America we go out of the way to attack success and we have a whole form of journalism based on gossip and attack. Apparently it sells magazines. Apparently it lets people get their frustrations out against the people they envy; famous people, whether actors or writers, or musicians. That's a very destructive journalistic trend. It literally destroys some of the people against whom it's directed – Jean Seberg, Marilyn Monroe, Truman Capote, Tennessee Williams ... the list is long. I do think it is an incredibly dangerous thing. Writers are best left alone. I don't think writers have much to learn from critics, truly. I mean I've never met an ideal critic. Sometimes I have had wonderful essays written about my work, usually by sensitive young writers or older writers, beyond jealousy, or sometimes academics who are particularly sensitive and who take my work very seriously (yet also playfully). I've been very grateful for that kind of intelligent consideration. But I never really learned anything from your garden-variety critic.

DCC: What are your prime considerations when you are writing a book review of somebody else's work?

EJ: [*sighs*] Oh dear! I always keep in mind how hard it is to write a book, even a bad book. Even the typing is a chore [*laughs*]. I realize that the stamina to sit down at a desk every morning at nine o'clock and to work in solitude isn't given to many people. It's not something to be laughed at, slashed at, made fun of. I'd rather not review a book than gratuitously attack it. I'm not much into attack. Because it seems to me that one so transparently reveals one's *own* smallness when one attacks. It may not seem that way to others, but when I read a vicious attack on someone's work I always see envy, envy, envy written all over it, and I can't help thinking, 'How can that person want to reveal to the world how envious and narrow and small he is?' I'm too proud to want to reveal those feelings. I have them just like anybody else at times, but I don't want to reveal them to the world. That doesn't seem like anything I want to be known for.

DCC: But aren't there ways of evaluating literature without being petty, vicious or mean? Aren't there ways of saying that this book is better than that book and this is why, without being small?

EJ: I guess there are, but you see so few examples of that sort of criticism. One has to write about the characters, one has to write about the language of the book, one has to write about whether the book has a heart or whether it's an empty shell. *Those* are the things that are important in a book. I can tell you in a minute when I read something whether it lives and breathes or whether it's dead. I can tell you, for example, that *Catch-22* lives and breathes and that *Something Happened* is a shell, although they were written by the same man, at different times in his life. *Good as Gold* is alive. That's what matters to me about books.

DCC: Many feminists today seem to respond best to a literature that reveals ideal role models: energetic, life-affirming women who are capable of taking their lives into their hands, as opposed to the perhaps more realistic portrait of women who are confused, and emotionally and philosophically ambiguous, or, in fact, complacent women who don't even care about these choices. Do you think feminist critics give bad reviews to writers who don't create these ideal role models; I'm thinking here of Roberta Tovey asserting in her review of *How to Save Your Own Life* that the ending endorses what she calls 'the power of the male'? I'm also thinking that *Fear of Flying* was what you called a saga of unfulfilment, so you were *not* trying to portray ideal role models; you were talking about one woman's life and the way she tries to sort it out.

EJ: I don't know the review you're talking about because I deliberately didn't read the reviews on *How to Save Your Own Life*; I didn't think I'd survive them if I did. All I can say is that there's a difference between literature and utopian inspirational prescriptions; and feminist activists (like the Marxists of the thirties) don't care about *literature*. They are looking for inspirational writing that will help women rise up from their despair. This is all very well and good but it has nothing to do with literature. I understand the *desire* for inspirational writing, 'I am woman, hear me crow, blah blah blah... I am strong, I am invincible, I will overcome, we shall overcome, blah blah blah.' That's useful at certain points in the struggle. There's a need for that. But it has nothing to do with literature. Literature has to do with accuracy and truth. It has to do with representing, with as much accuracy as you can tolerate, the situation of women as you see it. It cannot help but partake of the conflicts you perceive in your own heart. Do you have a fantasy about a man under the bed? Well then, you write a poem about it. You don't say to yourself, 'Is the fantasy about the man under the bed perhaps an expression of my oppression as a woman and perhaps a woman who is not oppressed will not have such a fantasy?' That may well be, but it is your job as a writer to write about the truth of the heart, not the societal changes you *hope* will come in the future. Find me a woman who is strong and invincible (who isn't a cartoon character like Wonder Woman), who you'd like to read a novel about. Let those feminist critics come out of their collectivist cowering in the closet and write a goddamn book about an invincible strong woman who is not dominated by men, and let that book be something that ten million women around the world want to read! Will they read it? I mean, will it relate to their lives? It sure doesn't relate to my life. My life has been a constant struggle of self-stunting stereotypes, of falling in love with men who were very sadistic, and then having to escape various cages of my own making, of educating myself to freedom because I was *not* born free. And I think I'm quite a characteristic woman of my time. I've had a great struggle towards freedom and a lot of women identify with *Isadora* because she is struggling. She is in conflict, as most of us are. Besides, with Utopian literature, there is another problem. If you start out with a heroine who is strong, invincible and not in conflict, what the fuck are you going to write about? Where's your story? From the simple point of view of the storyteller, there is no story without conflict; there is no story without struggle. There is no story without change and growth. I mean, what they're asking for is something you would only ask for if you had never tried to write a book. It's meaningless. It's silly. It's almost a giggle. I've been told by certain feminists: 'Isadora should not have gone back to Bennett at the end of *Fear of Flying*.' Well maybe she shouldn't have, but that has nothing to do with writing a novel. That 'should' and that 'shouldn't', has nothing to do with literature.

DCC: Are there any female writers now who don't seem to elicit the critical antagonism you do? Why?

EJ: Well, my father calls me up and asks, 'Darling, why don't you get reviews like Joan Didion?', and I explain patiently why, and I *do* understand why. Joan Didion is an excellent writer, but she doesn't really question the female role. Her women are invalids and cripples. She is a brilliant prose stylist; her essays are beautifully formed. I read them with great pleasure, I must say. Her novels interest me very little, because I'm weary of novels about women who are invalids, who are mental cases, who are self-destructive. But I think she appeals to a certain kind of male-oriented critic because she doesn't question the proper sphere of woman – the proper sphere of woman is to lie in bed and be an invalid. She says it about herself when she talks about her migraine headaches. She says, in effect, 'I am not robust.' In the patriarchal culture we live in, there are certain acceptable roles for women, and one of those acceptable roles is to be perpetually ill. And you will find that women writers who accept the invalid role, the sick, suicidal, self-destructive role, encounter far less controversy than women who assert that females are strong, that females are sexual, that females are whole. Mary Gordon's *Final Payments* is an example of a really fine piece of work that also does not question the traditional female role. And I think the book was praised not so much because it was excellent (which it was), but because it showed a woman submerging her whole life and identity in her father. Perhaps unconsciously, all those critics who were so shocked by sexuality in my work, *loved* the idea of a young, educated woman submerging her identity in her father. Often when books are madly praised, you must look through and see what is going on psychologically. This takes nothing away from Mary Gordon who is a wonderful writer, an extraordinary writer. But she is not a revolutionary one. The revolutionary writers tend to get axed.

DCC: How do you feel about Diane Wakowski refusing to be included in all-woman anthologies?

EJ: It's understandable, after centuries of oppression, centuries of denigration of women poets, that some women poets should feel that they don't want to be classed with the women poets! I understand her feeling, but I think it's a misguided attempt to remedy sexism.

DCC: Many women feel that art exhibitions like 'Retrospectives of Women through the Ages' are a negative thing, simply because they categorize women as 'female artists'. You don't see 'Retrospectives of Male Artists through the Ages'. When Sarah Caldwell was invited to Russia as a 'female conductor' to be exchanged with another female conductor, she wrote back and said, 'Look, I'm just a conductor.'

EJ: It's entirely understandable that these women don't want to be ghettoized; I don't fault them. I don't fault Wakowski, I know what motivates her. But essentially we're quibbling. We live in a society that is very oppressive to women, and women creators, and I think that any way we can make ourselves visible, we ought avail ourselves of. We should be pragmatic. We shouldn't get ourselves all screwed up in all kinds of ideological disputes at this point. We don't have the luxury to do that right now. Of course, to be known as a 'woman' artist is a denigration, but it's not as bad a denigration as being totally invisible, which is what has happened to most women artists in the past. I think we have to have a sense of humour about this. We can't *afford* to be purists yet.

DCC: I agree. You've talked about writing myths. You've said that you're writing 'a mythology of continuation'. What are the 'myths' that 'expand human consciousness' in your work?

EJ: When I was working on *Fear of Flying*, I was very struck by the fact that there seemed to be a 'proper' ending for women's novels, and that proper ending was always suicide or madness. If

you look at the novels by and about women (and I'm not just
talking about novels by women, but also novels about women by
great novelists like Tolstoy and Flaubert) you find that
womanhood inevitably ends in madness or death. I felt it was
very important to write a novel about a woman, that didn't end
in madness or death. And I feel that that was a very
revolutionary thing to have done at the time. And I honestly
believe that a lot of the flack that I've received has to do with the
fact that my heroines do not die and do not self-destruct. I refuse
to accept the idea that women must be cripples or invalids. You
can argue about whether women ought to wind up in the arms of
a man or in the arms of a woman but that's less important than
whether they wind up *alive*! I don't know if you've ever read
Wendy Martin's brilliant essay 'Seduced and Abandoned in the
New World: the Image of Women in the New World' [see
Women in Sexist Society, ed. by Vivian Gornick and Barbara K.
Moran, 1971]. Martin argues that women in literature usually
die for their one attempt at independence. The weight of
tradition is extraordinary when you start looking at it. I mean
you see it even in the 'liberated' women writers of the last couple
of generations. Look at Mary McCarthy's *A Charmed Life*.
Look at the independent, strong woman who has to have an
abortion and dies in the last paragraph of McCarthy's novel
because she can't decide whether the baby belongs to her
ex-husband or her present husband. Look at that as a 'myth' of
an intelligent woman destroyed by patriarchal values. Look at
that and weep, and then you will understand why *Fear of Flying*
created such a furore, such a ruckus, because on a mythological
level what I had said was that women can live, *women can have
sex and live, by God*! It's sort of pathetic that you and I can sit
here and have to say that that's a radical idea. I mean it's
pathetic and sad, but there it is.

DCC: You use the 'mythology of continuation' also in *At the
Edge of the Body*, which is quite different I think from what you
were doing before. In your excellent article 'Creativity Versus
Generativity', you speak of a literary history of childless
women. In what way would literature change, if women who are
mothers by choice and desire were writing to a much larger
extent?

EJ: Well, because patriarchy split women into the whore and the madonna, it became necessary (both for practical reasons and for reasons of sheer survival, both physical and mental) for those women who wanted to be creators to swear off family life or procreation, and for those women who were mothers to completely submerge themselves in motherhood. It need not be so. If we had a sane and rational society, we would be able to have babies and write books. There is no reason why we can't. Maternity is not a form of invalidism. I wrote like a demon while I was pregnant. I enjoyed my pregnancy. But I also had a husband who cooked and who did all kinds of things around the house and who completely assumed that the house was as much his responsibility as mine. I had enough money to hire a nurse for my baby when she was born. Because I was established in my career, I did not have to choose. So it was not easy for me to do both, but it was *possible* for me to do both. And it would be possible for most women to do both, but we've been really robbed by patriarchal culture. The waste of life-power, of woman-power is tragic. As a result, most of the women who have been creators have been so at the expense of their generative function. And consequently, they've been fearful of maternity, fearful of men because men might trap them into maternity, fearful of families because family life might smother their creativity, and all of this is quite understandable. I probably would have been the same had I lived in that age and had no contraception and no money and no legal rights and so on. But that doesn't mean that it's *natural*. I think that when you have a generation of women who have been creators and mothers both, there are going to be experiences in literature that we will not have seen before. In my novel, *Fanny*, which is an historical novel, I have a section dealing with birth and pregnancy and the kidnapping of a small baby that I think could only have been written by a woman who is a mother. In a way, it's the most moving section of the book. I could never have written about this as well, if I hadn't experienced motherhood. I could have written it, but I could never have written it quite the way I wrote it, from research alone, or from reading diaries of pregnant women. And I think literature has been pushed in the direction of male concerns for centuries, for twenty-five hundred years to be exact, and I think it is time for that to stop.

DCC: I've heard so often Karen Horney's point of view that men created because they couldn't have babies, which, as you've pointed out, are quite different experiences. Art is conscious. Giving birth is not.

EJ: Many women believe that and it becomes a self-fulfilling prophecy. My oldest and best friend from college (who's a highly intelligent woman) says, 'When I'm pregnant I can't do anything creative.' Now, she's a brilliant woman, but what it is that leads her to believe that (I think she's just been brainwashed by male culture) has created a situation in which she does stop work when she's pregnant. When I became pregnant, I feared a cessation of my creative drive, but in fact I was extremely productive, and I think I wrote better than I am writing now. I wrote with tremendous fire and tremendous passion because I felt almost as if I had the Muse inside me. Maternity is an amazing experience. And I secretly think that men and male culture have denigrated it because they can't have it. 'If we can't have it, it must be bad and it must impair your creativity', they said. I think, on the contrary, maternity enhances creativity, and we've been lied to. Moreover that lie has been enforced by sheer brute force; the throwing of women out of academies, the firing of pregnant women, and such atrocities. If women are so naturally weak during pregnancy, why all the obstacles? It's rubbish!

DCC: I like that. To change the subject, Karl Shapiro wrote that many American poets wrote prose, not poetry. It's another one of those statements.

EJ: I think it's kind of silly. Most poets in any age are not inspired by the Muse. I prefer Robert Graves' distinction to Karl Shapiro's. I think the test of a true poem (as Graves says in *The White Goddess*) is whether or not it is true invocation to the white goddess (the mother goddess who is the goddess of creation, of destruction, of provenance. The triple-aspected-goddess). One knows a true poem by whether or not the hair stands up on the back of one's neck. And, alas, 'tis true that, most poets in every country, in any age, do not write muse-poetry (in Graves' sense). They write clever anagrams, rhymes, verses. They write topical trivia, or prose, or fashionable cant. But it's not truly muse-poetry, for that is always a very rare commodity. And even a poet who has written muse poetry at some time or other, may not always write it, because the Muse comes and goes as She wishes.

DCC: What are the elements that constitute your decision to write a poem or a novel?

EJ: A novel starts out with a situation and a question. A novel is usually an exploration of a situation and a character, while a poem usually starts with an image and a poem is an epiphany. They are totally different kinds of writing. With a novel I'll begin by saying, for example, 'What if a young woman in conflict, trying to break away from her family, has an unsatisfactory love affair with an impotent man, travels across Europe, loses her husband, but finds herself as a result?' A novel starts with a, 'What if?' And then I say to myself, 'Who is this woman? This woman is very intelligent, very well-educated, but emotionally confused, tied to a conservative husband on the one hand, tied to a family who is trying to thwart her on the other hand, and at the same time she's an artist, she has longings for adventure, and so on.' She's tugged between two forces. She's in Europe, in Vienna, it's a psychoanalytic convention ... and then I work out the details. But a poem starts with a line and the hair standing on the back of my neck. I'll get an image from the blue and I know I'm on the track of some buried memory or something in the communal unconscious that needs to be teased out. The poem is a burst of insight rather than a working out of a psychological situation. They're so different that the two kinds of writing don't conflict at all. They satisfy different needs.

DCC: You've said that you're interested in mixed forms; the mixing of prose and poetry which you have done in your novels and your poems. What are the possibilities for that?

EJ: The possibilities are much greater than have been explored to this day. I've always particularly admired a novel of Nabokov's called *Pale Fire*, which is written in the form of an epic poem with footnotes. The whole novel takes place in the footnotes! I love that sort of thing. I'd love someday to write a book in which I use both poems and prose. I tried to use poetry to some degree in *How to Save Your Own Life*, because I think it is better to tell a love story in poetry than in narrative. Perhaps one can tell a love story more truly in verse.

DCC: In a review of Anne Sexton's poetry you said that two of her worst traits are 'repetition' and 'excess'. Do you think that there is any aesthetic value in both? Most great writers are uneven. In some cases their worlds are felt and lived in by the reader precisely because they are repetitious and excessive. The observation also seems contradictory because you've said that you use repetition in your poetry and that what you want particularly in the novel is 'excess'.

EJ: Maybe I criticize it in her because I see it in myself.

DCC: But it's something you like, 'excess' in the novel and 'repetition' in poetry. You see that as something positive in literature, yet still you pointed it out as a weakness in Sexton.

EJ: Perhaps I was being unfair. As Anne Sexton's work went on, she edited herself less and less. Which maybe isn't always a bad thing. I think perhaps her later work was too loose. But she was a great poet; I'm not saying she wasn't. In fact, when I told her she had 'excess' in her work, she wrote me and she said, 'Of course, I have excess, I am an excessive person.' Maybe I was really criticizing myself because, at times, I share that trait with her. Often, in our book reviews we are more subjective than we admit.

DCC: I don't think that if you criticize her for what you think inhibits the poetry, that this necessarily means that you are saying she's not a good poet. What is the balance between viciously attacking a writer for no purpose at all, and standing back and saying, 'Well, this isn't doing what you want it to do.'

EJ: Alas, there is very little good criticism around. There are a lot of reasons for this, too. One reason is the gossip-mongering mentality of most magazines and the low level of contemporary journalism. But this infects literary journalism as well, although the literary journalists claim to be above it. But they do exactly the same sort of thing in their own way. Witness those articles in the *New York Times Magazine* about John Gardner and Truman Capote and Norman Mailer. They make writers seem like buffoons! Even the article on Updike was regrettably gossipy. And the one on Mailer was so vicious that it made me want to hug him and say 'there, there'. But I do think there's another reason as well. Most writers have very weak egos, and they tend to like unreservedly those people who praise them. Writers and critics tend to group themselves into cliques. And much book reviewing is merely touting one's friend's books and smearing one's enemy's books. There are very few real literary standards being deployed. I have felt the pressure. Sometimes I'll be sent a book to review and it's a bad book by somebody I'm personally fond of. What to do? I turn the review down, because I can't honestly rave about the book. But at the same time I don't want to hurt the author's feelings if he's been kind to me in the past. That's why I often think we are much better critics of foreign writers whom we don't know personally. I notice, for example, that I always get a far more dispassionate appraisal in France, Italy, England, Sweden, Holland, and Japan than I do in this country.

DCC: I know that Isadora isn't necessarily your mouthpiece but she does make an interesting statement. She says: 'Mediocre poetry did not exist at all.' Now is that to suggest that mediocre prose is *not* a contradiction in terms? Was Matthew Arnold right in saying that poetry is the most perfect speech of man, for through poetry man comes nearest to being able to utter the truth? And of course, there is the Western bias that poetry is the greatest of the three literary genres and the novel is a sort of poor cousin.

EJ: I think they do different things. A poem can't tell you much about the relationships of people in families. A poem can't tell you much about the way society infringes on the individual. Not in the way the novel can. They're very difficult to compare because they have different spheres. I think that poetry is more precise than fiction. Poetry chronicles the *dream* life of an age; a novel chronicles its *social* life. What I meant really, when I made that distinction in *How To Save Your Own Life*, was that you can have a novelist, like say, Dreiser or Doris Lessing who is not a beautiful stylist but who's a great novelist none the less.

Whereas in poetry, a person who is a clumsy stylist wouldn't be good at all. I'm always amazed how graceless Lessing's prose is.

DCC: She's doing it intentionally.

EJ: I don't know whether she's doing it intentionally or not. I find her a rather graceless writer, but also a great writer. I can't think of anyone in our age who can so involve you in the world of her novels.

DCC: But that's her point. Because life is confusing, because it is graceless, because it is fragmented, we need a style that is commensurate to whatever is being discussed. So she deliberately sets out to be clumsy, fragmented, graceless. She feels it is pointless for critics to remark, as they did, that her style is clumsy. Of course, that raises the aesthetic question of whether the theory is better than the practice.

EJ: The last person I would feel myself worthy to criticize is Doris Lessing, whose achievement is immense. I look up to her as one of the great women of our age. But I would say that I have often wished that her novels were easier to read. It took me ten years to read *The Golden Notebook* because I was so turned off by the introductory dialogue in that novel that I kept putting the book down. As a novelist I try to lure my reader into my story more seductively. I don't want to be easy, but I do want to be seductive enough to the reader to be read. I don't see that as prostitution of art. I see it as enhancement of art. But every writer is entitled to write the way she wants to.

DCC: Do writers of even loosely based biographical portraits in any way feel exempt from such depictions? Would you resent anybody if they depicted you in a novel in the same way that you loosely based portraits on Anne Sexton and Henry Miller?

EJ: Both Ann Sexton and Henry Miller should be flattered at the way they've been depicted. I don't think anybody could ever maintain that either of those portraits is anything less than totally flattering. I remember Anne Sexton's closest friend, Maxine Kumin, saying that Jeannie Morton was a very touching portrait of someone like Anne. And Henry Miller's children thought that the portrait of Kurt was very much the best of Henry. If I lived for my critics, those people who did not find the portraits flattering, I wouldn't live long! I went through a very rough time after *How to Save Your Own Life*. I never believed there was that much malignity in the whole world. I am not a vengeful person. I've always had lots of friends who were loving and affectionate. I could scarcely believe the hatred that was spewed out against me. I went through a terrible time. I felt very misanthropic. I felt as if I never wanted to publish again. I also went through a period of total sexual isolation because I had been so typecast as a sexy writer that I didn't even want to have sex again as long as I lived! But that depression has receded and I've been left with greater detachment from praise and blame. I hope that now I'm healthy enough to say: 'Fuck you world!' The fact that I've stirred up controversy and denunciation is proof that I'm doing something worth while. I look back at the women writers who have been most attacked (Aphra Behn, Sappho, the Brontës, Kate Chopin) and they were all revolutionaries. If you look at the history of women writers you'll see how *horribly* they've all been treated. Look at the examples of our female geniuses and say: 'I'm lucky to be alive, I'm lucky they don't burn me as a witch. I'm lucky I'm not stoned on the heath!' In another age, I would have been totally silenced, like Kate Chopin. And, of course, they *have* tried to silence me. There has been censorship of my work in many places, including my own country. We're none of us beyond that and we're going back into a period of tremendous repression. It's a dangerous time.

DCC: You consider yourself a satirist. What do you mean by the term?

EJ: I think a satirist is someone who scourges the world in order to bring it to its senses. That would, of course, be Swift's definition. Swift said also that satire is 'a glass wherein people do generally behold every face except their own'. That's a fair definition of satire too. But privately, I think of a satirist as someone who's disappointed in mankind (because he once was an idealist) and who makes fun in order to bring it to its senses. A satirist hopes to ameliorate the world, although the satirist will always tell you that he doesn't believe any amelioration is possible (because human beings are completely, morally destitute). Yet the satirist keeps on trying to bring them to their senses! Swift, for example, is the ideal example of a satirist. I love Swift. I even like what I know about him as a person, crazy as he was. The world tries to wear artists down. The world tries to batter them. All those creepy little conventional journalists, all the Lance Morrows of the world, try to make artists tow the mark and be good girls and boys. What they're doing is not really any different from what your mommy did when she said 'girls don't do this' or 'girls don't do that'. What are they but spokesmen for convention and bourgeois morality? They claim to be spokesmen for literature, but they're not spokesmen for literature. It's doubly hard if you're a woman because you're trained to try to win approval, to smile, to be nice to authority figures. You have to *learn* the sheer strength not to let the bastards get you down. It's very hard. By God, it took me two-and-a-half years to get over my sense of hurt and outrage about the way *How to Save Your Own Life* was treated. But really now, when I think about it, it was a very cleansing kind of experience because it reminded me that I am a maverick, and that I shouldn't be seeking approval. The minute I get approval I should be worried that maybe I'm not telling the truth in my writing anymore. As a writer, my value is partly as an irritant. If I'm not an irritant, maybe I'm not telling the truth anymore. If I ever write a book to which Elizabeth Hardwick responds and says, 'Ah, that's what women really think', I'll be very surprised if it's any good. I think Elizabeth Hardwick is a brilliant woman, and her writing in *Sleepless Nights* and in her literary essays is beautiful. But I think she's another woman writer who doesn't question the female role. And I don't think she tells the whole truth. I think she's been properly socialized to the female role.

DCC: Did you read *Seduction and Betrayal*?

EJ: Yes, I did. There are some things in it that are very good, and some things that are totally wrong headed about women. When, for example, she says about Sylvia Plath that the problems for a male poet are the same as the problems for a female poet, she's dead wrong. But the giveaway to me is *Sleepless Nights*. A beautiful book with a totally empty centre. How can she write about a character named Elizabeth who lives on West Sixty-seventh Street and talk about everything about her life except the central fact of her marriage? The whole relationship with the man who shaped her life, to whom her life was, in one sense, sacrificed, is left out. It's as though her life as a writer were sacrificed to being a muse to Robert Lowell. But this sacrifice is *not* in the book, which is precisely why the male critics all stand up and say, 'Bravo Elizabeth, you never gave him away! You did the thing that women are supposed to do, you stood by your man.' What distinguishes her from Tammy Wynette? I mean, *really*? Except that she's a beautiful, beautiful writer. And some of the stories in that book just break your heart. The things about the old people and the bag lady and the crazy old hotels on the west side. You read them and you weep. And then you weep again to think that a woman of such great talent should have been sacrificed to the ideal of the 'angel in the house'. Who says that perhaps her gifts were not equal to Lowell's? He did *not* spare her in his poems. But, Freedom, as Camus said, is the right not to lie, and women writers do not yet have that freedom. We're not supposed to say things about our husbands in public; we are not supposed to say things about our sex lives in public; we may only write about those subjects that we are allowed to write about (i.e., old bag ladies and hotels on the west side). And those we write about beautifully; we pull out all the stops. But we can't permit this self-censorship to continue! You cannot be a writer and censor yourself at the same time. And to be a good woman in this patriarchal society is to be self-censoring and self-stunting; *ergo*, the woman writer, is perforce a bad woman.

DCC: Are there are any other writers, past or present, whose comic sense you like, other than Swift?

EJ: I love Mark Twain, Chaucer, Rabelais, Colette, Keats and Blake. I discovered a lot when I did my eighteenth-century novel *Fanny*. I discovered who I still liked and who I didn't like at all any more. And I found I didn't like Pope at all any more, though I had once loved him.

DCC: You did your Master's thesis on Pope.

EJ: But I can barely stand him now. Swift, however, I like better than before. And I now find Fielding very trying – very distanced from the reader. I used to love Fielding. Now I find I can't bear the way he puts a kind of screen between himself and the reader. I once adored everything about *Joseph Andrews* and *Tom Jones*. Now, when he says, 'Dear Reader, this is the meaning of this scene', I hate the Fielding narrator. I also find I like Smollett very very much. I like his vulgarity and I like all the things in Smollett that Dickens imitated (Dickens was always saying that he learned from Smollett). I like him far better than Fielding at this point in my life. Isn't that funny?

DCC: How about people in the twentieth century?

EJ: I like Salinger very much too. Henry Miller – I think he's funny and I think he's bursting with life, despite his sexism, his anti-Semitism, and all the other antisocial things that he does.

DCC: Do you like Mordecai Richler's humour?

EJ: I loved *St. Urbain's Horseman*. I thought that was a terrific novel. Rollicking and funny and full of life. And full of a nice kind of vulgarity. You see I think Lessing is right in the sense that a novel has to be as crammed as life. That's what the novel was born to do.

DCC: You said that *Fear of Flying* was a female picaresque in the tradition of *Henderson the Rain King* and *Tom Jones* and *Augie March* and the *Tropics*. In what way were you thinking that it is a female picaresque?

EJ: It's a story about a young person going on the road in order to find herself. That's a very old literary form, perhaps the most ancient. It's a way of organizing a hero's or a heroine's quest. *Fear of Flying* is clearly a novel about the quest for self.

DCC: I also found that there were many structural and thematic similarities to Joyce's *A Portrait of the Artist as a Young Man*. *Fear of Flying* was the portrait of the artist as a young woman. I was impressed by the structure, the use of flashbacks, and as you said 'recollections in tranquillity', the use of consciousness.

EJ: That was my original title for the book. All I can say is that *A Portrait of the Artist as a Young Man* was one of my favourite books. I think I first read it when I was fourteen. I loved that and I loved *Dubliners*. Of course, *Ulysses* is a wonderful book although it takes five years to read it. When you read *Ulysses*, you read two pages a night and annotate and try to figure out what's going on. I would like to read it again, but it is not something I would readily plunge into. That's why when I started to talk about structure before, I said narrative structure is a ploy. In a way, it is a part of the writer's bag of tricks, and it's merely a way of keeping the reader turning pages.

DCC: I find so many of your ideas about narrative structure interesting and one of the things that struck me in *Fear of Flying* is that you called the last chapter 'A Nineteenth-Century Ending'. I assume that this title was ironic.

EJ: Obviously. Nineteenth-century novels end in marriage while twentieth-century novels end in divorce. Twentieth-century novels usually begin with relationships breaking apart. I was playing on those ideas.

DCC: You've been asked before about your audience. You've said that a possible epitaph could be: 'She addressed her readers as if they were her friends and they become her friends.' Yet you have also talked about the perverts you attract. When I first read *Fear of Flying*, my reaction was that you were talking to me partly because the novel makes highly literary allusions to writers and artists; on the other hand, you have said that there are women in Texas with minimal education who feel the same way.

EJ: I've never really understood that, but it's true. Perhaps we literary types underestimate our readers. They are smarter than we give them credit for being. Some people who read *Fear of Flying* and *How to Save Your Own Life* had never read a novel before.

DCC: I like what you said in *How to Save Your Own Life*; '. . . the aim of my writing is to utterly remove the distance between author and reader so that the book becomes a sort of semi-permeable membrane through which feelings, ideas, nutrients pass'. Do you think that that happens with the reader from Texas with minimal education?

EJ: Yes I do. I don't really know why, but I do think that I found an awful lot of readers who had never really read before. I must say that I have a lot of readers who are not readers of novels *per se*, and who are not particularly literate. It comes as a great shock to me because I was really the most bookish sort of Ph.D. candidate and never thought of myself as the kind of person who would become a popular writer. Even when *Fear of Flying* was first published, the publisher thought it was a literary first novel (by a poet no less) which is why they didn't promote it or advertise it enough. Nobody thought of it as a blockbuster. Nobody thought of it as a sex-novel, by God, and it was only a year later that people were asking me in interviews, 'Did you put in the sex to calculate the success?' As if I had calculated it! I wish I could! So it comes as a great shock to me to have an audience that broad. But I like it. In a way I'd rather have an audience of people who have never read a single book before than have an audience of fabulators. Better fornicators than fabulators! [*laughs*].

DCC: What is it about the eighteenth century that you particularly admire? I loved *Fanny*.

EJ: It's before the nineteenth century and the horrible sexual hypocrisy of the nineteenth century. As you know, if you've read Boswell, life in the eighteenth century was far less hypocritical about sex than life today. Sexuality was much more in the open than it is today. The English in the eighteenth century were extremely coarse about hygenic functions, personal functions, shitting and pissing and fucking. When you go back to the eighteenth century, therefore, you go back to a period of great robustness and great vulgarity. But it is also the period in which our modern consciousness was formed. We, in the United States, have a constitution that is an eighteenth-century document. Our country has eighteenth-century ideals – 'The pursuit of Happiness', for example. So I take this wonderful time in which there was so much ferment about the slave trade and the rights of women (and yet the women were legally second-class citizens; they could not own property, they could not vote), and I say, 'What if a woman like myself had lived in that time?' And I was able to put all the problems of women in society in relief because I was dealing with a time removed from ours, and yet through it I could satirize our own time. It was a book I had always promised myself to write. For years I had wanted to do an eighteenth-century novel in which the heroine got involved with all the great men of her time: Pope, Hogarth, Swift, all of them. And it was great fun to write – and, I'm told, great fun to read. My desire to write *Fanny* came out of my perception that there are far too few great women heroines in literature. I wanted Fanny to be a female picaro, an innocent who is educated but not corrupted by the evils of an evil world. I use Cleland's Fanny as a kind of counterpoint to show that women can be far more than the whores of erotic fantasy. I have always had great affection for *Fanny Hill*, mostly because of the sunnyness of the writing, but there is no denying that Cleland's imagery of women is extremely reductive. I wanted to show that a woman might be reduced to working as a whore, but she would not necessarily forfeit her brain and subtlety thereby.

DCC: In your 'Afterword' to *Fanny*, you wrote: 'In many ways her [Fanny's] consciousness is modern. But I do believe that in every age there are people whose consciousness transcends their own time and that these people, whether fictional or historical, are those with whom we most closely identify and those about whom we most enjoy reading.'

EJ: It is one of the tragedies of the movement for feminine liberation (which spans the last three centuries) that each generation has to discover it anew as if the issues had never been around before. Our generation is no exception. In fact, Lady Montagu, Mary Wollstonecraft and others understood female bondage quite as well as we do. Their works are still tremendously timely. Society has not changed all that much, alas. But even with all their self-awareness, these women accepted their societal constraints as the price of their survival. Fanny does not. She has an unshakeable conviction of the importance of her own selfhood which is really rather modern.

DCC: Witchcraft is an important part of *Fanny* and you've since written a book called *Witches*.

EJ: One of the most attractive theories of witchcraft suggests that witchcraft is, in fact, the remains of an ancient matriarchal pagan cult surviving secretly in a Christian world. Although some scholars have quibbled with this theory, it seemed to me an important and richly evocative philosophical underpinning for a novel. I wanted to write a novel about female strength, female bonding, and using the witches exemplified these things underlying *Fanny* as a matriarchal myth. Women come to help other women in childbirth, in rape, in economic need. The men are incidental to the story. The male lovers are companions, but the primary importance is the mother–daughter bond.

DCC: Fanny often changes into male costume. This aspect of androgyny can be seen in opera, drama and literature. Shakespeare often has women playing men: Rosalind in *As You Like It*, Viola in *Twelfth Night*, and Portia in *Merchant of Venice*.

EJ: I made Fanny change into male costume throughout the book to emphasize the capriciousness of sexual roles and their immense variability. The sexual roles as we know them in our society are really metaphors for power and powerlessness. They are not immutable and biologically destined. By showing Fanny putting on and taking off roles with her clothes, I wanted to show that sexual roles are every bit as superficial as clothes – and as important.

DCC: You have said that with *Fanny* you wanted to 'try an epical novel, an historio-comic epic (as Fielding would say), in which I could show through the counterpoint between past and present, just how much had changed for women and how little'.

EJ: In the early seventies, it was very important for women writers to make sense of their own presence, to understand their own oppression and anger. As the feminist movement matured, it became important to see our own struggles in an historical context, to realize that the more things change, the more they stay the same, and to discover our own histories. The historical novel, like the science-fiction novel, has often been a satirical device for viewing our own world. In *Fanny*, I wanted to show both how immensely the world had changed for women, and how little. In general, I think writers tend to turn to the past for their material when the present seems overwhelming. The perspective of the past enables us to understand our own times more acutely.

DCC: What is your response to people who ask, 'When are you going to create a male hero?'

EJ: People always ask me when I'm going to write about men – as if writing about women were just a warm-up for the main business which is writing about men. The question has a sexist assumption about it, albeit an unconscious one. Male novelists have often used female protagonists to represent the human condition (Anna Karenina, Mme Bovary), but when a woman uses a female protagonist to represent the human condition, critics ask 'When are you going to write about a *male* hero?' It seems to me that we have had four thousand years of male heroes, and only about a decade or so of female heros. That means we still have three thousand, nine hundred and ninety years to go before we catch up!

6   Isaac Bashevis Singer

DCC: Saul Bellow is on record as having said that he finds the label of 'Jewish writer' intellectually vulgar, unnecessarily parochializing and utterly without value. Do you feel the same?

IBS: Well, I would tell you I don't feel so strongly against it. I consider myself a Jewish writer but as a whole I call myself a Yiddish writer, because if you call a French writer by the French language and the English writer by the English language and so on, I would prefer to be called a Yiddish writer. What Jewishness is, is not clear. It may be religion. However, Yiddish is a very clear notion, so I rather call myself a Yiddish writer. But I am a Jewish writer just the same, I am proud if people call me so.

DCC: There is some debate among various ethnic groups that artists should either emphasize the uniqueness of the group or transcend this limitation. Allen Guttmann has suggested that Arthur Miller's *Focus* and Laura Z. Hobson's *Gentlemen's Agreement* are respectively counterproductive and worse than trivial because both novels attempt to demonstrate that Jews and Gentiles are indistinguishable. It is necessary to affirm the Jews' difference to other groups.

IBS: I haven't read a single of these novels. The only thing I can tell you is that there isn't such a thing as what an ethnic writer should do or a writer generally should do. A real writer does what he thinks is right, what he pleases, not what some professor will tell him he should do. There isn't such a thing as an ethnic writer, all writers are ethnic, because if they are not ethnic, they are not writers. A writer does not become ethnic because he speaks a language which is spoken by five million, and he is not ethnic if he speaks a language which is spoken by a hundred million. Being ethnic means being rooted in one's

This interview first appeared in *London Magazine*, March 1984.

Isaac Bashevis Singer (*photograph: Trevor Clark*)

environment and in this respect every writer is ethnic, so this whole business with the ethnic writer is a complete misunderstanding. It is only the writer who writes in a language which is spoken by many people that likes to call the writer who writes in Bulgarian or Serbian, ethnic. But in what way is he ethnic? How many people spoke English in Shakespeare's time or in Milton's time and how many people could read altogether? So we are either all ethnic writers or none of us is.

DCC: There is an extensive bibliography on your work, most of which is contradictory. Irving Buchen sees you as a creator of an 'Eternal Past', Eli Katz sees you as a modernist, Robert Alter sees you as a maverick, Baruch Hochman sees you as a traditionalist, and Irving Howe sees you as an existentialist. Do you like this critical uncertainty?

IBS: I will tell you, maybe I am all of these things and maybe I am none of them. I don't know what these names really mean. Professors like to have classifications, to call a writer ethnic or what other qualifications you made. I don't know what an existentialist writer is. I studied philosophy but what an existentialist is, I have not the slightest idea. So I would say I am satisfied with the idea that I am a writer.

DCC: Do you feel that critics and scholars see things in the writer's work which he never intended? Do you think they obscure literature with arcane theories and an overabundance of analysis?

IBS: Actually it is a question of who is the critic and who is the professor. One of them may see things, another may just imagine things, one may try to obscure things, another one may try to clarify things. I would say in science generalizations are useful, but when it comes to literature and to art all generalizations are false. You have to judge every writer or every artist by himself.

DCC: When you lecture or write about literature, what is your critical approach?

IBS: My critical approach is only, is it good or bad? I think although many critics try to make a science out of criticism in literature, I think it will never be a science. In science, you don't say something is good or bad, you only state facts but when you write a story you want it to be a good story and if you read a story, you want it to be a good story. If you go to a doctor, you want the doctor to cure you not kill you. From a scientific point of view to kill or to cure, they are both events. Since art is not a science the question of good or bad is the main question. Of course, the critics and the professors, since they want to be scientists, they never speak in these terms, they say only that the reviewers speak about good and bad. They have to state how the writer came to this and in what environment he lived. Actually the question of good and bad is the real question in art. The same Picasso who painted good pictures in his young days painted miserable pictures in his old days. Although the professors can write a million books about him, it is still a fact that the good was good and the bad was bad, so, this is my answer.

DCC: You once remarked that if you have been ambiguous in your writing, if you yourself are not sure how things work, then why should the reader be sure. Critics and scholars sometimes see your ambivalence and your irresolute endings as a blemish in your work, such as in *The Family Moskat*. This ambivalence is, of course, contradictory to what they want to do. The commentators demand clarification.

IBS: How can they demand clarification if they themselves try so hard to be obscure? I say that so many events, they are ambiguous, but I never try to be obscure. Let's say if I describe a situation, sometimes the situation itself is ambiguous. As a matter of fact, there is ambiguity in almost all of our actions except in something as simple as eating and sleeping. The writer or the artist does not have to explain himself. The events themselves should make it clear, but I don't mean by clear, crystal clear. There is ambiguity in much of what the artist has done, in other words, he can judge a situation from the point of view of many levels.

DCC: From the critic's point of view or the scholar's point of view, what then would be the appropriate response?

IBS: The appropriate response would be, does a good reader enjoy this story or is it for him already obvious and tedious and doesn't give him any pleasure. I would say that good writers entertain good readers and cheap writers entertain cheap readers and very bad writers entertain no-one. But there must be some element of pleasure and if it doesn't give you any pleasure, it is just stuff for people to do research. It stops being literature. Just as a doctor, if he never cures anybody, he is not a doctor if all his patients go home and die. The same thing is true with a writer if all his readers just yawn and don't want to read him. Then he is not a writer.

DCC: You have said that sometimes not only the reader learns from good criticism but also the writer. Could you give me some examples where you have learned?

IBS: When I say good criticism, I don't mean only the criticism from critics but also the criticism of readers. I get letters from people and I read them. There are also critics who can tell you things, but I learn mostly by the simple kind of criticism that a reader will say to you, that you paint a false picture, or you are not convincing, or you repeat yourself. But from the kind of criticism where critics will write two hundred pages about me, about the environment and the political situation, I learn nothing. The political situation or the sociological situation does not really explain why one writer is good and the other writer is bad. It can rather be explained by his genes, and no one knows really how they work and what they are.

DCC: It's your belief that experimentation with literature takes place in the laboratory of humanity, not on paper, unlike some writers who emphasize 'form'; as you have said, whether to punctuate a poem or not to punctuate, whether to sign with capital letters or with small letters.

IBS: What I mean is that by sheer changing of words, or changing the construction of the sentence, by using special kinds of words like Joyce did, you are not going to create something new in literature. The real writer explores life all the time, not style. Style is important and every story has its style, but if you depend on style itself, you will never create anything of value. Just like a painter all the time looks at the model because he knows that the face of the model keeps on changing, and he can see there more than on the canvas. The same thing is true in literature. Millions of changes take place in life and its combinations and there is your laboratory, not in style. A good writer should have a good style but it is not average.

DCC: Romain Rolland's *Jean Christophe* and Thomas Mann's *The Magic Mountain* bored you because you said that they were works for critics, not readers. Do you think that readers today still seek that which is analytic and puzzle-solving?

IBS: A lot of readers have been spoiled by reading the critics and by reading books about literature and by trying to become writers themselves, although they may not have the talent. Since millions of people in this country have studied literature in universities, they become would-be professors themselves and they would like to find in literature always that literature should solve the social situation, the political situation, that the writer should tell them if they should vote for Carter or for Reagan or something like this, that the writer should free the proletariat, that he should make peace. They demand from the writer things which he cannot do, which he has never done. The writer, the painter, the actor, are entertainers, in either the lower sense of the word or in the higher sense of the word. He has to give something to the reader, but he cannot really give him the things which he doesn't have.

DCC: Is that what Aaron means when he says that writers are like magicians in *Shosha*?

IBS: I don't know what he means. The only thing I know is what *I* mean. I mean that when I begin to read a book I may find a lot of scholarship in it and a lot of the situation, but if I read three pages and I haven't enough I know that this is not a good book as far as I am concerned. No matter how friendly he is to humanity or how unfriendly he is, it doesn't bother me at all.

DCC: What are the binding limitations of narration?

IBS: If you will write a story on ten thousand pages, no matter whether it is good or not, no one is going to publish it and no one is going to read it. This is not true about science. If you really make great scientific discoveries, there are no limitations. Since literature and art have to innovate, please one reader, to entertain a reader, there are limits to what you can do and what you cannot do. So this reader, this artist who will give you a canvas as large as this room, and he will leave it all white, and he will say that it expresses some part of his soul; it may express his soul, but I don't give a hoot about it. I don't care about his soul and what it expresses.

DCC: You are a story-teller. Yet many modern writers seem to move away more and more from story-telling.

IBS: Take away story-telling from literature and literature has lost everything. It is story-telling. When literature begins to analyse life and also tries to explain the facts of life, if it tries to become Freudian, Jungian or Adlerian, it becomes a bore and meaningless. Because what Freud had to say he has already said and it's not my duty or your duty to write stories according to Freud.

DCC: Have you ever read Thomas Pynchon's *Gravity's Rainbow*?

IBS: I looked into it.

DCC: Do you like it?

IBS: Not at all. I like a rainbow but not Pynchon's [*both laugh*].

DCC: In 1974, when you won the National Book Award, Thomas Pynchon was the co-winner. He, of course, is quite a hermit and he didn't show up to receive his award, so his publisher sent the comedian Professor Irwin Corey. I wonder, how did you feel about that?

IBS: I was in Israel but I didn't hide like him. When I got the information that Pynchon got it, I mixed him up in my mind with another writer. There is an English writer who is also a critic and who has a similar name. Anyhow, I made a mistake because I didn't really know about Pynchon then and so I sent words of praise about the wrong writer. I don't know whether Pynchon is good or not because I don't understand what he is talking about.

DCC: You have mentioned that this century has not given us great gifts in fiction as the century before did. Whom do you admire among your contemporaries?

IBS: Who says that I have to admire anybody? I don't read enough really to know what is going on in literature. This is the truth. When I was young, I was nearer to the nineteenth century so I read the masters of the nineteenth century. When you get older, you don't read so much. So many books are coming out, that I don't know whom to admire or whom not to admire. I think this is true about many writers. They don't read enough because there is too much to read nowadays.

DCC: That is very true. We live in a time when reviewers claim a 'masterpiece' every month. These are, what you call, the false witnesses to greatness. How do you know when you are in the presence of a masterpiece, and how would you define the word or would you even use it?

IBS: I know that a masterpiece lifts up my spirit, it gives me the feeling of great joy, it gives me the feeling of discovery, while the opposite of masterpiece makes me feel that I see something which I don't want to see and which I have already seen and which does not interest me. So I would say the emotions explain it, I cannot really explain it by words. Let's say when I was a boy, I read *Crime and Punishment*; I didn't have any notions about art or how to define it because I just was delighted about it and I still enjoy Dostoevsky. I also know that I tried to read some other books, some Yiddish books, some Hebrew books, Polish books which never gave me any joy and this is enough for me to judge and I would say, this is still my measure today. If you will ask a man how do you define love, how do you know that you are in love with a woman, he cannot tell you if she has a straight nose or a crooked nose. If you are in love, you feel that you are in love and if you are indifferent you feel that you are indifferent. Of course, the critics have to find words for these emotions but basically it is the emotion, not the words.

DCC: What was there about Henry Miller's work that you particularly admired, apart from his freeing up of censorship?

IBS: I will tell you. I wouldn't say that everything which he wrote was good, but when he was good he was direct and he was clear, and he was human, and this was the language of a man and not of a stutterer. He left you with something, he gave you something. He did not all the time cry on your shoulder and complain all the time like some writers do.

DCC: Did you know him for a very long time?

IBS: I read him and I met him a few times, I got letters from him, and we were friends but mostly far away ones. He moved to California, I moved here.

DCC: You have admitted that Herman Broder in *Enemies, A Love Story*, is the way you would have been in his circumstances. You seem to feel no restriction at all in admitting your autobiographical ties to your work. Yet I find a number of contemporary writers hasten to disavow that their work is in any way autobiographical.

IBS: They are afraid to get a bad name. They are afraid that people who say, if you describe a thief, you are a thief yourself, but this is completely silly because Dostoevsky described a murderer but didn't murder anybody. I am not really afraid to say that my writing has many autobiographical elements because many of the things which I describe that happened to me are things which might have happened to me and literature is not history, not only about things which happened. The writer is free to write about things which might have happened and he uses imagination, his experiences. I am not afraid to get a bad name because of my life.

DCC: You refer to the Holocaust in your writing and the consequences of the Holocaust on your characters. But it is never central to your work.

IBS: I would say that people are entitled to write their memoirs. But to make fiction out of the Holocaust is not the right thing because you cannot write a book of fiction about twenty thousand people being burned or killed. This is because fiction is always about a few people. You cannot write fiction about millions of people. You cannot write fiction about the masses. It is true that the communist writers tried it but they never succeeded. Even in Tolstoy's *War and Peace*, there is neither war or peace, there is only a description of a few characters and they are those which remain with you.

DCC: You write short stories as well as novels. How does the short story occur in your mind as opposed to a novel or vice versa?

IBS: Well, a short story is a shorter story than a novel. A novel is a long story and a short story is a short story. Some writers will take a short story and make a long novel out of it, which means they will repeat themselves and analyse and go on, but this is not good. Sometimes he has a long story to tell so he cannot make it short. Tolstoy couldn't have made *Anna Karenina* a short story, it was a long story, and the same thing is true about *Crime and Punishment*. The same thing is true about *Madame Bovary*. The art of writing a short story is very great because given a short story's genuine characters and emotions and suspense and all these things which you need for a story, it is a great art. I would say that in a long story, a lesser talent can sometimes succeed just by heaping on a lot of facts and giving the reader reading stuff for many days if he prefers it. But in a short story, if you really don't have the mastership of writing, it would become nothing.

DCC: If the power of philosophy, as you have said, is an attack upon reason, if the human intellect confronted existence, and existence stubbornly refused to be systematized, what is this human impulse to give order to existence? Why do we not just move in step with chaos and dissolution?

IBS: Fear of death, because everything which has a life is afraid of dying. We all have this imagination that when you die you are still there, you lie in your grave and it's dark, and you are hungry and you don't eat, you are thirsty and you don't drink. We imagine that and we are afraid of it and the fear of death is what keeps human beings alive. When the fear of death ceases, a person really has a good reason to commit suicide and they do.

DCC: Aaron in *Shosha* says that literature helps to keep time from vanishing.

IBS: It did so for a long time. Now you can make movies and you can record speeches, but until about fifty years ago, literature was the only record of human life, a simple kind of life, not what the kings did, but what simple people did. Generally, I would say that bad writers always like to write about big people; they would take as their hero Napoleon. Actually, there are records of what they did. It is the simple people, the plain people, the unknown people whose life should be recorded. So the writer who always writes about Freud or about such people is really not doing literature a favour, because we know about Freud without a writer. We don't need any fiction writer to explain Freud or Nietzsche or Schopenhauer but we really need a story about Raskolnikov or Madame Bovary who were simple people and no one would ever have thought about them if these great writers had not told about them.

DCC: So many of your characters, I find, are running and having to escape. Tamara, in *Enemies, a Love Story* observes that Herman has the look of an animal 'surrounded by hunters and cannot escape'. But he perversely enjoys the danger and compares himself to the 'calculating gambler' who thrives on daily risk. Yasha Mazur in *The Magician of Lublin* also lives by risk. What is the value of living on the edge?

IBS: It is true. We need suspense in life. We cannot live without any suspense. The reason why you don't like to go to some far away village and stay there, is because you know that every day will be similar to the other. You will just get up, you will not know what to do with yourself, and such a life is to some people worse than death. It is true that the people who live in this village feel different because they have relations and friendships and quarrels, there is some suspense in their life. But let's say if you go there a stranger, you would run away. Why we need suspense in life, I don't know, but we need it in both life and literature. Some people, if they cannot get pleasant suspense will creative negative suspense, which is better than nothing, than complete boredom.

DCC: In *A Young Man in Search of Love*, you wrote: 'Weininger, Schopenhauer, Nietzsche and my own experiences had transformed me into an antifeminist.' Do you make a distinction between anti-feminist as opposed to anti-female?

IBS: When I was young, you know, young boys always have bad things to say about girls and girls have to say bad things about boys, but actually I am not an anti-feminist. You cannot be 'anti' half of humanity or more than a half. Of course, women are women and men are men and no movement can change it. In other words, the woman who thinks that by liberating herself, by putting on a pair of pants, she will become different, makes a big mistake. We have to stay basically as we came into this world, and I am not against women, I am against those who think that we have the power really to outsmart nature and change things completely, which is not true at all.

DCC: Is that what Herman means when he says to Masha that she is a modern woman through and through, with all of the modern woman's ambitions and delusions?

IBS: In a way, yes.

DCC: Although you write about the evil and weakness of men, the women seem so much worse. They, as a group, often are spiders and witches, they can be bought, they have no logic, no memory and they are principally vessels of sex, to paraphrase Otto Weininger.

IBS: I don't write just that they are witches; they are also sorcerers and murderers and thieves. I cannot write all the time about good people. As a matter of fact, good people are not good topics for literature. It's the bad people who create suspense, so for a writer to condemn himself only to write about good Jews or good women would be literary suicide.

DCC: What is there about Shosha that makes Aaron sure that she is the only woman who won't betray him?

IBS: We can never be one hundred per cent sure, but a girl like Shosha could not rush to have a love affair three years after she would marry. She would most probably be a decent devoted human being.

DCC: Part of the reason that Aaron trusts her is because she has a purity of heart. But she is intellectually stunted and she is stuck in childhood.

IBS: All the saints were children. By the way, this lack of intellectualism is not such a terrible thing in my eyes. To me, Shosha would be good as a wife or as a lover. I wouldn't be very much in despair by the fact that Shosha cannot understand Kafka or *Finnegans Wake* and all these things. I think that many of the so-called intellectuals are terribly stunted, although they have doctor titles. Some of them are, in my eyes, highly retarded.

DCC: Dostoevsky would agree with that idea.

IBS: He wouldn't have to agree with me, and I wouldn't have to agree with him. He is an older writer [*both laugh*].

DCC: When you were young, you said you saw a basis for ethics. Did you ever find it?

IBS: There is no intellectual basis for ethics, except Schopenhauer believed in a feeling of compassion for other people. He was the only philosopher who believed that compassion is the basis for acting. If you feel how terrible it is to be beaten, you don't want to beat somebody else. And again, there is no real explanation for this, some people have compassion and some people don't have it. So some men will jump into the water to rescue a child while another man with the same logic will take a child and throw it into the water.

DCC: In your introduction to an edition of *Aesop's Fables*, you wrote: 'The fable taught man that there is sometimes a deep truth behind an obvious falsehood. . . . Art in general has much to learn from Aesop, because art as a reflection of human character, can never undergo radical changes.' Could you give me some examples of this in your own work?

IBS: Let's say such a proverb as 'A chain is as strong as its weakest link', contains a lot of wisdom; not only is it true in literature, it is true in medicine, it is true in politics, it is true almost in all human relations. So, such simple words, call them fables or proverbs, sometimes contain deep truths and though they look like clichés, they are far from being clichés. There are such things as eternal truths. Although any woman in the market can say it, it's still profound, more profound than some of these aphorisms which contain only a half truth or quarter truth or they are false from the very beginning to the end.

DCC: In a world of faction–fiction, the novel as journalism, you still write about a world of wonder and dreams and spirits, an imaginary world that does seem only once removed from the true world.

IBS: I would not feel like writing what they call faction–fiction because if it is facts why call it fiction, if it is fiction why call it facts? However, in my autobiographies, I sometimes mix facts with fiction because I like to write about things which did not happen but might have happened. I also sometimes don't want to divulge truths about people who are still alive so I say in the preface that I write about things that are not to be taken as complete autobiographies. This is true about *A Little Boy in Search of God*, *A Young Man in Search of Love* and about my so-called autobiographic volume called *Lost in America*. This is the third part of it.

DCC: I'm asking this next question for all unpublished and published writers who don't have your success. Since your Nobel Prize do you ever get your work rejected?

IBS: Yes, all the time. I don't get it rejected myself, my agent gets it. The magazines, which accept the worst kind of junk, when it comes to me, they are very, very strict, as if they would feel here is a person who should give us something good. Why they feel that way, I don't know and I am very glad of this. Sometimes I don't always agree with their objection, and if I don't agree, I try to find another magazine who will not reject me. But the very fact that people don't assume that everything I write must be good is for me an omen that I am still considered a beginner which I like to feel I am.

7 Vasily Aksyonov

DCC: The American writer Harlan Ellison has written that 'The valuable writer is a night rider. A commando who slips in when things are most quiet, and turns the night red with explosions. Don't tell me what a nice story I wrote; I don't need that, I don't want to hear it. Don't hum at me, don't invite me to parties for pleasant chat. I want to hear the sound of your soul. Then I can translate it into the mortal dreads we all share and fire them back at you transmogrified, reshaped as amusing or frightening fables.' Does that mean anything to you?

VA: Just Mr Ellison's personal feelings. I always try to avoid such a bombastic way of expression. Each writer should be a sort of entertainer. I really consider that literature is a part of the human carnival. I prefer to create something like fireworks rather than Mr Ellison's dangerous explosions. So, please do tell me what a nice story I wrote and don't hesitate to invite me to parties for pleasant chat. I really need it.

DCC: Julio Cortázar said, 'My novels reflect what happened to me over the years.' Alternatively E. L. Doctorow has said, 'I don't take my characters directly from my own life or experience. I put them through several prisms. There is no calculation or intent beyond what a few images mean to me.' Do you lean to either of these views?

VA: From the very beginning I felt closer to Julio Cortázar's point of view. As far as I remember, among our friends and among our own people there was the opinion that you should be as far from yourself in your writing as possible. It's a sort of homework for high quality, professional skilfulness until you are finding yourself between two temptations. To write about yourself is to create a romantic image of the contemporary writer. On the other hand, to prove your skilfulness, your

Vasily Aksyonov (*photograph: Trevor Clark*)

professional ability one should write about somebody else's life, about some remote cultures – be cool, restrained, sophisticated. You can realize that everything is not so simple. Hemingway used to write about himself and he was reincarnated in all of his images. On the other hand Balzac credited the chain of different characters, women, children, older ones, young ones and others as being very remote from himself. In Hemingway's case, the professional writer, who wrote fiercely, and restlessly, was obsessed by writing rather than bullfighting or drinking wine. If you're looking at the ways in which his cultures differ you realize that all these faces are just the nebulous terms of his own face before the mirror. Leo Tolstoy is everywhere in his *War and Peace*. You can see him on the battlefield as well as in the bedroom of Natasha Rostova. So, writers are not gods to create new people. Every time we are trying to describe somebody else we replace this person by ourselves or the numerous masks of our own face. It doesn't mean that you have to follow only the events of your own life. To me it's boring to describe your own life events. The situation is paradoxical from my point of view, you have to be inside all of your characters and at the same time you should be somewhat aloof.

DCC: Your earlier work does not reflect the experiences of your youth – the Stalin terrors. Why did you choose to ignore it in this way? Was it a need to repress unpleasant memories? Geoffrey Hosking suggests that the barbed wire of Kolyma is as remote to the long-haired youngsters of your earlier writing as it was to Augie March or Lucky Jim.

VA: During the early sixties many times I asked myself, 'Why am I so reluctant to write about my terrible experience in Kolyma, about the fates of my own parents and others, and about this bloody Stalin's crimes?' I always considered this memory to be used as material for my main book, but I always postponed the start of this new book. Instead, I was looking for a so-called young hero in whom I presumed hopes for a better future. Now, looking back and trying to appraise my earlier writing I realize why I returned to these themes of secondary importance and was so reluctant to start the main book. I think that happened because all those years have been an endless carnival for our generation and probably unconsciously I tried to maintain this carnival mood in myself and in our circle of friends. That is probably why this memory of terror and fears seem to me out of place. So, year by year I postponed the writing of this main book as if I predicted that other times are coming, that our carnival will be over sooner rather than later and the different times will come serious enough to start this main book.

DCC: You have said that our greatest value was our old wounds. Does the artist need struggle? Is this Edmund Wilson's wound and the bow theory?

VA: Unfortunately, I am not familiar with the wound and the bow theory. It was the late Yuri Trifonov who said that old wounds are our hidden treasure. Something like that. I can quote another author, Aleksandr Blok. His words could be translated approximately this way: 'Those who were born during the deaf times failed to recall the past. We, the children of Russia's horror years cannot forget anything.' So, you see in the deaf times, the quiet peaceful years, that memory of literature is dead so that's why these old wounds are so important for the writer. I don't believe that the struggle against anything is necessary for writing. Maybe the suffering is more important for him. Struggling against the Soviets for instance, against censorship, against the totalitarian oppression, you'll always have the impression that you are doing something clumsy, something shameful, something humiliating which humiliates yourself. Maybe that sounds strange, but I never was proud of my struggle against Soviet bureaucrats. Probably because they are so ugly, even struggle against them becomes an ugly, ugly thing. I would say that the struggle against them looks like swimming inside the haystack. However, even humiliations like this are useful for you, the writer. Anything is useful for you: suffering and struggle, old wounds and fresh ones. And it's not necessary that you are a participant of some important events or a fighter in some historic battle. You could be an onlooker, but being an onlooker you can get a sharper sensation than the direct participants of the events can because you are a writer. Remember Dostoevsky's little girl. Remember the struggle of Polish solidarity; these events could be equal for a writer.

DCC: Hemingway wrote that among the casualties of the First World War were the words 'sacred', 'glorious', 'sacrifice' and 'in vain'. D. H. Lawrence and William Faulkner were both concerned about the loss of certain words. Have you lost any words?

VA: Our generation has not experienced war, but two decades of post-Stalin struggle in the Soviet society could be equal to war I would say. Now the paradox is that we gained some words rather than lost them. Among those words abandoned in Soviet society and gained after Stalin during these two last decades, I would mention the words like mercy, sympathy, enchantment. I would mention also the forgotten capital letter in words like God, Lord. You could not spell these words with a capital letter and when one started to write down these words with a capital letter it meant that the really new mentality appeared. Besides, we gained the tune of irony. So, these famous Hemingway words enriched the Soviet literature of the sixties. We could be called the 'lost generation' from the official point of view. But as a matter of fact, we were a sort of rediscovered generation because we rediscovered the forgotten words of the Russian language, the forgotten capital letter, and international irony.

DCC: Do you agree with Francis Bacon that 'histories make men wise'?

VA: When I hear sentences like this I can say right away, 'Yes, I agree.' Histories make men wise, sure, that's for sure. But on the other hand I can easily say, 'No, I don't agree.' Histories make men silly; as well I can say, 'Histories make men optimistic or, yes, histories make men despair.'.

DCC: You once stated that Russian writers abroad can help the writers at home to break out of their isolation, to shake the wall: 'We will return with a new experience, with the experience of America and Europe, of the whole of mankind.' How specifically will that change the writing?

VA: Our Russian culture needs to be returned to the family of civilized nations. So, if histories make men optimistic we have the right to fight for that. On the contrary if histories make men despair we would have the right to retreat. Presumably we are optimistic and Russia eventually got a chance to get out of its provincial, ideological seclusion. It can not but change everything. The restoration of our links with the European culture is probably what our ideological watchdogs fear most of all. That's why they encourage, nowadays, literature which proclaims the isolation of the Russian culture. It is called 'village literature' or perhaps it would be better to say 'rural literature'. There are some talented authors among the writers of rural literature but in encouraging them the ideological officials with their intolerance are trying to impose these rural goals as a normal way of Russian literature. So, in other words, they are trying to restore the reclusiveness and isolation of the Russian literature of today. Their goal is clear. No links with the West. You have to write only about the simple characters, about the so-called folk characters. You have to write about the simple human beings without any ambitions, without any ambiguity. As a matter of fact, the writers who work in the Western literary tradition are now ousted. So, if things change and we will be able to return to our country, personally or by our books, no doubt the situation will be changed in writing. The most important thing is that the spirit of tolerance will dominate, and the Western attitude toward writers will be established.

DCC: Your mother, Eugenia Ginzburg [author of *Journey into the Whirlwind* and *Within the Whirlwind*] chose these words from Aleksandr Blok's poem 'Retribution' as an epigraph for her autobiography: 'The twentieth century – more homeless still, a haze where terrors hide beyond our ken'. Can literature ever truly reach the essential formlessness of this?

VA: That's a good qustion about formlessness. Formlessness of that kind is a fear of prophecy. The experience of prophecy is always frightening. Every time I reached the edge of that formlessness I was frightened. I would prefer to be a writer rather than be a prophet. As a human being I would better avoid encounters of that kind, but it's inevitable that writing something serious you will touch from time to time something scary. It's not necessary for writers to be always inside these dimensions. There is no need for a writer to be a prophet, no need for a writer to be a psychic. However, the perception of this formless cloud should exist in your writing.

DCC: For those in the West who don't know about the '*Metropol* affair', could you tell me about it?

VA: This so-called *Metropol* affair has been the first attempt in the history of Soviet literature to establish an independent literary magazine without any interference from the party ideological officials. Our predecessors always tried to get the favour of the Party. The *Metropol* contributors never tried to do that and we even tried to avoid any relationship with the ideological operators of the central committee, or any relationship with watchdogs inside the Writers' Union. That was really a daring attempt and I cannot rule out that there was blackmailing from our side because we decided first to make the publication of *Metropol* in twelve copies and then to smuggle a couple of copies to the West and only after that to let the ideological leadership know about the affair. We were sure that if they were in the know beforehand, they would destroy the whole idea. On the other hand, there was not any sort of conspiracy in this case. When we were preparing our first edition the so-called literary Moscow was talking about it endlessly. These *Metropol* people could be divided roughly into three groups. First are the famous authors, among them are the writers like Akhmadulina, Bitou and myself who have been established in Soviet literature for a long period of time. Another group are the younger writers, who by that time had lost any of their hopes to get their works published in Soviet magazines. They were represented by the writers like Popov, Erofeev. The third group are the authors well known in the Moscow and Leningrad literary underground. These brilliant authors like Rein, Vakhtin, Sapgir and some others including the enormously famous Vysotsky. All these guys could not even dream of their works published in the official Soviet magazines. So we decided to combine all our efforts to establish this unique collection of contemporary Russian prose and poetry and philosophical articles, like the work by Victor Trosnikov. This unique character who used to be a physicist and the man of the so-called scientific revolution in the Soviet Union all of a sudden lost all his materialistic views and switched to religion, to the absolutely idealistic perception of the universe and human life. And side by side with him the philosopher of the, I would say the, positivist school, like Batkin with his thoughtful research of the meaning of contemporary culture. I would say that the basis on which all these authors were unified was ethical rather than aesthetic. These authors represented the great scale of variety in different artistic schools and streams. Some of them were the *avant-garde* authors and other ones represented traditional styles and so on. They are all unified on the basis of everybody's desire to get out of the party control. I don't say to get out of state control because we admitted the state control, the state censorship rather than party ideological censorship. It seems to me that the *Metropol* case is an unique one and maybe the first sign of the growing disobedience inside Soviet society. It's still underestimated by the world public opinion.

DCC: Why did Soviet authorities oppose the publication in the Soviet Union of *Golden Pieces of Iron*, a novel which from an ideological point of view I would have thought could only have pleased the authorities?

VA: If they were pleased from the ideological point of view with *Golden Pieces of Iron* they would print it. I went out of my way to get this novel published in the Soviet Union because I felt that this was a turning point for me. I deliberately tried to avoid painful questions like the cult of personalities and so on. My personal task in this novel was to achieve the full expression of my craft and skilfulness. I love this novel probably better than many others that are so-called more serious. It seems to me that the ideological watchdogs could see from the very first moment that this novel was out of their field, out of their zone and aesthetically it was far away from their kingdom. It was probably more distant aesthetically from their kingdom than the work of Solzhenitsyn or some other dissidents. That's why they were so negative to *Golden Pieces of Iron* because that was a book written about probably their worst enemy, the Soviet intellectual of the sixties. I have my own strong feeling that nowadays the aesthetic and let me say the style becomes the matter of ethics which could be from time to time even more important than the moral issues. Aesthetic alienation from officialdom is considered by political watchdogs maybe almost equal to political alienation from them. So, after I failed to publish *Golden Pieces of Iron* in the Soviet Union, I realized that I became completely an inner emigré in my own country. This was important for myself and the turning point in my destiny.

DCC: You have said that you don't believe that the novel is dead but that it exists for a group of people who are interested in it, but this group will *not* be in the majority.

VA: That's for sure. The novel is alive and it's not going to die although the circle of readers becomes narrower. It's impossible to write a novel for everybody in our time of the information flood. Each author has in his imagination the faces of his own readers. Nobody knows why even today, millions and millions of people throughout the world are looking for solitude from time to time. To get isolated, to be alone with this strange thing made of paper and to read it, instead of ordering some sort of mini-tube with colour pictures which can tell you what's going on it this thick, strange, object. And all these masses are divided by the different types of the desired solitude.

DCC: In Russia, are writers the media celebrities they are in North America?

VA: During the sixties the poets in the Soviet Union were as famous as soccer stars or even brighter. Recently Bella Akhmadulina became a TV star until her readings on the TV had been banned by authorities because of her independent public position. A different sort of celebrity exists in Russia. First there are the so-called official celebrities; they are the generals of Soviet literature. They're highly decorated with all possible orders and medals invented by the party and government and everybody knows their names because it's impossible to get rid of them. They're everywhere, in all the newspapers and on TV and so on, but they're terribly boring and people are looking for stars whose images are much closer to the Western meaning of the word. Secondly, there are the young poets of the sixties; they became the real stars and became the great celebrities for those times. And there is a third type of celebrity, the underground celebrity. To this type belongs the famous poet and singer, Volodya Vysotsky. After his death he became the real idol of, I daresay, all circles of Soviet society.

DCC: Your earlier writing reflects an interest in adolescence. You bid good-bye to adolescence with *It's Time, My Friend, It's Time* and *Golden Pieces of Iron*. One of the teenagers in *A Starry Ticket*, says to his older brother: 'Your life, Victor, was devised by Papa and Mama when you were still in the cradle. A star in school, a star in college, graduate student, junior scientific worker, M.A., senior scientific worker, Ph.D., Member of the Academy, and then . . . a dead man, respected by all. Never once in your life have you made a truly important decision, never once taken a risk. To hell with it! We are scarcely born when everything has already been thought out for us, our future already decided. Not on your life! It's better to be a tramp and fail than to be a boy all your life, carrying out the decisions of others.' Was this conflict between the generations reflected in much of the literature in Russia in the sixties?

VA: The sixties were the time of waking-up for Russia and probably that's why there was so great an interest in the adolescent characters in the literature, in the movies and in the theatres of Russia of that time. Yes, there was a great deal of literature dedicated to the so-called youth problems and my novels of the early period where in the stream of the literature of that time, along with the novels of Kuznetsov and many others, as well as the poetry of that time. I'm sure that there is much in common in different countries, inside different societies at the same time. There is something common to all mankind, especially for the countries with the same cultural roots. Russian, European and American cultures share the culture of the Bible and ancient Greece. In the late fifties and early sixties we hardly knew James Dean, the rebel without a cause or the beat generation of Ginsberg and Kerouac, or the angry young men in England. But once we got a chance to be acquainted with that, we were surprised to find so many common things in the literature of so distant countries and cultures. Later some fundamental differences between Russian and Western psychology became clearer. The morning period in Soviet life was too short. We've had too many horrible memories and hidden wounds. It was hard to maintain the spirit of the morning with a memory like this.

DCC: You have also said that in your writing you were mostly interested in the sociological aspect, not in stylistic mastery. Is your style now also your content instead of separate entities?

VA: That was typical for the time of our beginning. The prose writers of those times were always in a rush. We tried to express everything we knew as fast as possible, to speak out the more the better, as if we subconsciously perceived the limitations of this morning period of our culture. Probably that's why we were so little concerned with the style. The critics of those times used to write about *what* was written in the novel and never *how* it was done. Only when this hectic period was over did I begin to enjoy the writing itself. I started to think about my art and then I realized that I love Gogol much better than Dostoevsky. Gogol is a Writer. Literature is impossible without play, without stylistics. I share Nabokov's point of view that a writer is first of all an enchanter.

DCC:　In *The French Lieutenant's Woman*, John Fowles writes questioningly and ironically that 'the novelist stands next to God. He may not know all, yet he tries to pretend he does.' Others like Angus Wilson feel no embarrassment about adopting the 'God's eye view'. Where do you stand?

VA:　We are all God's children including the wisest philosophers or genius mathematicians. The wisest thinkers of mankind are naïve under God's eye and probably writers are the most naïve kids. A writer is always trying to save the passing time, to keep the moments flying past. In other words, to deceive Cronus who, as you know, devoured his children. It seems to me that literature is a very naïve attempt to replace the Cronus victims by some stones. Anyway, that is good.

DCC:　The rhythms of your prose remind me of jazz which you use over and over in your writing. Other writers have used jazz as part of the shape and structure of their writing? Could you expand on your use of jazz?

VA:　I love Julio Cortázar's story dedicated to Charles Parker. I'm sure that many writers either consciously or subconsciously are using jazz rhythms, especially *Ragtime* by Doctorow. You know that was my first experience of translation from English to Russian and I hope it will be the last. I didn't expect that it would be so difficult. Constant delving into the dictionaries drove me crazy. That occurred, incidentally, once in a Moscow house. We were talking about *Ragtime*. There was one of the editors of the *Foreign Literature Magazine* present. All of a sudden this lady offered me the translation. She said, 'Why shouldn't you try to translate this novel?' Anyway I set a task for myself translating this novel and I tried to keep these syncopated rhythms and the rhythms of *Ragtime* itself. It was hard to preserve this rhythm in Russian because the Russian language in general does not match jazz rhythms. That's why it's so hard to sing jazz in Russian. Anyway it seems to me I succeeded doing that and some readers told me that they, without any previous knowledge, perceived the ragtime syncopation in my translation of Doctorow's novel. Jazz was always my favourite type of musical art and for our whole generation jazz meant something extraordinary because of two things. First of all, jazz brought its improvisation. It symbolizes the idea of artistic freedom. In improvisation you are going out of lines; you are making yourself free from any rules, any restrictions, any limitations. You are partially outside your totalitarian government. That's why I guess Hitler and Stalin didn't like jazz. That's why jazz was forbidden in these countries. On the other hand, jazz for our generation was a revelation, a message from the other shores. It was a confirmation that the rest of the world existed and was always crossing the border. Besides, I was always impressed by the devotion that jazz musicians brought their art. They were faithful friends of their music whatever would happen and they would never submit to any political motivations. That's why I quite often chose jazz musicians as my heroes.

DCC: With *The Steel Bird*, you moved to a greater use of the grotesque. Fantasy and reality (or are they one and the same) mix and mingle in your writing; time is not linear but simultaneous and circular. It is a style of our time. Anna Balakian has written that surrealism does not propose escape through dream but rather proposes a revision of reality through dream in order to nourish and expand our understanding of it. Does that mean anything to you?

VA: That's a good idea about the revision of reality, but from my point of view I would say that I use the absurd as a matter of harmony in my writings. Reality is so absurd around us that the writer quite often is using the method of absurdity of surrealism, of the grotesque. In order to harmonize the absurdist reality, whatever you see around has different dimensions and it also has the dimension of irony. This irony is quite fragile but it's necessary for the writer of my time to use this fragile irony for expressing some thing, for making the reality clearer, more transparent.

DCC: Is your recent book *The Island of Crimea* a fable?

VA: *The Island of Crimea* is not a fable. It is a sort of false realism book. There are not any surrealistic tricks because the whole idea of this fantasy island is the story of a non-existent island. I chose an absolutely realistic way of writing. That's why I call this novel a false realistic book.

DCC: Why was Hemingway's *The Sun Also Rises* your 'gospel' in the post-Stalinist era?

VA: *The Sun Also Rises* has impressed me enormously. As far as I remember I was twenty-five or twenty-six when it was translated and a whole generation of young Russians started to read it and discuss it. That was obviously a sort of gospel for us, but let us say that was a lesson of solitude in a socialist society. It was a lesson of isolation, separation, alienation, and courage.

DCC: You said that when you wrote *The Burn*, you had Hemingway's *The Old Man and the Sea* in mind.

VA: I didn't use any stylistic or philosophical details from *The Old Man and the Sea*. I mentioned this novel because while writing *The Burn* I used to talk to my right hand in the manner of the old man, the character of Hemingway's novel, who used to talk to his hand. You remember this way of conversation with the hand or with the fish and so on. And I used to talk to my own right hand which was writing this novel, the novel which could change my whole life, and which did that. I understood quite clearly that it would change my life and from time to time I found myself a little bit scared. At this moment I used to say this with a smile, 'You! hand! should not stop, you should proceed, and so and so.' Then the KGB turned up with an inquiry about *The Burn* ...

DCC: Your early language innovations, words such as 'gudbai', 'Brodvei', and 'bugivugi', seemed so right for your characters. Will exile affect your writing?

VA: 'Gudbai', 'Brodvei', 'bugivugi', and all words like this, are from American idioms and contemporary Russian slang.

They are only a minor part of my usage of slang and that's what I really missed after immigration. I really miss the language of Moscow bums and tramps. That will probably affect my writing in the future, but I think so far so good. Recently I finished a novel, *The Paperscape*, which is set in Moscow of 1973 and it seems to me that I succeeded in describing the real life of Moscow's streets. The characters of this new novel are the people of Moscow's streets. It's inevitable that I will be more and more distant from the living language of contemporary Russia, but instead I hope to obtain the new linguistic idioms and innovations typical of emigré people which I already did in this new novel. The last part of the book is set in New York and there are some funny examples of emigré language. I was able to observe how the Russian language is changing outside Russia and how it is changed under the influence of English, the influence of alienation from Mother Russia. It seems to me that this view influenced by American life and language will not be incomprehensible for Russian readers because it is so close to the so-called 'clockwork orange' language reversed (remember Anthony Burgess's novel) which is used now by some city people of Moscow, Leningrad and other big cities of Russia. Probably, in two or three years I will try to play between two languages; you know probably some works by Max Frisch, the Swiss author, who from time to time writes some parts of his novels in English. Why shouldn't I follow suit?

DCC: You have said that the writer creates his readers in his imagination. Who are these readers? Why is it necessary to do this? A number of writers deny that they have any readers in mind.

VA: For sure my first reader is obviously myself. When I talked about my readers I meant that a writer always keeps imagining the faces of his readers. He is always trying to find these familiar faces in the crowd regardless of where he is now living. I can even spot some familiar faces in the crowd of American cities from time to time when I'm walking along the Washington streets. I'm playing a game to find some faces of my possible readers on the streets and I used to say to myself, 'Look at this guy who will *never* throw out my book.' In other words, writing in a sense is a search for spiritual relatives.

DCC: I'm interested in your reactions to several critics. Ellendea Proffer analysed your books *The Burn* and *The Island of Crimea* in relation to Thomas Pynchon's work as a literature of disintegration and paranoia. Do you agree with her that your work has a connection with Pynchon or the rest of her analysis?

VA: Well, I had never come across Thomas Pynchon's books. To be honest that was the first time I had heard this name in Ellendea Proffer's papers. Then I found one of his books and started to read it and I should say that I don't completely agree with Ellendea. I found little in common with Thomas Pynchon's book and I would say that we are maybe similar to each other, but no more than any other two contemporary writers. Ellendea brought out many interesting things in her analysis and she and some other American critics are quite close to my own point of view on my own writing. What can I say about the Soviet critics? The real critics could not express their point of view freely because of the well-known reasons, but I would say that I was quite correctly understood by the official communist critics and Stalinists who distrusted me from the very beginning.

DCC: Carl R. Proffer wrote that *The Island of Crimea* is more conventional than *The Burn* in form. Do you agree?

VA: In *The Island of Crimea* I used the so-called conventional form because the main idea of the novel was the fantastic, the surrealistic from its very beginning. It was based on the fantastic ground of unexisting territory, unexisting customs, unexisting culture, unexisting people, that's why I decided to avoid many of my favourite surrealistic ways of writing. That's why it looks like a conventional, realistic novel although the whole novel is a huge hyperbole.

DCC: Felix Svetov has said that in your novels you are in a hurry to say as much as you can about everything on earth. Whereas he feels that in your volume of short stories, *Halfway to the Moon*, you take the time to be attentive to your characters. Is this a fair assessment?

VA: Svetov meant my early so-called youth novels written in the early sixties. Those were hectic times and the young writers of those times were always in a rush and really tried to express as many things as they could. We were always anxious of our readers' eagerness. Then, I decided to make the number of my readers smaller and after that I went to depth rather than width. That was a period of writing short stories.

DCC: Elena Teypkin has written that in *The Island of Crimea*, you have only rarely been up to your main aspiration – to create a full scale, major anti-Utopia. She feels it is not close to *The Yawning Heights*, for example. Agree?

VA: *The Island of Crimea* is not an anti-Utopia in the usual meaning of the word. I tried to create a false perception of reality in this novel. I tried to create a sort of thriller adventure. I was not going to achieve the values of *The Yawning Heights*. I will never be fond of this type of literature. *The Yawning Heights* is not professional prose; this is semi-scientific and the expression of an irritated mind. It has nothing to do with style, with plastic words or plastic prose. I can appreciate the efforts made by Zinoviev to express his total disgust of the Soviets and the deterrent State but really I cannot accept a world where only mountains of shit exist. Even under the communist power man can see and want to see the sky, the clouds, the birds, the trees, the water, the flowers, the ducks and so forth.

DCC: How do you feel about being referred to so many times as a Slavic J. D. Salinger?

VA: I have never been close to Salinger except for a questionable closeness of my boys to Holden Caulfield. I'd written *Ticket to the Stars* a half a year before I'd heard the name of Salinger and at least a year before the translation of Salinger had been printed in Russia. However, the critics didn't care about this chronological nonsense. Probably, they supposed that there were some illegal connections with this American author. Yet, I didn't refuse this reference to him because I really admired some pieces written by Salinger. . . .

DCC: This question has probably been put to you *ad infinitum, ad nauseum*. What do you think of Solzhenitsyn's work?

VA: Frankly speaking, I miss Solzhenitsyn as a prose writer. In the name of his prophecy and reconstruction of history he sacrificed his great ability to write brilliant prose, but it's his way and I feel a great respect for his efforts. It's just not my cup of tea.

DCC: George Feifer in *Harper's* magazine found on a recent visit to Russia that 'most Russians who think at all about dissidents are more likely to despise them as sappers of Russia's strength and smearers of her name than to applaud them'. They see dissidence as 'the fancy of pampered intellectuals'. What is your response to this?

VA: Most Russians George Feifer met are duped people or are trying to find an excuse for their inertia and inability to express their sincere point of view. As a matter of fact, the people of Russia are exhausted by the permanent pressure of enormous propaganda.

DCC: More and more writers in North America and the West are concerned with censorship and various forms of oppression. How do you as a writer who has had his 'phone tapped, his mail opened, has been followed in the streets, and has now lost his Soviet citizenship, respond? Is their oppression relatively privileged? Is a comparison fair?

VA: It would be really and totally unfair to talk about Western censorship compared to Soviet censorship. Last winter I followed the first Congress of American writers and I know the laments concerning censorship in the United States. What kind of censorship exists in North America? Comparison of this kind is simply absurd, nonsense.

DCC: You said *The Paperscape* would be 'a thriller, part realism and part an excursion into fairytale'. What do the terms 'thriller' and 'fairytale' mean to you?

VA: The Russian word for 'thriller' has a negative literary connotation but I like it. It's still premature to talk about the future novel about the Russian newcomer to America. I have just finished a novel which is set still in Russia. The title is *Say*

Cheese. The heroes of this book are the photographers and that is the peculiar thing. There is a great psychological difference between American and Russian photographers. To take pictures here you ask people to make their mouth broader to show big white teeth. In Russia they ask people to make their mouth smaller to *hide* their teeth. To be pretty little us, that is a joke, indeed! As a matter of fact, this story is based on the *Metropol* affair.

DCC: People in the West have often said that Russia has no 'detective' or 'spy' literary tradition. Is that true?

VA: It's not true. There is a tradition of spy and detective story in Russia. It existed even in a pre-revolutionary time, and during the Soviet period it was flourishing. I would say the spy and detective literature in the Soviet Union is still waiting for its Western researchers.

DCC: In Eugène Ionesco's play *The Lesson* the professor explains: 'One must be able to subtract too. It's not enough to integrate, you must also disintegrate. That's the way life is. That's philosophy. That's science. That's progress, civilization.' I think this applies to you.

VA: The idea of Ionesco's subtraction is complete genius and I agree with that. I would just add that to be disintegrated you must be first integrated, just as to be cheered up you have to be first upset.

8 Elie Wiesel

DCC: In your preface to *The Testament*, you write of the Legend of one of the Just Men who visited Sodom, only to be ridiculed and then ignored in his efforts to end immorality. When asked why he persisted in his mission, he replied: 'In the beginning, I thought I could change man. Today, I know I cannot. If I still shout today, if I still scream, it is to prevent man from ultimately changing me.' Do you ever feel like this man?

EW: Of course. I know that this is the task, the mission, the vocation of writers in all times, especially today, and especially writers of my generation, and of my background. I don't think we are Just Men, but I think we are the ones that scream or that don't scream. I hope our silence itself will soon become a scream. And it's true that very often we go through periods of disenchantment and despair. But we go on shouting simply to remain what we are.

DCC: You once made a statement that man may not have the last word, but he has the last cry. That moment marks the birth of art. This idea is vitally portrayed in *The Testament* and most of your writing.

EW: It is not only the agony, sometimes it is the triumph of human existence. The laughter of human existence, the joy, but also the despair. It is a matter of how you approach it. Sometimes you approach it with tears, other times you approach it with laughter. It is always, of course, human existence that should be the texture and the magic of art.

DCC: I agree with you that it is crucial that we never forget the Holocaust. But the West, and particularly America, has moved from indifference and even suppression of information, to a

Elie Wiesel (*photograph: Trevor Clark*)

strange appetite for books and films about Hitler and the Holocaust, almost a death-camp chic.

EW: I am afraid there is something to what you say. Years ago when they showed on television the series *The Holocaust*, I protested against the trivialization of the subject. To make box office out of Hitler is a disgrace. I believe it should still be considered a sacred thing. Unfortunately, it's becoming so watered down. Everything is a holocaust, and everything is a death-camp and everything is a genocide, and everybody was a victim, and there is nothing we can do about it, except to continue to work the way we do. While it is true that not all victims were Jewish, all Jews were victims.

DCC: Your books often deal with the question of good and evil. In *The Gates of the Forest*, Gavriel says, 'the difference between Christians and Jews was that for Christians everything that comes from God is good and everything evil bears the mark of man; the Jews, however, press their search further and more blasphemously, crediting God with evil as well as absolution'. How does mysticism handle evil?

EW: This is of course a Jewish idea, it is not mine. The whole idea of mysticism is how to handle evil and I try to deal with it in my work. The idea of evil is present in the Bible. Since we do not believe that there are two Gods but only one, the question of evil actually involves God, the only one, and in the very beginning you are confronted by it. Mysticism tries to redeem evil since we cannot ignore it and we shouldn't ignore it; but it's hard to redeem it. There were great masters who really believed that even in evil deeds God is present; that means that no person can do anything without God being involved in his or her deed. The main problem in that case is that the human being is deprived of his or her free will. How do we deal with free will? So the problem is no longer the problem of evil but the problem of free will? There are all kinds of theories. One is that evil means the absence of God; it means that when we try to exclude God, even if God himself is not excluded, that he will appear. Another theory is that evil is only the other side of good. In mysticism it's important because we believe based on a certain Talmudic saying that the Messiah will come and either all evil will disappear or all good will disappear. It's either/or. This means that the world, time, space, soul, the myth will crystallize from an ingenious tapestry, so to speak.

DCC: Jean Améry, a survivor of Auschwitz, wrote the following of his book *At the Mind's Limits*: 'I had no clarity when I was writing this little book, I do not have it today, and I hope that I never will. Clarification would also amount to disposal, settlement of the case, which can then be placed in the files of history. My book is meant to aid in preventing precisely this.'

Do you feel this way about your books, given that scholars and critics often seek to clarify your work and so do teachers in the classroom?

EW: Absolutely, absolutely. I feel close to his approach to the problem. The fact that he committed suicide makes it more dear to me, and tragic. But it is absolutely my way, I don't believe in answers, I believe in questions. Every book that I write I hope to deal with the question or the interrogation.

DCC: The main critical impulse seems to be to clarify, to be coherent, to find answers. This is a total contradiction of everything really that you are doing.

EW: I am a teacher, but that is not my way of teaching. Questioning, always questioning. Always bringing up the question, and even the question of the question; that is the best way. The world is full of unanswered questions. All my life people ask questions and I don't give answers. Whenever I try to give an answer it is not an answer, it's simply another question. It's the meaning of that first question. The basic idea for me is to follow Rebbe Nahman of Bratzlav who was a very good master and whose disciple I would like to be. He says there is one person in one place who asks a question and many, many, many, many years later another person would also ask a question and he wouldn't know that the second question was an answer to the first. It really is a road that we are travelling from question to question. From the first outcry of a baby to the last outcry of the agonizing person, it's a life full of questions that we live.

DCC: Nelly Sachs wrote that her poetry is 'always intent upon raising the unspeakable to a transcendental plane, in order to make it tolerable'. How do you make 'the unspeakable' tolerable?

EW: I don't make it tolerable. I try not to make it tolerable. When I see that it becomes tolerable, I don't speak about it. That's why I have written so little about the Holocaust. That's why I moved away in my work, in order not to speak about it. In *The Testament*, there is half a page devoted to the Holocaust, that's all.

DCC: Many people have commented on 'madness' in your work. You have said that you write 'in order not to go mad. Or, on the contrary, to touch the bottom of madness.' In your play, *Zalmen, or the Madness of God*, Zalmen says: 'One has to be mad to believe in God and in man – one has to be mad to believe. One has to be mad today to want to remain human.' Madness has been seen to be many things: vision, poetic second sight, breakthrough into awareness, the devil's hand. In your work, 'true madmen are as worthy as true saints' [*The Oath*].

EW: Yes. I deal with madness mainly mystically. My madmen are not clinical madmen, they are mystical madmen. My madmen are not destructive, they are trying to reconstruct what has been destroyed. Therefore, they are mad because they live in a world of destruction. I deal with it in many of my works because I think this is the question of all questions, the problem of all problems, the tale of all tales. What are we doing with knowledge when knowledge no longer makes sense? What are we doing with experience which doesn't relate to our knowledge or to our lives? So, my characters are always madmen. But they are madmen in the ancient sense of the word. These are the nomads, these are the wanderers, these are the messengers who know a truth which will probably last longer than their lives and ours.

DCC: Isaac Bashevis Singer has told me that it is all right to write memoirs but it is not right to make fiction out of the Holocaust, for the most part, because fiction is about a few people, not millions. You have certainly expressed concern about creating fiction out of this experience but your concern lies elsewhere. Is it what Robert Jay Lifton, in *Death in Life: Survivors of Hiroshima*, calls 'creative guilt among the writers of the A-bomb literature'?

EW: I cannot write fiction about the Holocaust. I never have. And for obvious reasons I simply cannot see how one can write, 'Holocaust, a novel'; it doesn't go together. Furthermore, how can we imagine what was beyond imagination? However, that is for me. I cannot but that doesn't mean others shouldn't try, and some have tried. I am not insulted by that, I am not offended. It all depends on how they do it, if they write with respect or without respect. If they write with respect and they try, then good. If it's disrespectful then they shouldn't. But I never wrote fiction on that subject. I write to denounce writing because how can we retell what escapes language, a child's anguish on the way to a mass-grave or his father's rage and at the same time his powerlessness to save his son? I think in our case, it's different because the writers who write about this period feel guilty even afterwards. They feel guilty for writing not only for living. While those writers who wrote about the A-bomb did not feel guilty for writing it. They felt guilty for surviving. It is much deeper than that. I find Lifton's analysis went far enough but then he stopped there, he stopped at Hiroshima, he didn't go to the next step.

DCC: What constitutes the world of fiction?

EW: My fiction is about either before or after the Holocaust, but not during.

DCC: If it's not possible to fictionalize the Holocaust, could you write about other atrocities, such as the Inquisition?

EW: I cannot write about it, I didn't say others couldn't. Could I write about the Inquisition? Maybe, I haven't tried yet. I may try one day but then because of the distance. I described a pogrom in one of my books and it is possible to describe a pogrom, at least it is possible to try. It is easier for me to describe the destruction of the temple two thousand years ago than to describe the destruction of the Jewish people now. It doesn't mean that atrocities cannot be comprehended through language. I would say that this event is not like any other and therefore cannot be used in literature as fiction. We still cannot come to terms with it.

DCC: You have said that 'every writer today, no matter who, Jewish or not Jewish – but particularly Jewish – must write with the Holocaust as background, as criteria'.

EW: The means must be justified against that background. If I with my writing helped a killer, then I shouldn't write. If it helps the victims, then I should write and do nothing else. For it is really the only yardstick. The problem is that you cannot do with or without. If it's there, it paralyses you, if it isn't then you shouldn't do anything. Between paralysis and insensitivity, where do you go? It's not easy. I think it would be much easier to be an expert let's say in seventeenth-century literature, twelfth-century poetry and stick to it. Once you are aware of what's happening around you, you are a problem, not only are you open to problems, you become a problem to yourself.

DCC: William Styron, in *Sophie's Choice*, raises the question of whether or not writers should attempt to respond to the Holocaust. Your use of silence is far more complex than he suggests, and you have tried to deal with this atrocity, as he is trying to do.

EW: What he says is what he believes, and that's all right. I can accept this, but again it is a matter of humility; I feel more humble about it. I don't think I *can't* go beyond the silence, because then the silence itself becomes an expression. After all, he is talking about someone who has written about it. I tried. I use silence in the way I use madness, as a leitmotif, as a driving force, as a relentless call, coming from beyond the age.

DCC: The use of silence in your work reminded me of the number of people who have used silence in their art. I think of someone like Thomas Merton, the monk and the poet, searching for elected silence. I think of John Cage in music, and Peter Matthiessen in literature, using silence as an expression of their Buddhism, both structurally and thematically. I think of Henry Moore who has made the open gap, the holes in his works serve the shape and the texture of his sculpture. T. S. Eliot also said, 'Words after speech reach into the silence' ('Burnt Norton'). Even Thomas Carlyle made a grand juxtaposition of 'Speech is of Time, Silence is of Eternity.' Camus, in *The Myth of Sisyphus*, wrote that: 'The absurd is born of this confrontation between the human need and the unreasonable silence of the world.' Others have used silence in a purely aesthetic way. However, in your novels, you seem to reject art that is self-contained, outside history, or a hermetically sealed world.

EW: My silence is a metaphysical silence. It is not an artistic silence. I rather place my work through the Jewish tradition, the mystical tradition, the Hasidic world, the Cabala, the Talmud. If I do claim kinship with some writers like Camus, and so forth, it's really on the artistic level. There is the craft, I'm trying to learn that, the approach to words, the cadence of the sentence, and the structure of the novel and so forth, but my inner attachment is really a Jewish one, the Jewish collective memory that nourishes and feeds my work. In *Somewhere a Master* I speak of the school of Worke, a poetic kingdom, another face of the Hasidic movement. There people journeyed to the end of language, another universe, where silence was the only language available to men. For God, there is no conflict between silence and language; they both point to harmony and no creation can be complete without them. Silence is sinful when it means indifference, when it denies language, when it makes you an accomplice to evil. But silence can also appease, can carry melodies and dreams and it can also open you to anguish and sadness and anger. Silence is both a disturbing and creative force. As Reb Mendel explained: 'Silence is good even if it is empty – not so with words. When they are empty, they remain empty.' For him silence was a world to explore, a way of life.

DCC: I am interested in the technique of communicating silence. In *Gates of the Forest*, you wrote that perhaps silence is the 'language' of 'a new era'. And George Steiner says that we have 'to create new forms because the ineffable lies beyond the frontiers of the word'. If you think of writers in the eighteenth and nineteenth centuries, it's difficult to imagine what Balzac or Dickens would have done in terms of form and language with ashes and chimneys. You embrace this problem with dreams, parables, legends, riddles, metaphors, allegories, and sparse language.

EW: Maybe I am still fighting; I am still researching. I am fighting words with silence, I am fighting silence with words, and hopefully one day I would be able to fight silence with silence, but then that would be the end of literature. I tell stories to escape an irreducible silence. Some experiences lie beyond language because their language is silence. Silence does not necessarily mean an absence of communication. Imagine a great dancer motionless, for one hour, on stage; imagine a gifted painter staring intently, for one day, at the white canvas. This is the evocative descriptive silence of the artist. If you use silence, you are no longer silent. There is a mystical concept meaning talking less or using less words, surrounding words with silence or introducing silence in to the word. You can introduce silence into a word by waiting before the word comes to life so that it carries its own silence.

DCC: Some people have called your writing a literature of silence.

EW: Some of it is, but not all. Again, it is a literature of madness, of fire, of ecstasy and so forth.

DCC: Perhaps it's that impulse to genres, to categories.

EW: Oh, that's terrible.

DCC: You said that you entered literature to write, to bear witness. Camus entered literature through worship and Céline through anger. In *The Testament*, Paltiel Kossover writes 'in order to vanquish evil and to glorify that victory . . . to justify the thirty or forty centuries of history' that he bears with him.

EW: That was Kossover the Communist, not Kossover the has-been, the former Communist. The next Kossover was ready to bear witness. Kossover the Communist is not the same as Kossover the prisoner.

DCC: I have found in talking to several contemporary writers that they object to the question 'Why do you write?', because 'purpose' and 'meaning' seem somewhat suffocating to them.

EW: No, I don't dislike it, I don't mind being asked.

DCC: Through all the years I've been reading your books, they have the effect that Kafka believes to be most important. He said that 'a book must be an ice-axe to break the sea frozen inside us'. Do you agree with him?

EW: Absolutely. It is not only the ice; it is the ice, it is the night around us, it is the indifference in us that must break. Books are there to disturb, not to soothe, not to appease.

DCC: You have mentioned to me that your books are 'tales' and not novels. What is the difference?

EW: A tale has something to do with timelessness, while novels are always set in time. Tales are imaginary but yet they have some relationship to a different reality which is reality, while a novel is reality and imagination but of a different kind. A tale is linked to an event but only through its substance, while the novel is, I think, linked through the form.

DCC: In *Messengers of God*, you asked: 'Where are questions allowed to remain unanswered?' The answer is 'in art, particularly in literature'. Is it for this reason alone that literature and the act of imagination, better than psychology, history, sociology, or memoirs, convey the ideas that you are interested in? Perhaps this is what Günther Grass called the 'substantial reality that throws a shadow', a form without defining meaning, illumination without explanation.

EW: I tried everything. I tried actually not only novels, I tried essays, I tried to invent a new genre through the dialogues. Every dialogue of mine is actually a story and a drama and a tragedy and an essay and so forth. So, of course, I am trying to explore every area of literature. I will not be against writing a book on psychology even though that isn't my field. But that is not the reason why I chose literature. I chose literature for some other reasons, very profound reasons. There is my love for literature, for tales, for ancient stories, for legends. And in addition, besides that, it allows questioning.

DCC: You wrote also that 'there is no such thing as a literature of the Holocaust. . . . The very expression is a contradiction in terms. . . . A novel about Auschwitz is not a novel, or else it is not about Auschwitz. The very attempt to write such a novel is blasphemy.' This is close to Hermann Broch's idea of the 'immorality of the work of art' in an age of gas chambers. I suppose by the very act of creating within that kind of structure, you transfigure what happens.

EW: I wrote only one book about Auschwitz really and that is *Night*. It is not a novel, it's a memoir. It's a fragment of truth.

DCC: That is something that deeply concerns me. The phrase 'the aesthetics of atrocity' disturbs me. Is it wrong to get aesthetic pleasure from literature such as this? Other people have written poetry, short stories, novels, and plays about the Holocaust, and people will often respond, 'what a wonderful story, what a beautiful book'; these words seem totally wrong. Sometimes when I read your books, I want to say, 'beautiful, devastating, wonderfully written', but I am never sure what is the right vocabulary, what is the correct word to use.

EW: I don't know really. The only hope I have is to pass on some of my bewilderment, some of my puzzlement, when I am faced with one of my own stories. Words desert me in the face of that terrifying mystery called the Holocaust. I don't use aesthetics. I wrote so little about that period but even then I tried to reduce language, to reduce words, to write soberly and with as much austerity as I could. As for the response of the reader, 'thank you' is proper. I believe in that. I believe in gratitude.

DCC: N. Bliven has written that you write 'less to create a fiction than to create a disturbance in the minds' of your readers.

EW: I agree but, of course, it's fiction; it is a different kind of fiction. The reality of two thousand years has become my fiction. That is why I prefer the word 'tale' because it's always the same tale, an ancient tale inserted in memory. The key word is memory, the endless, collective, bottomless memory.

DCC: As you know, there has been a large amount of literary criticism written in the last few years in response to your books and others. Alvin Rosenfeld feels that we lack a phenomenology of reading Holocaust literature, a series of maps to guide us; that older critical orientations – Freudian, Marxist, formalist, structuralist, or linguistic are inadequate; that a search for Oedipal symbols, class struggle, revealing patterns of imagery and symbolism, mythic analogies, or deep grammatical structures, would be a radical misapplication of method and intentions. Have you any suggestions as to what that phenomenology would be?

EW: No. I know that the era is an era of darkness and it calls everything into question. Whatever was sure before is unsure now, whatever was white before is no longer white, whatever was clear before is no longer clear. And therefore, really the Holocaust (the word, because it is a word) right away makes all the other words shake. There is no way of penalizing a story, a novel, or a poem, where the Holocaust plays a central part because the moment you *analyse* it, you go away from it. Like a Hasidic story, it has to be told, not studied. The moment you look at it, you are no longer in it. The whole idea is to pull you into the story, to pull you into the experience. Now, this is the dialectical dilemma. We know that this experience cannot be repeated and cannot be communicated vicariously. How do you give what nobody can receive?

DCC: So the very act of reading is itself challenged.

EW: That is a challenge. The way I see it is that that person should know that he or she can never enter the gates of the burning ghetto or the gates of the death camp, but they can come close to the gates. And through reading one comes closer and closer to the gates but that's all.

DCC: A number of critics have said that they do not care whether or not your tales are great or even art because they are important evidence, great documents; they bring the horror to our awareness. For me, this is a contradiction because only the best writers could make this material as vital and absorbing as you do. Do you dislike this separation of your tales as either art or compelling history?

EW: I am on your side. Unless you write well, you cannot communicate. If my stories were written poorly, then they wouldn't be read, nobody will read them, nobody should read them.

DCC: Exactly. I was quite annoyed when I read Jeffrey Burke's review of *The Testament* in the *New York Times Book*

Review. He said that you have a tendency 'to sacrifice the demands of craft to those of conscience'.

EW: He is wrong. But that's a personal thing. The editor of the *New York Times Book Review* is carrying on a personal vendetta. He is obviously looking for negative reviews.

DCC: Critics seem to influence one another because I find that one picks up a notion and others carry it on. For instance, Curt Leviant along the same line said that he felt that you should permit the novelist to subdue the sage. Do you read the critical books of the Holocaust?

EW: I do because the subject is important to me, and that is why I read everything on it.

DCC: Do you think they are useful?

EW: It depends what one says and how one says it. When I am confronted with even the memory of the memory I am in awe. Some people take it just like another subject of the seventeenth century or the twentieth century. But the Holocaust is something else and, therefore, I can't understand these people who approach the subject just as though it was another subject. I don't like that attitude of the reader or of the writer.

DCC: It has been suggested that there is a predominance of women writing about the A-bomb and the Holocaust. Lifton feels it is because of women's close identification with organic life.

EW: Not in this case. In this case it has effected both men and women alike. Lifton didn't make a distinction between the A-bomb and Auschwitz. It was a mistake because there is a difference. The difference is that there were no men and women in the time of Auschwitz. Somehow the Germans managed to create a new being, all men looked alike, all women looked alike, children were old, old men looked just like children. They were all ageless, colourless, nameless and that is different. At that point it affected everybody and men had the same desire to speak or not to speak as women.

DCC: Why was your first book written in Yiddish and no others?

EW: It was called in Yiddish 'And the World Was Silent'. Then I rewrote it in French. My first book had to be in Yiddish, a tribute to that language which was mine. Since then I have written Yiddish articles. Why I wrote in the language is clear, it was a tribute, it was a sentimental act. Why I moved away was because it was a challenge to take something new which wasn't mine and to give that language a form, not just of words but also of life. To take a language and fill it with something that is so unlike it. It became a challenge. I needed a challenge.

DCC: W. H. Auden has spoken of the writer who has taken the role of 'the less exciting figure of the builder, who renews the ruined walls of the city'. Do you feel any affiliation?

EW: That is beautiful. My role is really to recreate; it is not to create (we cannot create) but to recreate the ruins and with the ruins to create what was before them. To invent, why invent? But to reinvent, that is more difficult. To bring back to life one child is more difficult than to give shape and form and substance to someone that I've never met. So this is what I try to do really. I like what Auden says. But my way is more Jewish. However, the idea is a challenge.

9 Toni Morrison

DCC: I have read that you once said that the progress of black American writing is marked by five stages. First, comes the heat of protest, and then the more reflective search for personal identity. This is followed by an exploration of culture, a refinement of craft, and finally, a wider vision of the world. Claude McKay, the Jamaican novelist and poet, insisted that there should be no double standard of appraising black artists' literary products. He said that his daemon, as he called it, urged him toward the mainstream. The famous clash between Irving Howe and Ralph Ellison reflects the call to clenched militancy, on the one hand, and to universality on the other. Do you still hold with your original statement about the five stages?

TM: Well, those were not my stages. That quotation was distorted. That was a description of a book I had published called *Giant Talk*, which is an anthology of Third World writings. That book was edited by two people other than myself and that was their thesis. I was describing the way in which Third World literature can be taught, and those five stages suggest a way in which one discovers that evolution of Third World literature from one place to another doesn't have anything to do with the *writing* of literature. It has something to do with the pedagogy; that is the simple and at the same time complex and very fruitful way in which to handle the course. Most courses are handled rather badly when Third World literature is taught. The real question you're asking is whether the Third World artist is universal or is he by definition parochial and limited? This is a question that always offends me deeply because it is inapplicable to anybody, it seems to me, except ethnic people. I never would require Tolstoy to be anything but what he is and I never would suggest that he be universal. He should be a Russian. So should Dostoevsky. So should Camus be French. So should Shakespeare be an Englishman. No one assumes that

Toni Morrison (*photograph: Trevor Clark*)

Shakespeare was writing for a little coloured girl in Ohio. It would be absurd to suggest it. Only black writers, it seems to me, are required to be larger than Shakespeare or Tolstoy or Dostoevsky. It's a racist question, it always provokes racist answers, and the quarrel between Irving Howe and Ralph Ellison is not really about that. No-one suggested that Faulkner stop being parochial and writing about the South. But they have implied that about black writers. The question does not deserve an answer. It's the wrong war; a writer can write any way he wishes. He can write totally political things, he can write Jewish things, he can write black, he can write anything he wishes and no one has the right to decide which is more universal and which is not. What they're really asking is, 'Are you going to accuse us or not?' Irving Howe says you ought to be more militant. I suspect he probably ought to be more militant if *I* want him to be. But you can't go to a writer and prescribe. The question doesn't have anything to do with anything of any interest at all about literature; it has something to do with the racist response to black writing. And sometimes, when I go to a university, people say to me the most unbelievable things like, 'You know, I did not relate to your characters because I am white and middle-class but I really found your book wonderful', which is another way of saying exactly the same thing. It means they had a problem with *Beowulf* and have a terrible problem with Jesus Christ and the Bible. But there is no suggestion of the possibility of making that leap without apologizing or explaining that they don't belong. But they don't do that with anybody else.

DCC: Similarly, Claude McKay has said that when he was urged to submit only poems which did not reveal his racial identity, he, of course, rejected this. He felt that in the poetry of Byron, Keats, Blake, Burns, Whitman, Heine, Baudelaire and Rimbaud, he could feel their race, their class, their roots in the soil, growing into plants, spreading and forming the backgrounds against which they were silhouetted. He could not feel their reality without that and, in a sense, that's what you've just said. 'Place' in your novels – the town, the community, the neighbourhood – becomes a character, like the people. Your use of 'place' reminds me of something that Eudora Welty wrote about place in fiction. She said that 'place is the named, identified, concrete, exact and exacting, and therefore credible, gathering spot of all that has been felt, is about to be experienced. . . . Location pertains to feeling; feeling profoundly pertains to place; place in history partakes of feeling, as feeling about history partakes of place.' Do you relate at all to what she has said?

TM: Oh, quite! I guess I never thought about place in her work because it was so closely woven with everything else. I think about it more analytically in my own work because as a writer the possibilities are infinite, but I would have no quarrel whatsoever with her description of what place means. It is a feeling, it is a perception about the past, a matrix out of which one either does come or perceives one's beginnings, or one's place from the long distances. Sometimes it's just a wild preoccupation with Dublin in spite of the fact that you lived the rest of your life in Paris or it might be some clarity that you acquire as an expatriate or just a way from the city back to the country. It has very little to do with its geography and it has an enormous lot to do with what was meaningful about it then. And it is a huge distortion. But that's only a distortion of facts, it's not really a distortion of the truth. You get closer to the truth when you sometimes ignore the facts of the 'place'. And it must function that way in those books. I'm not sure that it will always be as important to me as I write other books but certainly in the ones that I have written, it was vital that it be clear where those people lived and who they were and what that neighbourhood was like.

DCC: Some readers have criticized that you omit active, strong, fully drawn white characters in your books. This is hardly a legitimate response, given that white writers are never criticized for omitting strong, fully drawn black characters in their books.

TM: I suppose they're saying, in a way, that they would like me to do it and perhaps I write well enough that they would like me to write about white people. I can't imagine any other logical reason for making that observation at all. Any other comment I would make about that, would be pejorative so I will leave it as a compliment.

DCC: So many of your characters are not bound by society's rules or limited by convention. They are even 'lawless', to use your own language – Cholly Breedlove in *The Bluest Eye*; Hannah, Sula and Ajax in *Sula*; and Pilate in *Song of Solomon*. In *Song of Solomon*, an important part of Milkman's search for his past and maturity is tied to the search for himself. Is it only possible to find out who you are by creating your own life, by moving outside the strictures of society's rules and expectations, by taking risks?

TM: Well, yes, but that's a double-edged sword. It is certainly not the only way. The American dream of success is a lawlessness. You can't become extremely rich, like the very rich people in this country, without being lawless. They did not abide by the law to become Vanderbilts and Rockefellers. They broke the law or they made the law. It's not possible to do it by being a law-abiding citizen. The hero, whether it's a mystery hero or cowboy or millionaire, is a lawbreaker in this country, period. On the other hand, it is expected that less fortunate people abide by the law. A black man who abides by the law is safe, presumably. If he breaks the law and does not feel sorry for it, even though he may be imitating the success story, he is uppity and renegade. It means different things for different people. In my books, I was much more interested in the laws of the community itself as a distinguishing factor from the laws of the country at large. I wanted to know who the black community respected, and what they considered an outlaw, as opposed to what the 'legal' outlaw was. And what could a person do to become an outcast in that community, not an outcast in the society at large, so that I could say something or reveal something, rediscover, recollect something about the civilization as it existed among black people underneath or in spite of or parallel to the other civilization that other people know about. The only way I can do it since I cannot write, or do not wish to read, books in which there is a lot of rhetoric about that, is to simply dramatize it. Sula is hated merely because she breaks the laws of the *community*. She put that woman in an old folk's home and that's not acceptable behaviour. She never does anything, as far as America is concerned, worse than her grandmother does; she didn't kill her son. But she is much more hated because love never informs her sensibilities. So that's what I was really trying to show, the differences between those perceptions of law – what is right. There are differences in cultures, enormous differences. I don't see much point in absorbing another culture until you know what your own is, so you can pick and choose that which is valuable and get rid of that which is wasteful. There are lots of things that are wasteful and lots that are useful. But there are other things that one must be aware of. It is not possible for generations of people younger than I am, to hear things anymore, perhaps, in some parts of this country. They are as alien to their oral history as somebody from another country. Because it isn't recorded, you see. I don't write books that pull from the future, only those that, at the moment, pull from the past.

DCC: Many of your characters push the boundaries of human experience because you are not interested in ordinary lives as some other writers are, for instance, Ann Beattie. Your people are very intense. Sula 'lived out her days exploring her own thoughts and emotions, giving them full rein, feeling no obligation to please anybody unless their pleasure pleased her . . . hers was an experimental life'. But, because she is uncontained, she gains not only freedom but also a kind of imprisonment, a kind of bondage as well, within her own lack of restraint. And I wonder, what are the dangers of the experimental life? I think I understand what the positives are, but what can we learn from this exploration in literature?

TM: Well, I found Sula frightening. Her definition of freedom is do anything one wishes, and I personally would be frightened by this freedom. I think freedom is being able to choose your responsibilities. It's not *not having* any responsibilities, it's being able to choose the ones you wish. She seems a very contemporary woman for that reason. I find her unusually attractive to very young girls though she's not that attractive to me. I mean, as a character, yes. If you don't have any connection with other people, you cannot nurture, which she doesn't do. Her few efforts at doing it were failures. On the other hand, Nel is always there. You can leave her, and she will pay the gas bill and there will be supper, you don't have to think about that. She will nurture. And it seems to be those two aspects of femininity that are important; not just that experimental quest that Sula is involved in but also that nurturing aspect of Nel. It seems to me that both of those prongs make a complete woman.

DCC: As an extension of that, I liked what you said in *Sula* about the artist with no discipline. Creativity needs to be disciplined. It's not good enough to have a metaphoric mind, to be able to see colour.

TM: If she is fickle, then she is like a child, extremely bright, very hypersensitive, who is in an environment that does not provide any route by which she can explore all of that. Those people are fickle people. They end up rather badly. If that is their bent, if they really hear music all the time and they have no instrument, then they can't concentrate. And if they're in a society in which there is no room and no way for that to happen … hers is a little more complicated because a woman in her situation, normally, I suppose, could join the Cotton Club [a nightclub in Harlem in the 1920s], or something, but she doesn't have any talents like that. An art form would suggest and imply its own rigour and she would have that if she were going to be a ballerina. Then she could be experimental, adventuresome, rigorous, and disciplined, and not play around with other people's lives where play or creativity is not necessarily constructive. You can't take great leaps of imagination when other people can get hurt that way. But you can do that with paint. It can be as wild and as disciplined as you want. Or with writing. Or with dancing. Or any other form. She can do it with a guitar. But if you have that interest and that compulsion and you don't have the *means* by which you can channel it – you see, part of it's channelling, part of it is having no limits. But we do it within the confines of form. She can't do that, so she's running around playing out her art form on other people. That's dangerous, you know; it's like Svidrigailov in *Crime and Punishment*, who has absolutely nothing but his own interests to fulfil and then eventually he becomes boring. I was interested in trying to project a person who could be conceived of as generally evil without actually being evil. Sula only does some socially unacceptable things.

DCC: Well, she does kill a boy.

TM: She has an accident. She's playing with him in a very fond, affectionate way and having a good time with him. It's Nel who doesn't want him around. Sula swings him around and he falls, and she is upset and wants to call somebody and it is Nel who prevents her. She doesn't kill anybody (and her mother doesn't commit suicide, by the way, she doesn't do that). But Sula does something worse in the eyes of the village. She does not feel strongly about anybody's demands. And she really does have characteristics which can be described as genuinely evil. Not like the people we normally think of as evil, as simply greedy or acquisitive or mean. She really is wanton. If you look at *The Exorcist* and you see the child possessed by the Devil, that child does absolutely nothing except break social codes: she says dirty words, she masturbates, she defecates, none of which is evil. It's just repulsive. She has no manners. But genuine evil is something we like to escape. It's really evil because it has no order, and it doesn't need you, and it doesn't want anything. You know, you can predict what a dictator will do.

DCC: Walker Percy talks about the search for pure evil in *Lancelot*, evil that has no crutches, no causes in chromosomes nor environment. To deviate, you've mentioned that painters are a greater influence on your work than writers, for example, Edvard Munch. His painting, *Spring Evening on Karl Johan Street*, conveyed the atmosphere you wanted for a scene in *Song of Solomon*, the one in which Milkman is in a small Southern town – anxious, feeling lost, out of place. That particular painting conveys all of this, I think. But I find it interesting that as the pedestrians are walking towards the spectator with ghostlike faces, Munch himself, is the one figure walking away from the spectator. Have you ever, as the artist, injected yourself, as Munch did, into your work?

TM: . . . That painting had the feeling of vulnerability and anxiety which I wanted. Milkman had that scene where he hit his father; he is very vulnerable and he is very anxious and he is hurt. He feels separate. And he's looking for his friend. In order to convey all of that, I either had recourse to a lot of language about it, or, I could describe a scene. This is all very visual to me; if I can't see it then I really cannot write it. The colours are important in this scene. It's very important that the opening have all that blue, red and white. If I can't visualize it, I can't move forward. When I was trying to visualize it, I began to write about him walking down the street that way with nobody being on the other side of the road, and then I remembered instantly that that was Munch's painting. That was helpful because I could simply reproduce not the painting but the situation and the feeling of the painting. I am very conscious of that. Sometimes there are simply things I have seen, you know. For instance, I may have seen a woman walk down the street with nothing in her hands in a country town. Years later it will come back and be useful for a particular scene. There's a horse that Munch has painted. It is cheerful and green and Christmasy and very powerful. But it's very frightening. So, in something else that I was writing, I was looking for a way to say that this person is afraid; I had to catch hold of the reins of that horse. That's my job, to describe an experience in such a way so that it conveys fear, to hold it. That doesn't come from anything that I've read, that comes from my impression. I have no idea what Munch had in mind but that's not important. His painting was full of all the most wonderful, cheerful, Christmas colours and it was terrible, at the same time, and frightening, at the same time. That is what I mean when I say I really remember being influenced by paintings. I never read anything when I write; if I thought I were being influenced by a writer, I would stop. Nevertheless, there are writers whom I envy.

DCC: Who?

TM: Gabriel García Márquez.

DCC: Is he the only one?

TM: Yes, I think he is the only one. I wish I could have what he knows; I wish I could have all of that in my head. I don't try to write that way but I envy that magic.

DCC: Have any other painters particularly stimulated images or influenced your work?

TM: Magritte used to. I could only look at one painter at a time. I mean, I could only love one painter at a time. And I could only love one musician at a time and right now I'm in love with a musician and I only listen to his music and nobody else's. And that's the same thing with a painter, I could only look at their paintings and I don't look at anybody else's. I finished with Magritte about seven years ago. I had no one and then I went into the Munch Museum in Oslo. And I fell in love over there although I had seen prints of Munch. There was never anything much written about him, and the art criticism didn't seem to know quite what to do with him. But I'm not at all eclectic. You can't really know anybody until you've stayed with them for a while. I read the same way. I would just read the stories I like over and over again and I keep going back to the same books. When I was introduced to Márquez, I did that with him. And I read everything he writes. One does that with the Russians, I've done it with the Italians over the years. And then you find one person who you stay with for a long, long time. It happened to me with Chinua Achebe and once I read a book that I couldn't get out of my mind for a long time which is *The Radiance of the King* by Camara Laye. I read that and for about three or four years that was what I read. Now at my age I feel I can stay with a writer longer but it puts me in an awkward position of never having read all sorts of important people.

DCC: Language is one of the most powerful forces in your novels. Are you in love with words in the way that Dylan Thomas was or are they ever weapons as H. L. Mencken's sometimes were?

TM: Weapons, I don't really think of them in that way. I want the reader to come with me, I want to make a space and a language so that he can step in and I will shut the door. I want him to feel comfortable because he's going to walk in terrain that is scary for him and for you because the characters are going to be in life-threatening situations and they will be operating under duress. We are going to find out who survives and who doesn't, and how and why, but I don't want the reader left outside; he must participate with this whole process of the book. And in order for him to participate with you, then I have to give him something to do, so I don't use a lot of adjectives because I don't have to. I can make it possible for him to supply that, at the right moment. If I want the reader to feel sexy when I describe a sexual scene, such as with Ajax and Sula, I will provide the broadstrokes: he is horizontal, she is vertical. And there is no sexy language in there at all. I think 'breast' is really the only physical word. While they are making love, he isn't saying anything that you can hear, but she is thinking things that have to do with loam and stuff. Nothing scatalogical. I rely on the readers' awareness of something that is much more primitive – mud – which is something you associate with childhood when 'dirt' was all right, and you could really make a mud pie. So that's the image that controls the sexual scene. The reader brings his own sexuality into it which is always sexier than mine. That is to say, one's own sexuality is always sexier than anybody else's, because it's yours. Which is why clinical descriptions of sex are usually boring, if you have any sex life or imagination at all. The writer doesn't do a lot. The function of language is not to shut out the reader or even to say only what I mean. The function of language is to drop down, when it should drop down, pick up when it ought to; it's to hold and maintain this experience that I, as a writer, and the reader, have. The intimacy must never be broken by the narrator. The responsibility of language is not to kill. Nor is it just the delight in words for their own sake. It really is to make it possible to have an intellectual and a visceral response to the book.

DCC: That's so true and it's so hard to do.

TM: The book should not appear *written* in that sense; it should look effortless, and a little sloppy and a little meandering in a sense, not written. And that's what's hard.

DCC: You have said that it's important to you that the effort doesn't show, that the 'seams' can't show.

TM: But, in the beginning, it's hard to stop twisting everybody's arms and telling them what to think, and analysing … you know what I mean? It's hard to get out of the book and to let it lie. I can do it better than I used to.

DCC: Do you revise very often?

TM: All the time, all the way to the printer.

DCC: I know John Fowles said that they literally have to take the manuscript out of his hands because he's revising to the minute. Have you ever wanted to do the kind of thing he did in *The Magus*, rewrite one of your other books that's already been published?

TM: I may do it. Oh, yes.

DCC: Really! Which one?

TM: All of them! I would rewrite *The Bluest Eye*. I wouldn't have the mother, for example, speaking. That wasn't any good because she didn't know enough. Then I wrote it with the Narrator speaking. That wasn't any good, it sounded pompous. So I mixed them, and that's a cop-out because I couldn't do it right; now I know how. And the ending wouldn't be that way. I mean, it would have that information but I would have more courage there.

DCC: As an extension to what you were saying about language, you have said that the writer has to use the words he does *not* use in order to get a certain kind of power, like a painter uses white space, or a musician uses silence. And certainly, in literature, writers as early as Mallarmé were trying to find the silent spaces in their poetry as Beckett has done in drama. The novelist, Peter Matthiessen, has used white space in *Far Tortuga* to set up reverberations in what is written, to make the reader receive things intuitively, to create more air around the words.

TM: That's the reason for it, it's not just aesthetic, you know. In some instances, aesthetics is enough for restraint and white spaces and silence. Just because it's more beautiful that way. My use of it can't be merely beautiful because I have a friend I feel some responsibility toward. That's the reader.

DCC: I know that writers don't necessarily start with the beginning of their books firmly in mind. Often it is an image, a scene, a metaphor that initiates their vision. But I'm intrigued that you always know the endings before you start; even the words, the sentences.

TM: I don't know how anybody would do it any other way, because the way in which one arrives at the idea in a book is via the words and the sentences and the dialogue. It's like knowing what the notes are in the last chord in music. You can hear it and know where you're going. You might not know how to begin but you would know where you were going, because that would be the essence of what it is you're talking about. I would know that Milkman has to fly and I could see that. Then I would know what the resolution would be. The last sentence in the book is the idea of the book, is the point you're pursuing, is the *raison d'être*.

DCC: The ending of *Song of Solomon* is replete with possibilities, and some have suggested, ambiguous. Do you consider the ending ambiguous? Do you want the reader to supply the ending?

TM: No, it's just that my notion of an ending is probably a little bit different from the traditional notions. Most people think of an ending as a close; a curtain drops, or a door shuts. I don't think of it that way because an ending is not like life, and it's not like the source out of which the material comes, which is highly oral, a sort of peasant literature, where the possibilities are infinite. It's an opening out of possibilities; it's not about 'meaning' or the final solution. That's a very post-industrial age concept of how to write a novel, where there is a conclusion and a final solution and a judgement. Oral literature has no judgements. The whole range of human possibilities is what the whole story means. I don't write in a comic mode where there's a union of the sexes at the end, but rather in a tragic mode in which there is an epiphany. The end is the epiphany. You know there's more after *Oedipus Rex*, and there's more after all of the tragic books, but at the highest moment in which some character realizes something which he would not otherwise have realized, the mere possibilities have tripled because of this knowledge.

DCC: Do you think this is a problem with critics in that they are looking for judgements and conclusions; that the literary methodologies today don't have an openness, don't allow for the possibilities that you are talking about?

TM: Well, for traditional literature they are set up perfectly. There is literature that's written for that criticism, and there is criticism that adjusts itself to the literature. It is not perhaps designed structurally for the kind of writing that I do. Recently there has been some effort to design a criticism for the kinds of work that some post-modernist people do. Structuralism and deconstruction are attempts to deal with that, wherein the critic himself is equally as important as the book. The text itself resists a 'final' reading.

DCC: *Song of Solomon* is embodied in metaphor and myth. How are you using myth?

TM: When myths are changing, people assume that the world is being demythologized, that the old myths don't work anymore. This may be true of white Western people. However, their mythology is not the reliable source of information in my work. The Western myths that are in my book are fairy tales. It's usually to show misinformation when I use them. Whenever Milkman is on the right track, he's pulling from the myths of his own people. And the Bible is also used the same way; names are given that have nothing to do with the biblical characters at all. The first name was chosen by a man who couldn't even read the Bible. It has nothing to do with an analysis of the Bible. The very first name was chosen by an illiterate; he just liked the shape of the letters. I wanted to show the distorted way in which people use the Western myth. The flying has nothing to do with Icarus at all, it has something to do with African flight which is probably older than the Icarus myth.

DCC: I find what you're saying about misinformation very interesting because a lot of reviewers and critics referred to your use of Greek mythology and tried to draw parallels. And you are saying that they are wrong. In one sense, your writing is a scholar's dream in that it's full of metaphors, linked images, and so on. Do you think that criticism, as a discipline, ever responds faithfully to the artist's work? Can criticism ever capture the essence of art?

TM: I don't take the trouble to explain my thoughts to anyone, I just answer questions if they're put to me. If I wrote critical articles about my work then that would be clear, but I don't do that. I don't do that deliberately because that's not my job. And the other reason I don't do it is because I know that when I want to understand something in Emily Dickinson or Shakespeare, I go to their sources because I want to understand it fully, and in the same way I want critics to go to mine. Somebody someday will take the trouble to be as fastidious with the work of black writers as they have been with Western writing; that's all it requires. I'm very well versed in Greek mythology; I know how to use it in many subtle ways. The Solomon part was problematic for me because it made the biblical reference too obvious. But it was a literal meaning. It had to be, because that's really what the book was about; it was about that man Solomon, and the fact that it was also a phrase used for the *Song of Solomon* was unfortunate. A critic can enhance a book. Wilson used to do it all the time, Pritchett does it constantly. So does Elizabeth Hardwick. Something in the work is enhanced by the criticism, for me, and made more intelligible. Some critics really do make a book richer or clearer through analysis. The critic's work is serious work; I wish they would take it really seriously again, but you need a wide vision for that. The great translators were the great poets, and the great critics were not just avaricious readers; they also wrote literature. Today there are expert persons who create a response that is obscure, only because it leans on its own discipline, not on any other, and the practising writers are not involved in it. The great poets these days are not the great critics because there is a kind of specialization going on in literature, so that you have very good single 'sight' but not good 'vision'.

DCC: One critic, Chikwenye Okonjo Ogunyemi, discussed the triadic patterns in *The Bluest Eye*: the reproduction of the initial passage three times; the three themes of sex, racism and death; the scapegoat mechanism with the cat, the dog and Pecola; the three family women – Geraldine, Mrs MacTeer, and Mrs Breedlove; the three prostitutes whose names symbolized for him the helplessness of France, China and Poland in the face of rape by more powerful forces in the Second World War. Is this far-fetched, or was the triadic structure in any way a conspicuous pattern in your mind?

TM: I wasn't aware of it. I would respect the triad as described by him and as you describe it, because it's there. I trust the tale, anyway. But I would be sensitive to that analysis. That would be something that would enlighten me and I would say, 'Oh, I did do that.' But I can't say that I had the rape of France, China and Poland in mind. I just know prostitutes named after countries.

DCC: You used to teach at Yale, and several prominent scholars there are working with various literary methodologies. Are you aware of the literary criticism practised by scholars?

TM: I've become interested in it very recently because I was doing some lectures. It's interesting; however, everybody's very uneasy about it, just as people are uneasy about the new architecture. Things are changing, the city is changing, the responsibilities are much wider. The city doesn't want to be a city anymore, it wants to be a village. But anyway, yes, I am aware, but never in my writing. It's not helpful, it's hurtful. I found teaching, which I like, something I can't do when I'm writing, because it requires a different kind of thought pattern. Criticism requires analysis and a kind of tearing down to examine parts. It's just a mode of thought that is not helpful for me. Some people I think can do it; the novelist, John Gardner, taught and wrote. He could draw from it in a way that I cannot.

DCC: Very often criticism does seem to obscure the writer's work. Terms like 'semantic gestalt', 'perceptual closures', 'undecidable significations' are forbidding. Does this really have any relationship to the creation of art? Is it possible that scholars and critics have moved away from their previous job of making difficult writers easy and now make easy writers difficult?

TM: It's very job oriented, I'll tell you. The nicest thing I ever read was that piece by Gore Vidal, which is so acid and horrible and excessively clever. He said that English teachers always envied maths teachers who always put those little formulas on the board, and the English teachers always wanted something to write, little dots and things [*laughs*]. They are in competition with science because the scientists are the nobles and the lords on a campus, and the English people feel inferior. They used to run that shop years ago; the Liberal Arts Colleges were the heart of the academic world. Now they are not. Instead of developing perhaps keener insight into what was going on, critics have simply tried to develop an obscure language and equations, so that they could sound like physicists [*laughs*]. More important than that, they used the text for such criticism, used the text very much the way scientists used cells and rats as something to observe and experiment with. Criticism can be obscure; it certainly isn't helpful to a writer. But there are writers who pay close attention; I think Barthelme does. The point of the criticism has nothing to do with the *writer*, it has to do with the discipline of criticism. It's about itself and the commentary is about itself; it's not about the writer's work, so that the writer and the text are subordinate. That's what makes me very unhappy, but it's all right. It's interesting, this projection of the critic on to the centre of the stage, a *prima donna* kind of thing, and it's sort of sweet in a way, you know. The worst thing that I've ever heard said about criticism is what you've just said: that it does some damage to the thinking process and it may in fact do that. In which case it may work some harm, but if the work is any good, it'll survive.

DCC: One of the things that scholars always want to know, is whether or not you have a particular aesthetic theory? But perhaps theory is not the right word.

TM: I have not articulated a theory. Obviously I was brought up in the New Criticism and I learned to think in high school and college. Marxist aesthetics were very attractive to me for a long time, and in a way still are, because they're harder to deal with and ought to be possible. It's the 'ought' that is attractive to me. I am interested in that although I'm not a Marxist. Yet the idea of making a work of art uncompromisingly beautiful and still socially responsible is all that I'm interested in. Now when I say that I like this literature, it means that I have to listen to what the characters, who are the people, say. They are the ones who verify it for me. I mean it in a very strong sense of community. I could make a book to which one has a visceral response and is exciting to non-readers, and at the same time has a lot of food for people of fastidious intellect. That's what I'd like to do, to do both, which is why I'm attracted by Marxist criticism. That's what it's supposed to do. Generally, Marxists have gotten so hysterical about art that they always stop people from doing anything. They betray their artists in many ways, or make bad art, institutional art; that is sort of dumb. But I think that will change.

DCC: It has been suggested that a Toni Morrison novel generally resembles a beautifully patterned quilt. One begins by admiring the intricacies of each square, and ends surprised and delighted by the way the disparate fragments combine to form the grand design of the whole. How would you describe the form of *Song of Solomon* since a number of others have tried?

TM: I like that word 'quilt'. They wouldn't say that about a man, would they? They would say chess game or something.

DCC: That's absolutely true [*both laugh*].

TM: I have sometimes spatial perceptions about a book. At first, they seemed to me to be hermetically contained in a room, and then they go and spiral. *Song of Solomon* did not. It seemed to me to be linear, although it went back and forth. It had for me the overwhelming rhythm of a train. It did sort of build up steam slowly in the beginning. It drives itself very fast and comes to a screeching end, a kind of explosive end; very much unlike the other two books, and that seemed to be very masculine. It had a driven quality. But when I think of it in terms of the way it was put together, I do not think of a quilt. What they mean is not inaccurate, however. It is a way of saying it, except that it's flat, because the book is trying to scoop up that which is in the past and apply it to the present. There's a movement back and forth and I try to make the way in which the information is revealed, one; the narrator must stand by the reader. Things are revealed pretty much the way things are revealed in life. You don't know today if already the most important thing is going to happen; you just look and it's already occurred. This morning you won't know it, you won't know it until next month, so if we mention it now, it has a quiet effect, and then two chapters later it will be the thing that appeared to be minor. Subsequently, the thing that looked like the most important thing turns out to be unimportant. Trying to distinguish between the significant and the insignificant is problematic in life. There's that kind of meandering understatement about life and you put your arms around all of it so that you don't lose any of it. Then you can see the connections. It's not designed to make it all so terribly clever, it's just a careful way to reveal the information so that the reader's not surprised. He does, however, experience dread, or hopes this does or doesn't happen, and that's the way I wish to get the emotional participation of the reader so that he cares about some of the characters. One of the ways for the reader to care is to have that feeling of 'maybe it'll be all right', although he knows it's not, or that maybe it won't happen. This feeling can only occur if you really are involved in the lives of the characters.

DCC: The pattern of symbols in your writing is always carefully done. Many writers have talked about the creation of symbols as an intuitive process rather than a consciously deliberated one. Is there a greater measure of rational construction in yours?

TM: The symbols are usually intuitive, yes. I wouldn't trust a symbol that wasn't, it would be too heavy-handed. Some of the symbols are grotesque, but when they work, they work. I never considered the absence of a navel in *Song of Solomon*, it just appeared with the woman, and I toyed with it for a little while. It seemed a little lunatic for a lot of the time, but I didn't let it go, and it began to work in other ways. Structurally, it established certain leaps in the imagination immediately, so already the reader has got to know, about fifty pages into the book, what the world of the book encompasses and its possibility. So the reader is prepared for anything to happen. Then, of course, the absence of a navel defined her character very specifically; it made her invent herself. I simply started out with a woman who more or less represented the difference between herself and her brother; he would be 'property' and she would be 'earth'. Generally speaking, the symbols chosen are usually accompanied by something in the character; in *Sula*, it is the birds. They are based pretty much on some natural distortion; nature seems excessive or dramatic in some way simply to echo the characters. I'm more careful about metaphors; those are very carefully thought out. I'm very careful of that, as well as the cleanness of the dialogue. As I said before, the book should appear effortless, not laboured and *written*. Also, *I* am not there. It is difficult to keep the author out, so there's a lot of rewriting in order to get that feeling. I don't want a story being told by a narrator, but just a story being told.

DCC: 'Singing' appears in several forms throughout your novels: Claudia's mother has 'singing eyes' and sings often in *The Bluest Eye*; people have names like Singing Bird; and your language has the rhythms of music, particularly the Blues. What is the importance of the Blues thematically and structurally in your writing? Do you think of the 'flat' note, the 'blue' note?

TM: Oh, yes. There are two things that are important. I was telling somebody today that I used to hear singing because people used to sing. That is, my mother would get up and sing; it was a way of talking. People sang all day when they were at their chores. I was constantly hearing somebody sing, all of the time. They were singing to themselves, or as a way of thinking or being. Therefore the Blues impact is not so much the sound as the Blues idiom. It is that particular kind of love song in which somebody has left somebody, but there is no bitterness or even vengeance, only sorrow. Nobody has hurt anybody. It is a compassionate, wide, spirited kind of thing, as opposed to certain kinds of country music in which people are bitter about it, and there's a suggestion of vengeance. There's an absence of that in Blues songs. It's not hopeless, although the singer is not optimistic when it's over. The quality of the music is generous.

DCC: Violence is also a part of your novels, and very often it's between members of a family whose relationships are brutal and death-giving. Concurrently, there's also love. What is the relationship of pain to the quality of life? How do we remain whole?

TM: Pain is information. When pain is bad for you, you go under. When you use it, you survive it, you are better. People don't sublimate anything much in my books; many do talk, and they act out, and they cause each other a lot of pain. The purity of their love is great because it survives all that business. They are willing to inflict pain on themselves, make huge sacrifices for each other and do without. But their inability to either express or rise above emotion is what's important. I like the reader to feel. Shame is more important that guilt, since guilt is what you feel when you can't feel something else. It's a substitute feeling for the real thing. You can't feel the real thing so you feel the guilt. If you can feel the shame, the hatred or the anger, then you don't have to feel the guilt. In *Sula*, it's much more explicit because the people of the town use all of the wickedness they perceived in Sula; they use it to make themselves better. As long as she's around, as long as evil is around, they can get themselves together. But when she's gone, they don't even have that to rub up against and they fall into disrepair. As long as she's there silently accusing them and questioning their values, they begin to take them very seriously. The horror is having it slop over into some sort of Christian symptomatic mentality of how people have to suffer, so you never have to devise some suffering for yourself; it's a form of flagellation.

DCC: You have said that the novel is the most demanding and challenging genre. What can you do in a novel that you can't do in a short story, or a poem, or a play?

TM: It becomes a way of life if you make the acquaintance of a novel's characters. I suppose long, long, poems do this too. Poems are hard because you have to distill the world into something very small. In a novel you take something that's very small and make it bigger and bigger and bigger. There's so much room and the possibilities are infinite. That's why I find it the most challenging form. The possibilities are not infinite in poetry. Once you have decided on your form, the challenge is trying to get all that done within that confine. That's the challenge. Some doors are shut; it can't be an epic, it can't be a sonnet. I'm overwhelmed by all the space in a novel, all the possibilities, all the ways in which the characters can turn; but the novelist can still try to contain all of this and let the characters breathe.

DCC: When you were a young girl, what writers particularly impressed you? I would assume that you were a tremendous reader.

TM: I've read a lot all the time, it's just that I don't really remember who they were. It was a major education. The first were the Russians, and then I read, but did not relish, William Faulkner; I appreciated him but did not relish him. I also read Hemingway, Fitzgerald, that whole genre. I was not stimulated by any of that. I read a lot of Italian novels for a long time, like those of Ignatio Silone. But the writers that I used to read a lot, over and over again, were George Meredith, who I always found just right, and, you'll laugh, Italo Svevo who wrote *Confessions of Zeno*. He was kind of a protégé of Joyce's, I think, at one time. Then later I used to read by countries. I did that with African novels, and then recently with Latin American novels. And I remember Dickens particularly, and Austen when I was young, because they were nice and long. [*laughs*] You could sort of stay in that world forever. And at that time I liked long novels of manners; Trollope, people like that. I also used to read a lot of plays.

DCC: Since a number of people have responded to *Tar-Baby*, could you tell me about it, in your own words?

TM: It is different from all the other books in a couple of ways. One is that the structure is more conventional and the times are contemporary. It focuses on a young man and a young woman, and a love relationship surrounded by other people, so in that way it's different. There's also more dialogue. The violence in the book is very bloody but it's not physical violence, it's just the kind of violence people do to one another with the best intentions in the world [*laughs*]. It hinges on that phrase, 'Tar-Baby', which is part of the story of the Tar-Baby, and this is the point of departure for the book. Tar-Baby is a pejorative word, a racist name that people call black girls. There are mythical origins of tar, since tar-pits are holy places, precious places before cement. People made pyramids out of it. Moses' little boat was held together with tar. Tar has an ancient connotation, and in Africa there is a demi-goddess who is the 'Tar Lady', so that the tar element has the ability to hold things together. It can hold a civilization together, hold a building together, hold a boat together, and hold something that's going to fall apart. I regard this as a feminine function; how this woman in the novel approaches or falls short of that is really what is meant by the Tar-Baby. You may be the only human in the world who knows what I'm writing about [*laughs*].

10   Colin Wilson

DCC: Throughout your work you refer to 'vastations' and 'peak experiences', terms used also by William James and Abraham Maslow. Could you discuss their importance to your life and work?

CW: The most basic question that you could ask about any writer is how far he is optimistic. One of the essential realities for everybody from the moment we are born is the fact that we are day-by-day, minute-by-minute, to some extent facing defeat. All of us could be brought to the point of a nervous breakdown by a little easy psychological conditioning in the way you give dogs a nervous breakdown by frustrating them. Psychologically speaking, human beings are not very strong. This means that if they are also born with the feeling that life is basically against them, or that beyond a certain effort it is just not worth pressing on, their feeling about existence is likely to be rather dull. Now this has always interested me because it struck me at a fairly early stage that the most interesting things in life are the moments when you seem to remember something. It is almost as if something explodes on the senses and you say, 'Of course!'; this 'Of course!' is like a memory of something which you'd discounted. Again, when these experiences occur, of what G. K. Chesterton calls 'absurd good news', you get an odd feeling that the terrific efforts you have made to fight your own tendency to pessimism were somehow pointless in a funny sort of sense because everything ought to be much simpler. I said it was almost like taking a taxi and then realizing that the place you asked the driver to go is only a single block away so that you feel 'God, I could have walked.' Now Maslow, of course, was also interested in the 'peak experience' and he found out that exceptionally healthy people always seem to have these flashes of sheer joy. But Maslow said that he did not believe that the peak experience could be induced by any kind of mental effort;

Colin Wilson (*photograph: Trevor Clark*)

he thought that it came when it wanted to and it went when it wanted to and there was nothing you could do about it. And even then, when I first corresponded with Maslow about 1959, I felt that this was a mistake, that somehow we must be able to do something about the peak experience. In fact, I felt that this was a contradiction of what Maslow really stood for. Because having said that he didn't accept the Freudian view that human beings are helpless puppets in the hands of a horrific monster called the unconscious which can twist you around, and about which you can do nothing whatever – having rejected this view, Maslow still clung to an element of the old Freudian pessimism in believing that there was nothing you could *do* about peak experiences. You see, what has always interested me was the recognition that in the peak experience we ourselves contribute an enormous amount. But I was also fascinated by the fact that as soon as Maslow began to talk to his students about peak experiences, they began remembering peak experiences, which they hadn't really noticed at the time, which they then recalled in retrospect. And they also began having *more* peak experiences. So as soon as they got into the habit of thinking in terms of peak experiences, they began having peak experiences. Obviously, the peak experience is due to auto-suggestion. I remember as a child in the cinema suddenly thinking when the film finished; 'Why am I feeling so happy? Oh yes, of course, we broke up from school this afternoon and it is a holiday tomorrow.' I had totally forgotten that, but, nevertheless, the feeling of happiness persisted like an underfloor lighting. In other words, I had said consciously earlier, 'Thank God, we have broken up from school. How nice!' And then in the cinema I forgot about this, my own subconscious remembered and my own unconscious continued to glow and be happy, even when consciously I was completely absorbed in the film. Coleridge was fascinated by a case of a certain girl who in delirium began talking in Hebrew when she had never learned Hebrew. They found that when she was a child, she lived in a house of a pastor who used to walk around reciting the scripture in Hebrew. Her mind had simply tape-recorded all this, and out it all came when she was in delirium – although consciously she did not know a single word of Hebrew. So this aspect of the unconscious mind, you see, is really fascinating. When Sperry began to do these experiments in the split brain in the nineteen-fifties, and sixties, it suddenly became clear that we literally have two people inside our heads. It became clear that, in Thomson Jay Hudson's terms, the right brain is the 'subjective mind', and the left brain is the 'objective mind'. The right brain deals with our inner world, so to speak, and it appears to be in charge of our energy supply. In fact, the right brain deals with visual impressions, with patterns. The left brain deals with language. We don't need this feedback between the right and left brains for getting through everyday life. But Mozart would soon notice if you split his brain – or an Einstein – because they were continually turning intuitions into words or language; ordinarily we don't.

DCC: Would you consider religion a peak experience? You once said: 'My deepest interest is religion. My deepest need, to create my own.' Have you done this in your life?

CW: What I was really talking about was, I suppose, the problem of allowing your deepest inner urges to get to the surface. It seems to me that an enormous number of people don't want to allow their inner urges to get up to the surface. In fact, they have created a complete defence system against them. Philosophers like Bertrand Russell are marvellous verbalizers, but somehow if you try to draw them into the realm of feeling they hate it. And what's more, you find that – like Russell – they are nearly always immature little bastards who fuck every girl they can lay their hands on. Obviously, they haven't integrated that part of the brain. Now Alfred North Whitehead, although he worked with Russell on the *Principia Mathematicia*, was nevertheless the sort of person who was fascinated by the inner religious impulses; he states that philosophy should try to cover every possible kind of experience: drunken experience, sober experience, mystic experience, practical experience and so on. I am, just at the moment, reviewing a book by Arthur C. Clarke in which he spends half his time tilting against people who believe in UFOs, but what you miss in this book is any real contribution by Clarke to imagination, to thought. You feel like saying to him, 'Okay, fine, we have agreed on the whole that the Bermuda Triangle was probably nonsense, and that UFOs are probably a delusion to some extent. But never mind that. Tell us what you believe. Never mind what you don't believe.' This is the interesting thing. Once you try to develop what you *do* believe, then I think you are amplifying your deepest impulses. In a poet like Shelley, who regarded himself as an atheist, you can see the way in which over the very short course of his career he began to use the word 'God' quite freely, simply because obviously he experienced these tremendous upsurges of emotion, and only by using a word like God could he express what he was feeling. Does this mean that Shelley believed in God? I don't know, it doesn't matter. But what it does mean is that people who shudder at the very word God, like Bertrand Russell, somehow never really amplify these deep feelings, and never as a consequence grasp the whole of reality with the intuition. This is what the philosopher ought to be doing: grasping the whole of reality.

DCC: From your youth, you have believed that man could become a god, regain the powers we have lost. When you were nineteen, you wrote in your diary: 'I would be God.' How close to that state have you come?

CW: Nijinsky wrote in his diary, 'I am God, I am God.' It is obvious that what he meant was that there were certain moments when he experienced the sensation of 'fire blazing into the head' (W. B. Yeats' phrase). This is the sudden sense of a tremendous rush of sheer joy and vitality into the brain. The pineal gland is a very peculiar part of the brain, because it is the only part that is not double; all of the rest of the brain is like a mirror image; one side's a reflection of the other. Evidence seems to suggest that the pineal gland may be the source of sexual ecstasy too. In the moments in which joy floods into the brain, there's also a curious feeling of 'grasp', of insight, as if a fist was clenched in the brain. And the grasp appears to give you a deeper hold upon the reality of the external world – the reverse of when you get up in the middle of the night feeling rather ill, and the world seems unreal and dream-like, and you have a strange sensation of being unable to grasp reality. So, in the moments of great intensity the world seems to become solid and real, and in a funny sort of sense you feel as if you can hold it and keep it. Normally the mind's experience of reality is rather frustrating, rather like trying to start your car when it's stuck in mud or ice, so that the wheels just spin. You get a feeling that there's no grip. And in moments of intensity the reverse is true – you get a feeling of grip, as if suddenly the mind is actually digging into reality like the iron wheels of a tractor. Now this is what I mean by the feeling 'I am God.' And so the obvious questions are, 'What can the mind do to grip reality? What is the technique for learning to induce this feeling of gripping reality?' The one thing that's for certain is that most of the nineteenth-century romantics had entirely the wrong attitude towards it, with a kind of passive drifting, the desire to be wide open to experience. . . . Rilke is one of the most interesting late examples of it; the feeling that the poet ought to be infinitely sensitive. And the result is that he spends all his life taking the temperature of his own feelings; waking up in the morning and saying, 'How *do I* feel today? Am I happy or miserable?' The answer should be: 'Who the fuck cares? Get on and do what you've got to do.' And when you get on and do what you've got to do, then, suddenly, the stupidity of the emotions ceases to be important. *You* take over, the 'central you', 'the presiding ego'. The interesting question of course being, 'What is this central you?'

DCC: Exactly. But clearly all human beings do not have the desire, nor do they have the ability to be gods or visionaries. Is there more involved than what the serpent in George Bernard Shaw's *Back to Methuselah* says, that 'every dream could be willed into creation by those strong enough to believe in it'? Do you believe that everyone is capable of the intense vision of reality that the mystics have?

CW: Oh yes, everyone's capable of it because we have the physical equipment. We have the pineal eye, for example. In most people though, you need to induce it by drugs or other external stimuli.

DCC: But what about the 'will'? And not everybody wants that vision, do they?

CW: No, because if you haven't seen it, you're not likely to want it. If you went to the east end of London to some of the slums, and asked the people there whether they wanted to go to the Continent on holiday, most of them would reply 'no'. In fact, if they had any experience in going to the Continent on holiday, they'd be hooked on it and want to go every year. If you haven't the experience, you won't want to do it. And this is the central point. It's the moments of intensity that act as a learning experience, that you need to grasp and get back to; if we believe firmly enough in the moments of intensity, it is possible to get back to them. But you need to be obsessed by them. It is a matter of living by them and refusing to accept compromise. Much more difficult to do, I agree, for people setting out in life. I, myself, having left school at sixteen, found it tremendously difficult to believe in myself enough to say, 'I am a writer. This is what I'm going to do with my life.' And even then, once I'd published my first book, *The Outsider*, it was difficult in a certain sense to stick to what I wanted to do, rather than writing the kind of books that people would have liked me to write. Somebody wrote to me the other day and sent an essay called, 'Is Colin Wilson the Jesus Christ of Modern Mysticism or its Judas Escariot?' implying that I obviously ought to have done something which I haven't done.

DCC: You often write about the difference between 'reality' as we think we know it, and the 'true reality' of the mystics. What is this reality of the mystics? Is it possible to be coherent or give it a framework in language?

CW: I've always thought so, yes. The mystics have always insisted that you can't do this, that it's ineffable. I've never accepted this point of view. Anything is inexpressible when it's new. So that you couldn't describe, shall we say, a new shade of green that you've seen, unless you could refer to other things and say that it's midway between grass-green and olive-green or something of the sort. In other words you need to have other solid points of reference. And if you're talking about mental states, then certainly you've got a hell of a job producing solid points of reference that everyone can understand. Still, it can be done. I've always believed that language will be able to express these things eventually. It's simply a matter of being willing to do it by what seems to be an extremely dreary method, the method that naturalists use, labelling butterflies. I agree. It seems ungrateful to label your most intense experiences in this way.

DCC: Or you could talk about a sect, like the Sect of the Phoenix. To what extent did Jorge Luis Borges influence your novel *The God of the Labyrinth*?

CW: Oh, that was only in technique. I don't like his work basically because he's a pessimist.

DCC: Do you think that the so-called magic realism used in contemporary Latin American writing best utilizes the 'vision' that writers are capable of having?

CW: The only Latin American writer that I like very much is Machado. He strikes me as being enormously important. Apart from him, I think that most of them are interesting but I feel rather as William Faulkner did when he was asked what he thought of contemporaries like Norman Mailer and he said, 'They write good but they got nothing to say.' [*both laugh*].

DCC: You have written: 'My critical books are essentially my vision of the world: just that and no more. If it has any sort of validity for our time (and I do not assert that it has), it is only because it is in some way typical of this age; not because it was supposed to be an academic examination of the problems of our age.' Yet critics have quarrelled with your lack of synthesis and analysis. They insist that you do something that you are not setting out to do. Would you agree with Emerson's description of the wise writer, that 'the ends of study and composition are best answered by announcing undiscovered regions of thought, and so communicating, through hope, new activity to the torpid spirit'?

CW: That quote from me sounds like the kind of thing I wrote twenty years ago. In which case, the real problem then, you see, is that when *The Outsider* came out, I was twenty-four years old. Young writers have the feeling that critics are of terrific importance – that they can really make you or break you; you get the feeling that the academic people who write about you and say 'Why aren't you far more academic?' may well be right. Iris Murdoch always wanted to send me to a university [*laughs*]. You therefore tend to exaggerate their importance. As you get older this ceases to bother you. You realize their opinions don't matter a damn. That you've got to get on with your own work anyway. Of course, it's just possible that by trying to give your work some kind of general, universal framework, some philosophical framework, you can actually make it better and clearer. But very often this is not so. Very often they simply misunderstand what you are trying to do. As I've gone on producing a body of work, I feel that it tends to be self-explanatory. You know, one book explains another, or throws light on another. It eventually becomes fairly clear that I've been preoccupied with the same question from the beginning, and that all of my books have explored it in different ways. So I don't see that it's really necessary to take into account these opinions. I agree with Emerson in his essay on self-belief. You see, every individual writer perceives the world in a completely individual way, through his own spectacles. As you read G. K. Chesterton, he's very obviously seeing the world through completely different spectacles, from say, Aldous Huxley, or Graham Greene. The spectacles are what makes the writer individual. Eventually, they're also what makes a writer valuable. Yet in really great writers like Tolstoy, you don't have an impression of a pair of tinted spectacles, as you do with Aldous Huxley. You're always aware that it's Huxley writing. But with Tolstoy at his best, you're not. There's a strange *impersonality* about the whole thing. And this is what I admire most. I think that all of us possess a personality, but we also possess what is far more important, an impersonality. It's the impersonal part of us that responds to the impersonal in the world around us. Einstein once said his aim was to see the world by pure thought, completely impersonally. This is what's important. Your personal view is not very important at all. Great writers are like medieval craftsmen – as if they were doing their work in a church, completely anonymously. And what's essential still comes over. That's why so many of these writers you've mentioned today don't seem terribly important.

DCC: In your critical writing, you have indicted modern writers for allowing their disgust with life to become a literary climate, a sense of defeat in their work, and a notion that the sensitive, intelligent human being is ineffectual and that the world belongs to Shaw's 'hogs'. What has been your most important contribution to change this direction?

CW: I think basically the fact that I'm of an optimistic temperament. I'm also of a scientific temperament. In other words, I think that my work is, in a sense, singularly objective – my mind's singularly objective – and this is what I admire in Shaw. Whenever I read Shaw, I get a breezy, wide open feeling – you know, as if you've opened all the windows and the wind is blowing through. Whereas when I read Graham Greene, I feel as though I'm in a stuffy, damp cellar. It's the objective feeling that I love.

DCC: You have cited Christopher Isherwood as one of the few modern novelists who has escaped the slide into defeat or negation. Who else would you say has escaped this slide into defeat?

CW: Very few people of this present generation. You see, the difficult thing to understand is that once you've made this premise of defeat – the Freudian premise that human beings are basically hopeless and helpless – then you've automatically negated your own work. You may have an interesting atmosphere, you may be able to build up an obsessive kind of suicidal intensity, but at best, I don't think you can go very far. The only living writer that I admire in that sense is Ayn Rand [she has since died]. She seems to me very interesting and important – even if at times rather bigoted and silly.

DCC: This defeat is often a result of boredom, of ennui. In his autobiography, Graham Greene describes his experiments to escape boredom, such as playing Russian roulette. This idea of going to the edge and experimenting is something I find in your books as well. Gerard Sorme admires Austin Nunne's wish to experiment in your novel *Ritual in the Dark*. You have also defined existentialism as 'the need to treat life as an experiment'. However, experimentation sometimes leads to murder, sado-masochism, destructiveness. Where are the limits of experimentation? Should there be boundaries on human experience?

CW: As soon as you begin to deliberately treat life in this way, as an experiment, to do so, as it were, consciously, intellectually, and in an orderly manner, the experiment itself begins to define its own boundaries. In other words, there's no possibility of spilling over into murder. A policeman came to interview me the other day to see if I was the Yorkshire Ripper. I pointed out to him when he left that no writer in history has ever committed a murder. Ben Jonson killed a man in a quarrel but that's about all. Writers are just not killers because they're using their creative energy in a completely different kind of way. I think that the moment you begin to use your energy creatively, to think, to analyse, then the possibility of your using it pointlessly and violently disappears. I think this is always true. But the most interesting thing that I've come across recently – and it is the answer to that question I brought up a few minutes ago about the 'central ego' – occurs in the work of an American doctor called Howard Miller. Miller, I think, has made the most interesting discovery since Freud. He sent me a paper about a year ago, called 'What is Thought?' in which he said that if you close your eyes and conjure up an image, you are aware of *you* conjuring up the image a split second before the image occurs. This 'you' he calls the 'unit of pure thought' and says that it is in charge of consciousness. Miller said that in spite of the fact that this inner monologue goes on all the time so that the brain appears to be a giant computer, *you* are nevertheless in charge of it. When I first read this essay I felt: it's interesting but not important. So I wrote him a nice letter and then forgot all about it. Well about three months later I'd finished a hard day's work and I was taking a walk on the cliffs. I discover that the main problem, after I've done a hard day's writing, is that it's very difficult to relax and unwind; you know, your mind's still grinding on with the day's ideas. You just can't get them out of your head. I discovered that the answer to this is not to try to open up and relax because it doesn't work. The machine grinds on. What *does* work is if you can concentrate hard enough on something else, put all your interest into it. Then you suddenly find that when you relax after that, things are fine. Wordsworth told De Quincey that when he was totally concentrated on something that had nothing to do with poetry, only then he relaxed. In the same way Graham Greene with his Russian roulette story – he points a gun at his head, pulls the trigger, and then when there's no explosion, he goes, 'Whew!' and relaxes. When I relaxed I found that I was enjoying nature again, things were getting through to me. And I asked myself: 'What precisely am I *doing* when I do this? What part of me, in other words, is giving the order to concentrate and then relax?' And then I suddenly thought, 'The ordinary left brain ego is doing it.' Then I thought, 'No, no, that's impossible. That can't be the answer to the problem. The ordinary left brain ego – No! Surely we're really talking about the unit of pure thought, or the transcendental ego or something much bigger. Not the ordinary left brain ego.' But the more I thought about it, the more I recognized that 'Indeed, it is the ordinary left brain ego!' What happens is roughly this: Graham Greene's left brain ego has become miserable and discouraged and defeated, and has therefore ceased to make any kind of effort. As soon as he points the gun at his head, the left brain ego leaps to its feet, shrieking, 'Oh no don't do that!' And the shriek wakes up the right brain ego which promptly floods you with energy. So in fact, the part of you that gives the orders, that brings about 'primal perception', is the left brain ego. Well that fascinated me. Then I remembered Miller's essay. I came back and reread it, and I saw there was an extremely important passage which I'd noticed at the time but not really grasped. What Howard Miller says is this: that the unit of pure thought fails to recognize that it is the presiding ego; it is, as it were, sitting in a corner of the brain, listening to this terrific racket going on all around it – the noise of the computer – and it's like being in a cinema – you know, images are flickering across the screen, music is playing, voices jabbering – wondering why the whole thing seems so meaningless. And the reason is that the presiding ego ought to be in the projection room doing the projecting! And what you're getting, in fact, is completely accidental – running of the film with all kinds of accidental shots and sounds and noises that have no kind of logic at all. And what Miller is saying is that as soon as you get up there in the projection room, quite suddenly everything becomes orderly. Then I remembered that story by Hemingway called 'Soldier's Home', which I quote in *The Outsider*, about this soldier who comes back from the war to his home town and is bored stiff, and plays billiards and gets fed up with himself, and then Hemingway says that he remembered 'all those times during the war, those times under crisis, when you did the one thing, the only thing, and it always came out right'. And it's true again, it's the Russian roulette. Under crisis, quite suddenly, the left brain ego realizes that it's supposed to be in charge, and leaps to its feet, otherwise it forgets that it's supposed to be in charge, and the result is that you get the film running in any old order; what Miller calls 'the phantasmagoria'. Well this suddenly struck me as a revelation. The image I used was this: imagine two Irish navvies, sent out to do a job by the foreman, and each one thinks that the other one has been put in charge. And so each one is waiting for the other to give an order. And one of them takes up his pick, and the other one thinks, 'Oh, he must intend me to pick up my pick', so he picks up his pick too, and the other one thinks, 'Ah, he's picking up his pick, I better show I intend to work', so he puts his pick down and spits on his hands. The other one thinks, 'Oh dear, he's putting his pick down', so he puts his pick down too [*laughs*]. And because neither of them knows who's the boss, nothing gets done.

DCC: You speak about crisis. One of the things that I find interesting in your work, and a number of other contemporary writers, is this idea that murder becomes a 'more life' theme. You've mentioned Graham Greene. James Dickey, Saul Bellow, and Walker Percy, all deal with it in one way or another. Murder or violence becomes a kind of respite from boredom or insignificance. You also explore murder as a perversion or inversion of the creative instinct, in some way aligned to the creative. Sometimes it's an insight into freedom, sometimes it's seen as a god's prerogative. And you have referred to Jack the Ripper as an artist in embryo, though of a disgusting kind. I think the idea of murder in terms of freedom, creativity, transformation, vision, needs further clarification. Could you put us straight once and for all?

CW: I took the theme from Dostoevsky's novel *Crime and Punishment*. I felt that Dostoevsky had recognized something important, and that is what William Blake meant when he said, 'When thought is closed in caves, then love shall show its root in deepest hell.' In other words, when thought becomes frustrated, then it tends to turn to violence. Blake also said, 'Rather murder an infant in its cradle than nurse unsatisfied desires.' Any kind of crisis will snap you out of your state of boredom. You see, this is an evolutionary problem. Let me dismiss that murder thing first. I don't think it's of any significance at all. Murder is just one form of violent stimulation, and because murder is socially forbidden, it becomes an interesting form of stimulation in the same way that certain people want to fuck nurses, or women dressed as schoolgirls, or whatever. In other words, they're using the fact that it's socially forbidden as an additional stimulus and, therefore, it has a tinge of violence. But basically it's the same mechanism as Hemingway and war, or Graham Greene and his Russian roulette. Anything, in other words, that will make the real 'you' get into the driving seat. But the interesting part about it is *why* the real 'you' should get into the driving seat. You see, I think that Julian Jaynes is right about one thing, that there has been a basic change in human consciousness so that we now have this compartmentalized brain with 'you' living in the left and with another 'you' living in the right-hand side. But what seems to have happened, as far as I can see, is something like this. To begin with, when life appeared on earth, there was no death, so these little amoeboid things swam around in the sea and lasted forever. But on the other hand they didn't evolve. Then after a certain point, life discovered a way in which it could evolve; it invented what I call the 'robot'; that is a genetic way of storing information, knowledge. Life then proceeded to use this information-storage system in conjunction with death because otherwise there would be far too many of the things swimming around. But at least it meant that the things could now afford to die because the information could be coded and preserved. This, I must say, tends to confirm my basic belief that life is somehow independent of matter and utilizes matter for its own purposes. Life is the great chessman up there somewhere, moving the things around on the chessboard. Once life had invented death, which I think took a billion years or so after its first appearance, then it also invented the robot. You now had an interesting combination; life had now become dual. Once upon a time it was just pure instinct, the pure instinct to survive. Now you have an interesting alliance between the robot and instinct, and this instinct–robot alliance dominated life for the next half billion years. This instinct–robot alliance is very useful, because instinct tells you what to do, you reach out for things, you know, for food and all the rest of it... You encounter various problems in the course of doing this. You solve these problems instinctively, and the robot codes your solution and remembers it. And so this instinct–robot alliance was a marvellous one, and it lasted for a long time. But it has one very serious defect. It was extremely shortsighted. This robot–instinct combination is fine, provided the level of emergency is great enough. So, the robot–instinct combination is ideal for creatures living under very difficult conditions. (And of course, life on earth was extremely difficult for an enormously long time, until, little by little, things improved.) And this is the problem: that as soon as things begin to improve, then the robot–instinct combination no longer works so well because creatures get automatically lazy; this is what killed the dinosaurs. And so at a certain point in evolution, life had the interesting idea of introducing a third element into this combination, the element called consciousness. Now the point about consciousness was that it could see further, and therefore had foresight; foresight was the all-important element. And this ought to have solved the problem superbly. Unfortunately, you find that even human beings, who possess reflective consciousness, are nevertheless quite capable of lying down and dying of sheer boredom. I mean this is what modern literature is about, ever since Kierkegaard. You know, we've had this mysterious problem of boredom. Artzybasheff's novel *The Breaking Point*, which is one of the great modern novels, describes how most of the people in a small Russian town become so bored that they all commit suicide. The real problem is this. Although consciousness has been introduced, and ought to solve the problem, consciousness does not recognize that its purpose is to solve the problem. In other words, consciousness has been introduced as a third partner in this triple alliance. Unfortunately, it thinks it's the office boy instead of a partner. It's basically passive by nature. It still leaves all the big decisions to instinct. It just doesn't have the self-confidence to carry off this position that it's been put in. And this is the real problem. In other words, consciousness thinks that its business is merely to be an observer, and that all the real work ought to be done by feeling and instinct. Consciousness ought to be at the helm, and instead it spends half its time in the crow's nest. Now, this would be a very serious defect if it couldn't be corrected. But in point of fact, the interesting thing about consciousness is that it can make a decision and stick to it. In other words, we have reached a point in evolution where consciousness has to take over a completely new position. It's got to take up its real role as the third full member of the triple alliance – of instinct, robot and consciousness. And what's more, not just as the third member, but as the leader of the triple alliance. Now this means that we're going to have to stop spending so much time brooding about our feelings; they don't matter a fuck.

DCC: Isn't that against the cultural movement of the last two hundred years?

CW: Absolutely. And this is because the whole drift of the last hundred and fifty years has been absolutely vicious. I mean twits like Freud, Whitman and D. H. Lawrence...

DCC: 'I feel, therefore I am.'

CW: Yes, quite. And of course, one of the few people who stood up against it was a weird man of genius called Wyndham Lewis who hated Freud, Lawrence, and this whole tendency. Unfortunately, he was also such a neurotic twit that nobody ever listened to him [*laughs*]. But he was right and the others were wrong.

DCC: You also explore the idea of consciousness and energy in your novel *The Space Vampires*. You write about positive vampirism where there's an exchange of energy. You cannot take someone's energy or will or life unless they will it consciously. And if you fight it, then the vampire cannot take you over, so it can be a positive thing. This is against the usual negative interpretation of vampirism. You have converted it into a positive and creative possibility.

CW: Yes, what I am saying is absolutely against the whole current trend. But, you see, D. H. Lawrence himself just made an honest mistake. He felt that as in moments of primary perception, you suddenly have this explosion of feeling, of instinct. And as the kind of people that he disliked intensely, the Bertrand Russells and all the rest of them, tended to dwell much more on impersonality than on instinct, he felt the answer must lie in trying to give instinct its full freedom. But you can see that Lawrence himself died in his early forties with TB, and died a very unhappy man, because he had simply gone for the wrong solution. He wasn't really giving his instincts total freedom. In fact, in a way, he was the most egotistical little bastard ever. You've only got to read him to see this 'I, I, I' in the prose all the time. And he was negative, simply because he got the wrong solution.

DCC: It's an honest mistake perhaps, but he was interested, I think, in the right things.

CW: Except that again and again, Lawrence wrote stories like

'The Woman Who Rode Away', which seem to me to be utterly bloody stupid – they seem to me to show how far he'd gone wrong – this idea of sacrifice and violence. A book like *The White Peacock* or a worse book like *The Plumed Serpent* seem to me to be utterly infuriating with their emphasis upon instinct and the way that instinct should be allowed total freedom. Because in the early work, it meant simply that he admired stupid people – big healthy males. And he did this mainly because he was a homosexual and admired big strong men. But in the later books, like *The Plumed Serpent*, it just turns into a silly sort of fascistic violence, which is no answer at all. If you read books like *St. Mawr* – about the horse – or *The Virgin and the Gypsy*, the thing that you feel most strongly is that after originally saying that all these people who use their minds too much are no good, what's more interesting are these simple creatures like gypsies and horses. Then suddenly, in both cases the story turns into something completely and utterly negative. *St. Mawr*, particularly, turns into something nasty and bitter. Because obviously he does not know the solution and what he's proposing is not a solution. You know, give way to instinct. All right, so the horse is more instinctive than the human beings in the story, but, where does that get us? We don't want to become horses, or the cows Walt Whitman admired. You see, Nietzsche understood it when he said that we envy the cows their happiness but if we wanted to ask them, 'Why are you so happy?' they couldn't reply, because they'd have forgotten the question before they could give you the answer.

DCC: I realize that you dislike Bertrand Russell, but wouldn't you agree with him that man created ideas so that he wouldn't have to think?

CW: [*laughs*] I sympathize entirely. Russell was rather more wide open than you'd suppose. He also wrote in that letter to Constance Malleson that, 'What I really want to say, what I've never yet said, is not something personal, but something' – I forget what he said exactly, something like – 'A vast wind blowing from far away, bringing the immense passionless force of non-human things.' This is what science is about. It's also what the greatest art and religion is about. So Russell did understand it – in flashes. It seems to me his early philosophical work is the most interesting. His later social theorizing was short-sighted and personal.

DCC: In your book *Introduction to the New Existentialism* you have written about 'life-devaluation': 'Our lives consist of a clash between two visions: our vision of this inner freedom, and our vision of contingency; our intuition of freedom and power, and our everyday feeling of limitation and boredom.' Various characters in your books, like Gerard Sorme, explore this, but others like Austin Nunne and Manfred Lytton in *The Schoolgirl Murder Case* explore it to destructive ends. If you are not an artist, philosopher or scientist, is it possible to reconcile this?

CW: What I do believe is that a small percentage of people are infinitely more influential and creative than we recognize. And that's what I said in *The Outsider*. These outsiders of the nineteenth century tended to die of TB and commit suicide and feel immensely self-pitying. What they had to face, whether they liked it or not, was that they should be the leaders. If only they could take up a proper role of leadership and accept that *they* ought to be the intellectual leaders of society then everything would be fine. Not only for them but for society. It's really the betrayal of the intellectuals, of the outsiders, the betrayal of their proper position of leadership that has led to the present mess. And then of course, twits like Samuel Beckett accept the notion of complete meaninglessness that arises from this confusion I've been talking about – from letting your feelings and emotions dominate your life. Read that biography of Beckett and you see that when he was young, one of his problems was that he stayed in bed all day because he could see no reason to get up! [*laughs*]. This is the problem. He looks inside himself and says, 'Why should I get up? I can think of no possible reason.' If someone had come and pointed a gun at his head, it would have been the best thing that could have happened to him [*laughs*]. Simply because it would have made him aware. In all our moments of intense happiness, the conscious ego, the left brain ego, suddenly gets behind the steering wheel and drives. And if it doesn't get behind the steering wheel and drive, then not only do we become victims of pessimism – for some reason the right brain is far more pessimistic than the left – not only do you get a basically pessimistic orientation, a basically trivial and personal orientation, you also get this complete destructiveness that you find in the culture of the past century. You get an increasing tendency to a negation, you know, for people to lie down and die. Beckett imagines he's saying something of universal significance. He's not.

DCC: Do people find him profound because he reflects a general malaise?

CW: Absolutely. What he's doing in a way is simply confirming this misery and self-pity in most of his readers.

DCC: You believe that literature should be concerned with the 'how' of living. In *Eagle and Earwig* you wrote that the existential critic challenges the author's overall sense of life. The question is not 'What do you see?' but 'How broad do you see?' So the ideal aim of the existentialist is to surmise life finally, its ultimate affirmations and negations. You once wanted to write a novel that deals with life with the same directness that we are compelled to live it. Have you achieved this?

CW: No, no, not at all. What's more, I said it in the preface to one of my worst novels, *The Man Without a Shadow*. No, I don't feel I have. *Ritual in the Dark* comes close in its techniques, and *Lulu* would be much closer to it.

DCC: Do genres restrict the novel from exploring the largest possibilities of life?

CW: I believe in deliberately using diffrent genres as exercises. I have used science fiction and the detective novel – even spoof pornography – in the hope of achieving the same kind of alienation effect that Brecht tries to achieve in his plays. The underlying implication is that this is *not* really a science fiction or detective novel. What I'm really saying is something about ideas. The reader and myself, sort of wink at one another but what we're really exchanging is ideas: in the same way Brecht's plays seem to say to the audience, 'Well we both know this is a play, don't we? However, what we're really talking about is the coming revolution' – or whatever.

DCC: Truman Capote's *In Cold Blood* was considered a literary innovation of the time. But you were convinced that it was inadequate as a non-fiction novel, or as they say, 'faction–fiction', and you decided to write a better one, namely *Lingard* [*The Killer* in the first British edition]. In what ways did you think that *In Cold Blood* was inadequate? What did you try to rectify?

CW: I just thought that there was a certain confusion in Capote – imagining that he had invented a new literary form. Balzac was writing 'faction' long before Capote. All good literature is faction in that sense. Zola spent an enormous amount of time exploring the background for his novels. So bulldozing a pile of facts into a novel is nothing. What is important in a novel is the novelist's arrangements of the facts. He uses fact to impress you that he's saying something real, that he's not telling you a fairy story to get into a receptive frame of mind. But he's getting you into a receptive frame of mind for his own purposes. In the case of Bertolt Brecht, his purposes happen to be Communist propaganda. And so in *Mother Courage*, he's saying to you, 'Well, here it is, this is war – this is what the thirty year war was really like.' And once he's got you convinced that he's really talking about the thirty years' war, he slides in his Communist message. But at least he has a Communist message. And in *Galileo*, you're impressed that this does really seem to be like the life of a real scientist and his problems and once again he slips in his silly Communist message. Actually, Galileo was a dreadful man. Not the least like the person Brecht tries to portray. He was an egotistic little bastard who did all these things for his own glorification, not for the glorification of knowledge [*laughs*]. But the point is, you must have a purpose in doing it. Capote has no purpose, he just uses fact for its own sake. In point of fact, nobody could write pure 'faction'. It would be like trying to make a movie that was pure reality, by just having a hand-held camera and photographing crowds as they walked past in the street. It would be fact, in a certain sense, but it would be meaningless. One obvious thing about Capote is that he's never really had a controlling ego. He's really a woman writer, that's why.

DCC: Why do you dislike women writers so much? Is it just because you believe that they emphasize the personal and emotional as opposed to the objective and impersonal? In *The Outsider* you commented on the scarcity of female outsiders, particularly in fiction. One example is Emily Brontë and Catherine Earnshaw in *Wuthering Heights*.

CW: I dislike women writers because they think about their feelings all the time. At the moment we tend to watch our feelings and our bodies and our sensations far too much. We tend to allow them to be the guides to what we do. When I tried to reread *Wuthering Heights* a few years ago to write an article about it, I hated the book. I thought, 'What trivial rubbish!' Indulging her self-pity and her emotions and rolling around in them [*laughs*]. I hated the book. It's to do with the right and left brain again. For some odd reason, women are much more mature than men. It starts in the womb. They're already several weeks more mature than the male foetus at the age of about five months. And they maintain this advantage in adulthood. The differentiation between the right and left brain is something that occurs about the age of seven. And women achieve an ideal balance of right and left much sooner than men. This makes them much more practical, much more down to earth. But it's the difference between right and left which makes for genius. This means that men like Beethoven tend to be capable of greater inspiration than women like Jane Austen, simply because of the imbalance between the hemispheres. The inspiration, don't forget, the intuition, originates in the right brain. Mozart said that he didn't know where his musical ideas came from – that they just floated into his brain all the time when he was feeling healthy. If he was happy and riding along in a coach, musical ideas just came bubbling into his brain. Well, obviously the right brain learned to express itself in musical ideas, and sent the ideas into the left brain in the way that it sends strange images into your head when your're on the point of sleep. These strange notions startle you because they don't seem to come from you. They don't, they come from the person in the other side of the head. Now this kind of thing, I suspect, doesn't occur in women to the same extent. It's interesting that Joy, my wife, is an absolutely typical right-brainer. Also, she's left-handed, and they've discovered that people who are left-handed are much more intuitive than people who are not.

So Joy's a kind of double right-brainer, which is the reason you know she suits me so well. Because I'm almost a double left-brainer.

DCC: You've said that you've always thought of yourself as a kind of scientist, rather than a novelist. What draws you back to the novel?

CW: I don't know, it's just the fact that novels are enjoyable to write. You may as well say, 'What's enjoyable in masturbation?' And the answer to that, of course, would be that in masturbation you can sometimes catch the reality of a situation that never would actually happen to you with such beautiful precision that it becomes real enough to evoke all of the sexual feelings which of course are basically right-brain feelings, even to the point of orgasm. Now in the same sort of way, you can involve yourself so deeply in creating the characters and situations in a novel, that once again it almost becomes a kind of self-running movie. You're astounded that these things begin to walk around inside you because you have actually created a new state of consciousness, or rather a new degree of control of your own consciousness.

DCC: You've written plays but you are really drawn, I think, most completely to the novel. Why do you write novels as opposed to poems or plays or any other form?

CW: I don't write poetry because that's a completely different thing. Writing poetry, for me, is supposed to be the essence of what you have to say. If W. B. Yeats had decided to write novels and critical books, he wouldn't have been a good poet, because in order to make one good poem you have to boil down, so to speak, a whole novel. I don't want to be a poet because I'd have to throw away too much; boil it down. There are no examples I can think of in history of people who have been really good poets and good novelists. Someone like Valéry, for example, was a good critic but not a good novelist. His only novel is atrocious. They are just totally different talents. Dostoevsky could never have been a poet although maybe if I was allowed to just write poetry in the way that D. H. Lawrence did – with no discipline whatever – I'd write poetry [*laughs*].

DCC: At one time you regarded Henry James as the greatest English novelist, always the observer, never the participant, watching the world from 'outside', which goes back to the your stress on ideas as opposed to the stress on emotion. What do you sacrifice in the novel of ideas, if the emphasis is on ideas? For instance, do you sacrifice style?

CW: Oh, probably style, yes, but I never bothered much about the style. I always felt that style was simply saying what you can in the shortest and clearest way possible. So if I achieve style ever, it's simply because my ideas are so compressed that they express themselves in a form that looks aphoristic and stylish. I think to actually aim for a style when you're not really trying to say that much, as Camus often did, is a kind of fake. I used to admire Henry James very much, simply because he seemed to me to be an ideal combination of a person who actually lived and observed, but also a person who then tried to reason about his living and observing, and to translate this into terms of fiction. What I now find is that I'm put off far more by Henry James's shortcomings as a person, by his timidity and by the pessimistic orientation of his work. When I was younger, I didn't mind the pessimism. I can't read Balzac for the same reason. I greatly admire Balzac, and yet if I ever try to read a complete novel I get so annoyed with his stupid pessimism that I can't go on. And I get the same feeling with Henry James. I admire him to a certain extent, and then, when I find all these pointless characters of his wandering around in circles not knowing really what to do with themselves... You know, Strether in *The Ambassadors*, says, 'Live, live, it's a mistake not to', but James doesn't actually show Strether living. He didn't have any capacity for showing you people living.

DCC: In other words, you would consider John A. Weigel's statement that you are not a stylist, that your most significant effects are seldom achieved with delicate nuances, or with pastel epiphanies, of no real importance.

CW: There's a chapter, for example, in *The World of Violence*, about Uncle Sam, in which he says he's gone on strike against God. I often read it aloud because stylistically it is a bit like Camus. I think it's well written but that's not very valuable.

There's nothing I'm proud of. In other words, I don't think that style's of terrific importance. Your style is basically your own way of thinking.

DCC: You've said that the best way out of the so-called 'cul-de-sac' that the modern novel has gotten itself into is to deliberately try to achieve the Brechtian alienation effect. Since you have utilized this same technique, and as early as *Ritual in the Dark*, is it a technique that you still use today?

CW: Oh, yes, very much. *Lulu* was intended to use exactly this technique, and that's why *Lulu* is defeating me technically. That is, this device works beautifully for short periods. *Ritual in the Dark* only covers about thirty-six hours.

DCC: You mentioned to me before that your novel *The Black Room* was a particular favourite of yours, and I noticed that you told Joyce Carol Oates that *The Space Vampires* was also. What is it about those two novels that you particularly liked?

CW: I can't remember why I said *The Space Vampires*. I'd have thought *The Mind Parasites* or *The Philosopher's Stone* much more. I may have said *The Space Vampires* because I'd just completed it, and I thought that this whole business about psychic vampirism was an interesting one. *The Black Room* is my central novel. The whole question of what we should do if we were placed in a non-stimulus situation is the one that has always fascinated me. It's what I called 'the original sin' in *The Outsider*. When confronted with any kind of difficulty or crisis, human beings are magnificent. the moment you place them in the situation of freedom, once again, you're up against the business of 'it's heavenly to *become* free, and boring to *be* free'. Obviously what we need in a way is a spring to give us a positive sense of freedom, so we would count our blessings and see them actively. The obvious real problem is that the strength of consciousness, the strength of the spring, is not powerful enough. So in the central scene in *The Black Room*, Butler has spent his first session in the black room and comes out and talks to Gradwohl. Gradwohl tells him about the time when they climbed the north face of the Eiger, and how it suddenly struck him when he was half-way up the face of the Eiger that all of those people down there lying comfortably in their beds took life for granted, and he felt he ought to make a kind of vow never from this moment onward to take life for granted. Because, stuck in this particular position, he could, as it were, appreciate with the utmost precision any situation, measure its value, so to speak. This is the interesting thing, the kind of value measurement of the situation. It's rather like that story that Robert Ardrey tells in *African Genesis* about Carpenter's monkeys. When the monkeys were placed on board a boat to take them out to an island where they were to be studied in a restricted environment, they could no longer have territory, and they morally went to pieces. The mothers no longer protected their children, and the husbands no longer protected their wives. The infant death rate soared because the mothers would fight the children for a scrap of food. As soon as they got on the island they split into bunches, and once again each bunch had its own territory, and once again the husbands would die to defend their wives, and the mothers would die or starve to defend their children. It's an odd business that you could pull out what you think would be the moral values of the monkey from under it, and completely reverse its normal conduct. So, this is what has always interested me about human beings. But it's boredom that does it to human beings, not being stuck on a boat without territory.

DCC: According to *The Times Literary Supplement* you are among the most discussed English authors in Moscow's literary circles. Do you know why?

CW: No. There's a friend of mine, a professor at Moscow University, who's written a book about English writers in Russian, and there's a section on me in there. I've known Valentina for years, and her students read me in Russian. One of them did her thesis on me, and I still correspond with her. At the period when I wrote *The Strength To Dream*, although I had always been anti-Communist and I still am, I was rather pro-Russian, having spent a week in Leningrad and found everyone so very nice. The result was that I wrote an appendix to *The Strength To Dream*, defending Russian culture, and particularly Russian populist culture, as well as Russian music. This, I think, rather put me in favour with the Russians, and I remember Sir Charles Snow saying to me once, 'I don't know why your books aren't all translated into Russian. You know, you're the sort of thing they admire, optimistic and all the rest of it.' And I said, 'Well, see what you can do the next time you're there.' And he said, 'Don't you worry my boy, I'll fix it', but he never did [*laughs*]. I think that the basic individualism of *The Outsider* would sort of choke in the throat of the Russian officialdom. As it is now, when I try to send my books, such as *Mysteries* to Russia, they don't get through. The KGB stops them. The result is that when I write to friends in Russia, I carefully never mention politics, so as not to cause them any trouble or embarrassment. The KGB reads all letters.

DCC: You've talked openly about your belief in your talents, your genius, your greatness. Do you consider yourself one of the greatest or perhaps *the* greatest writer of your time?

CW: I suppose so. The question has to be qualified. When I was a teenager, at the age of thirteen, the thing that interested me most was science, particularly Einstein, and I wanted to be a scientist. It was apparent to me then, in Leicester, in this working-class environment, that I was by far the cleverest person around because nobody at school, not even the sixth formers, were reading Einstein. So there was always this enormous gap between me and the others. It was a purely impersonal assessment that obviously I was one of the most talented people I'd ever come across. On the other hand, the people I mixed with in Leicester and so on, obviously weren't willing to acknowledge this for a moment. Their tendency was rather to take me down a peg or two and say, you know, 'All of this is illusion, there're much cleverer people than you in the world. It's just because you're so ignorant of the larger world' [*laughs*]. So really, I needed to grit my teeth and dig in my heels and say, 'I *am* a genius!' At the age of fourteen or fifteen it was the only way to preserve my self-confidence. And then when *The Outsider* came out, the same thing happened all over again. After a brief period of people suddenly saying, 'Ah yes, young genius Wilson', and all the rest of it, and comparing me to D. H. Lawrence and Plato and God knows who else, quite suddenly it was all over. Once again critics were saying exactly what family and friends had been saying in Leicester; 'Oh, he's just a sort of ignorant polymath.' Well this sort of thing made me think 'I'll show the bastards.' I still feel that in a way. Respectable critics dislike my work because it is implicitly a criticism of them for being too involved in the personal, in triviality. The older you get, perhaps the less you care about whether you are the greatest writer of your time or not. When you're younger I think you care about it. I suspect that I probably am the greatest writer of the twentieth century but I don't care about it anymore. It doesn't worry me one way or the other. I'd just be very interested to find somebody who was greater, so to speak. If I did, I'd be extremely interested, genuinely, because I'd really want to know what they had to say.

11   Mary Gordon

DCC: As a young writer who is relatively new to the literary 'scene', how do you feel about the critical response to your work? Did you find it particularly perceptive?

MG: I thought Wilfrid Sheed's review of *Final Payments* in *The New York Review of Books* was perceptive. And that was about it [*laughs*]. I think that the reviewers decided that since somebody wrote one favourable review, therefore they would all write favourable reviews. Every now and again somebody says something that you like to hear because they've noticed something that you're glad *somebody* noticed, but only the Sheed review was instructive to me.

DCC: What is the function of the critic?

MG: The most important function is to make known good things that are around so that people want to read them. I don't think about criticism in terms of setting standards. First of all, there's not much criticism written in America at the moment outside the academy. There is very little criticism written about current novels; there are reviews, but to my mind there's a big distinction between the 'reviewer' and the 'critic'. For me, the ideal critic would be Virginia Woolf; someone who says, 'This is wonderful. You should really read this for this particular reason.' That's the most important thing that a critic does. As far as cutting people down to size, I don't think any of us is on very sure ground about that. It seems to me that the much more important thing is the educative process of simply making it known that, 'This book is one you should really pay attention to.'

DCC: Should the novelist be a critic herself?

This interview first appeared in *Commonweal*, 9 May 1980.

Mary Gordon (*photograph: Trevor Clark*)

MG: It's good for a novelist to sometimes write criticism because it uses up another part of your mind. If you are always dealing in a fictive realm, there's a part of your mind that makes judgements on abstractions which are at the same time real, and that you don't use. I really like having to read other people carefully on occasion, and to have to make the kinds of judgements that are formed by my reading of the literature of the past as well. It's quirky that some people may be very hurt by writing criticism and some people might be helped. I enjoy it when I'm not writing fiction. I can't do both at the same time easily because to me it's a very different frame of mind. I'm not going to be remembered for criticism but it's a lot of fun. It's just fun to write about something that's not coming from your own soul.

DCC: What is the function of the novel? I'm thinking of your statement that 'novels are an important form of moral education'.

MG: Pleasure. If it has a function, it has a function to be beautiful. If it's accidentally instructive, that's all to the good. But the novel's main function is to be beautiful and, in some sense, true in a very large way that I can't even begin to explain. Again, Virginia Woolf said: 'What I want to do is to tell the truth and to create something of beauty.' I think that's what the novel is supposed to do. I don't think it makes people any better. If that were true, English departments would be the moral paragons of this or any other age. And anyone who has taught for two minutes knows that they are not.

DCC: How true [*both laugh*]. Goebbels had a Ph.D. in Romantic literature after all. When you talk about 'beauty', are you referring to some sort of objective standard, or do you mean that beauty is simply in the eyes of the reader?

MG: I don't know. I'm not an aesthetician. I can't say that there are any standards. I am very attracted to formal beauty. I like a well-made piece of work. I like balance; that's very important to me. I'm by nature a Classicist. I am by nature anti-Romantic. Novels that I like have to have a kind of shapeliness and a kind of balance and have to have beautiful sentences. It's important to me that novels be full of beautiful sentences. However, I know that there are some terrific novels that are written very badly in a particular way. I was reading *Shirley* by Charlotte Brontë last year, and it's a terribly written novel, but it's marvellous. Nobody in our age could write a novel where in the last ten pages the whole denouement comes out. Balance, form and care are essential.

DCC: That concern is reflected in your obvious care for language, what your characters, Isabel and Eleanor, call 'the perfection of the outward form'. Given that, I would think that certain notions of what is 'religious' in art, would seem sloppy to you. Paul Tillich, the Protestant theologian, defined the 'religious' as something of honesty and ultimate concern. He said, for example, that a rock by Cézanne is more religious than Christ on the Cross by a sentimental German painter named Uhde. How do you feel about that definition of the 'religious'?

MG: I think it's nonsense because it devalues both the religious experience and the experience of Cézanne. All beauty is *not* religious in its nature, and all aesthetic or heartfelt responses are not religious. You're right, I don't like that kind of sloppiness. For me, the religious novel would be one which had a relationship to God at the centre of it. No, I don't think that swimming in the ocean is as religious an act as contemplative prayer, which is not to say that one is more valuable than the other. It's simply to say that the comparison is a kind of messiness I don't like. If you call everything religious, then nothing is religious. It seems to me that the religious experience is very singular and very odd and entirely interior.

DCC: Do you consider *Final Payments* a religious novel?

MG: It's certainly not a religious novel in the way that one of Mauriac's novels would be, or one of Bernanos's, but I think that Isabel is searching, trying to come to terms with her religious life. I would not say that her path of self-identification is a religious path, but in that she is so importantly formed by her religious experience and really sees everything in metaphors of Catholicism, *Final Payments* is a religious novel.

DCC: To continue that point about using Roman Catholicism as a metaphor, do you think that the more secular world that we live in today has anaesthetized people to the symbolic world, to the understanding or the sensibility of the symbolic? Has this changed writing styles?

MG: That's very interesting. What's happened doesn't have to do with secularism, it has to do with communication. A symbol has to have a kind of thickness to it. It is something that has to build up over time for people really to be able to respond to it.

The symbol of our age would have to be something very evanescent because we're not interested in things that accrete over time, that build up meaning over time. I don't think it has much to do with religion, I think it has to do with the speed at which we live and our disregard for history, because a symbol only takes on meaning as it attaches to the past.

DCC: Wallace Fowlie has stated: 'American literature is quite thoroughly non-Catholic. There has never been in this country anything that would resemble a Catholic school of letters or movement in literature.' Do you agree?

MG: Yes I do. It makes a lot of sense. The Catholic church in America is an immigrant church. Immigrants were worried about making money and surviving, and they didn't encourage learning; learning was a threat to the family. The more you learned, the more likely you were to leave home. The Catholic church in America is and always has been phenomenally anti-intellectual. To go to school and to study philosophy or literature or art is very different because it's learning that won't get you anywhere, except out of the community. And they're right. What is touching and moving is the loneliness of the immigrant experience – always feeling an outsider, always defining yourself as 'not Protestant', and even later on as 'not Jewish', knowing that you somehow never had access to the real power, and kind of looking in with your nose pressed against the window. I think that's very much a feature of Catholicism in America. American Catholicism is also a profoundly anti-sexual tradition, in a way that the French Catholics really aren't and the Italian Catholics really aren't. Irish Catholicism is very anti-sexual, and the sexy people get out of the church; they have to. What you're left with is a marvellous ascetic type who stays in the church, or a person like Flannery O'Connor who's a virgin through and through, one of those wise and fierce Antigones. They can stay and be quite interesting and quite admirable, but the sexual people have to get out.

DCC: I find that that suspicion of the flesh, that Jansenism, pervades the writing of French Canada and Ireland as well. What are the cultural elements that contribute to this sensibility?

MG: It is a deeply Puritanical tradition. I guess what I feel about Irish Catholicism in America is that it took all the charm of Ireland and left it there, because the people who came to America couldn't afford to be moony and romantic. The ones who stayed here had to be very practical. We inherited the problems of Ireland, which are the problems of poverty, and centuries of intellectual oppression and centuries of distrusting learning and literature. I don't think all literature has to be written against the orthodox tradition, but I think in America it's almost inevitable, and in Ireland too.

DCC: The best writing seems to be in opposition to the orthodox forms of the church. Is it as simple as this, that the conflict stimulates greater questioning, greater probing and therefore greater art?

MG: What you say is true in America but it's not true in Europe. Writers like Bernanos and Mauriac, although they were of different political castes and different sensibilities, both defined themselves as loyal sons of the church. I think it's a peculiarly American thing, or maybe an Irish thing – Joyce had to rebel – in that I believe the American church to be mainly the Irish church, which people tell me is wrong, but I still think is right. At least, the east coast is certainly the Irish church.

DCC: Who are the best Catholic writers?

MG: Bernanos, I think, is the greatest. Mauriac is also very great and so is Graham Greene. I would include Flannery O'Connor, although she's a Catholic writer who never writes about Catholics.

DCC: How about Evelyn Waugh or Muriel Spark? Do you consider them Catholic writers?

MG: Well, they'd like to be considered Catholic writers. I don't know. I have a lot of trouble with Muriel Spark. She's awfully thin to me. Waugh was a brilliant stylist, and I even like *Brideshead Revisited*, which about three people in the world do. . . . On the basis of *Brideshead Revisited* I consider Waugh a Catholic novelist.

DCC: The Christian in our society must confront certain essential paradoxes of her faith. On the one hand, she is taught the need to lose one's life in order to save it. The lives and writings of saints and ascetics illustrate this impulse toward retirement and withdrawal. On the other hand, the Incarnation, by which God became man, and dwelt among men in the world and in history with all of its evils, defies this withdrawal. Therefore, the Christian lives both in heaven and earth. Does the character of Isabel in your novel *Final Payments* in any way embody this paradox?

MG: Yes, that's wonderful. You saw that, very few people do. It's something I think about all the time. It's a terrible paradox; it's the paradox of having a body even as Christ had a body with affections and needs and connections and yet knowing or sensing somehow that there's this angelic realm that you might almost have access to if you just give up this body. It is a paradox; there's certainly no way of resolving it. But it seems to me that the impulse of charity comes from the Incarnation, comes from going out. I've always wondered how a contemplative can fulfil his obligation in charity because in some ways it's a profoundly egocentric life. You spend all of your time getting rid of your flesh and the hell with everybody else's flesh; if they're starving and leprous, that's their tough luck.

DCC: Carl Jung believed that religion binds humanity together. Do you agree?

MG: No. I think it probably separates men, one from the other. If you've got two people together talking about religion, they'd usually disagree, but if you've got people talking about the way they felt about their children, they'd probably agree. Human affection is much more universal than religion.

DCC: Father Cyprian, in your novel *The Company of Women*, is so different to Father Mulcahy in *Final Payments*. Father Mulcahy is kind and loving. But Father Cyprian is cruel to, and contemptuous of, the women who make him the centre of their lives. He refers to them as 'goose girls'. They are brood hens circled around the dying cock whose struts they revered.

MG: They represent two very real types of priest. Father Mulcahy is less forceful, less intellectual than Father Cyprian. Father Cyprian has an almost gladiatory ideal of the priesthood. One is much more interested in the 'ideal' than the other. Father Mulcahy is not so attracted to this ideal as he is to a fantasy of the way people are. Father Mulcahy is more impressed with the merciful side of God, whereas Father Cyprian is impressed by the 'just' side of God.

DCC: Does Isabel's life in any way echo the saints as Doris Grumbach suggests – the fall, return, reconciliation, rescue?

MG: I think the lives of the saints on the whole are pretty good narratives. Maybe Isabel's life does echo the saints. That pattern is certainly not unusual in literature. Yes, I mean her to be a kind of saint.

DCC: What is the meaning of Isabel's sacrifice? She has given up her life for her father but she makes that statement 'not with self-pity but with extreme pride'. However, sacrifice in the book, especially the one Isabel makes for Margaret, seems to be more than the 'pride of sacrifice', the 'romance of devotion', or the idea of martyrdom.

MG: It was very important to me to make the distinction between genuine sacrifice motivated not only by love but also by affection which seems to me to be of immense importance in life. The sacrifice that Isabel practised in relation to Margaret is a kind of theft, sacrifice for its own sake without any movement of the heart. Sacrifice as an abstraction is hateful unless you really want to. Certainly there would be times when the person is physically appalling to you. But unless you have a memory of a stirring in the heart, I think you have no right to sacrifice yourself.

DCC: So beware of the person who loves humanity *in toto*. They are unable to love the individual. What do you like best and what do you like least about your work?

MG: What I like best is that sometimes I write really smashing sentences. What I like least is that there are certain things that I just can't do. I fear a narrowness of range. There are just some experiences I can't ever write about. I can never write about physical violence. I'm not very good at writing about young men, men who have a sexual identity. And I wish I were better. Flannery O'Connor has said that everything that is important to a writer she learns before the age of eight. I was brought up in a very female-centric world so that makes sense to me. But I wish – I find men so incomprehensible that I can't write about them very well.

DCC: We can see that 'female-centric' world even more clearly in your second novel, *The Company of Women*. It has been suggested that the best men and the most convincing ones in *Final Payments* are the invalid father and the alcoholic priest, both of whom are 'unsexed'. Do you agree?

MG: Yes. I have to do something terrible to my sexual men in order to understand them [*laughs*]. I can't write sympathetically about a normally-sexed man.

DCC: In both *Final Payments* and *The Company of Women* you are drawn to closed worlds. Both Isabel and Felicitas spend long periods of time in a world that offers suffocation, but also definition and even promise. How do you create a novel? What comes first?

MG: What comes first is a character in a situation. I usually have a shape which I then feel free to violate. But I have to have some idea of situation first. To me, character and situation are not separable.

DCC: You write both short stories and novels. What are the elements that constitute your decision to write a novel versus a short story?

MG: I feel that the novel has to be written *about* something, so that I can answer the question in my own mind: 'this novel is about –'; whereas a short story can be a situation, a character, an incident. I do feel that novels have to have themes. I don't think short stories do.

DCC: I would like your opinion about various attitudes toward the contemporary novel. First, what do you think of the Death of the Novel debate between, for example, Cheever and Fowles who assert that the novel is alive and well, versus Vidal and Capote who maintain that it is a dying art form and that journalism and magazines are taking over?

MG: I haven't thought much about it. I think that Capote and Vidal write journalism because they can't write novels, and they infinitely would rather be writing novels, but they can't, they're blocked. I suppose people don't need novels very much now, and that's sad. I think it's their attention span.

DCC: What about structural fabulation? This is the world, the Barth-theme world, that would go beyond and ignore historical reality in order to create self-sufficient worlds like those of Pynchon, Gaddis, etc.

MG: Let them do it as long as I don't ever have to read it. I just find it totally boring. I'm interested in the novel as a form of high gossip and the more the novel gets away from gossip, the less I'm interested in reading it. I want to know about Jane and Mister Rochester. I want to know about Dorothy and Elizabeth Bennett. I want to know what happens to Sue Bridehead. I don't particularly like the Barth–Vonnegut–Barthelme trip where literature is *about* literature. I wouldn't want to say that they are wrong, that that's not the way novels are to be written. I could change my mind in ten years. But I never want to read *Finnegans Wake*; *Finnegans Wake* is about language, it's not about people. And I think novels should be about people. I'm not interested in novels that are basically tricks to show us what writing a novel is really about. On the other hand, Virginia Woolf's my favourite novelist, and it seems to me she does all the stylization you could ever want to do, but doesn't move away from character. I think if they're crabbing they should just go and read Virginia Woolf and shut up [*laughs*].

DCC: How about Anaïs Nin and her notion of abstraction and the future of the novel?

MG: She's such a dumb... I just can't understand all that.

DCC: Which writers in the past do you admire?

MG: My favourite novelist is Jane Austen. I also love Charlotte Brontë, Thomas Hardy, George Eliot, and Ford Madox Ford. Ford is one of my favourites. I think I'm going to have to put him third after Woolf and Austen.

DCC: Are any of these writers important to your writing?

MG: Virginia Woolf. I was writing a dissertation on her when I was writing *Final Payments*, and I was copying out – I never finished it – but I was copying out passages of one of her novels in the afternoons. I was writing my own work in the mornings, and I learned so much about prose writing from her. I've stolen her use of the colon. I really learned a lot about colons and semicolons. Yes, I learned a lot from her …

DCC: Who do you admire among contemporary writers, given that you have said that this is a time of thin and trivial fiction?

MG: I admire Eudora Welty, Margaret Drabble, Toni Morrison, John Cheever, Doris Lessing when she's not being visionary, and Gabriel García Márquez who is a great genius.

DCC: Elizabeth Hardwick advised you to change *Final Payments* from the third person narrative to the first person. In what ways did it change the book?

MG: It allowed Isabel to be more intimate and more self-exploratory. I had done an awful lot of rumination and I realized that the direction of the novel tended to be quite ruminative.

DCC: Has Elizabeth Hardwick had a major role in your life?

MG: Yes. She's one of the most important people in my life. I also think she's one of the best prose writers writing in English just in terms of beautiful sentences.

DCC: You liked *Sleepless Nights*?

MG: I adored it.

DCC: Does your writing draw heavily from your own life? I'm not only thinking of your novels but also your short stories like 'The Thorn', 'Now I Am Married' and 'The Other Woman'.

MG: I feel freer to be autobiographical in short stories than in novels. Somehow talking about yourself for ten pages is okay, but talking about yourself for three hundred pages is a bit much. *Final Payments*, and I've said this a million times, is not about me. The point is that if you write a good novel, who cares where it comes from. Virginia Woolf says about Charlotte Brontë: 'always to be a governess and always to be in love is no advantage in a world in which most people are neither'. On the other hand, we have *Jane Eyre* and *Villette* and I'm terribly glad we do. I don't care that she was being autobiographical. I care about the novel.

DCC: I didn't necessarily mean physical autobiography. I meant a spiritual, emotional, and psychic affiliation to the worlds you create. Writers like John Cheever and John Irving have both come out very strongly against the novel that is what they call 'crypto-autobiography'.

MG: But what is *The World According to Garp* but crypto-autobiography?

DCC: In her review of *Lovers and Tyrants*, Sara Sanborn says that 'first novels produced by American women lately . . . seem to have only one real character in them: Me. A procession of erotic Dorotheas, without the rest of *Middlemarch*.' Do you agree?

MG: I don't think I did that in *Final Payments* but generally it probably is a bit of a tendency.

DCC: So much has been written about mothers and daughters, yet you focus on the father/daughter relationship in both *Final Payments* and 'The Thorn'. Why?

MG: Well, I did mothers and daughters in *The Company of*

Women [*laughs*]. But the father/daughter relationship is so romantic. There is always a kind of distance, a kind of glamour. The sexual difference makes a kind of formality almost inevitable and, as I said before, I'm interested in formality. It's a very touching relationship in which so much *cannot* be said.

DCC: Are traditional forms of writing controlled by a male sensibility or are all great minds androgynous?

MG: Novelists are very lucky because the novel was considered not respectable; therefore, women were allowed to write novels. But almost from the beginning I feel that the novel has been an androgynous form.

DCC: Except that Virginia Woolf, for instance, said that there's such a thing as a 'female' sentence. Unfortunately, she never expanded the idea. Also, there are people who are trying to create a feminist literary criticism. A lot of female artists insist that female metaphors, for example, are very different from those of male writers.

MG: It might be true, but it's nothing to think about. I mean, I wonder about it, but I certainly don't wonder about it while I'm writing. I think it's much more simple than that. Women have a proclivity, women are trained to be more associative, and they're trained to be more interested in human relations, and so they tend to write about these things in their novels. That's what I'm interested in, and because I think other things are trivial, I'm perfectly happy with that. I don't read many novels that don't have women in them; I don't read many novels about men shooting up other men and finding out what their penises are for. That bores me to death. I'll read about what happens in the drawing room in Somerset by the hands of Jane Austen for fifty years, but don't ever ask me to read Conrad again.

DCC: Really? I love Conrad.

MG: He's a wonderful stylist but I don't ever want to read him again.

DCC: Did you encounter any particular problems as a woman writing novels or short stories?

MG: I had no problems with the response to my writing. However, I encountered lots of problems with people asking me, 'What's a nice girl like you doing writing?'

DCC: You have met with tremendous success, and Graham Greene has said: 'For the serious writer as for the priest, there is no such thing as success.' Can you relate to that?

MG: That is so true. The only thing that matters is what you're doing in front of the page, and this has nothing to do with what anybody thinks about it. Nevertheless, in practical terms, if you have some money you have more time, and that's important. But on a profound level what Greene said is perfectly true. I love that quote.

DCC: I know that the actress Diane Keaton took an option on *Final Payments*. Can mediums be transferred? John Cheever doesn't believe they can.

MG: I don't think about it. If they make a movie, I will have nothing to do with it.

DCC: Some writers, such as Patricia Highsmith, like to be involved in order to make sure that her story is not aborted. I believe that John Fowles was involved with the making of *The French Lieutenant's Woman*.

MG: If it means that I could buy a house in Cape Cod, I would like to have a house in Cape Cod. Because film is a different medium, I feel no responsibility for it. I would feel terrific responsibility for anything I wrote. Even if they did the film well, it wouldn't be mine anymore, so good luck to them. I just don't want to hear about it.

DCC: What is the role of an editor? You have published in the magazines *Redbook*, *Mademoiselle*, etc. Is there any kind of critical help on their part? Or is it a *fait accompli* when the story is submitted?

MG: You have to be very tough. If they say they are going to cut out the whole middle paragraph because they have an ad. for shampoo there, you just have to say, 'Well, you can't do that.' They cut things up and you just have to be ferocious.

DCC: That's outrageous. I'd like to go back to *Final Payments*. Maureen Howard felt that Isabel's sojourn in the big world is a lot less interesting than her bondage. Do you agree?

MG: No.

DCC: Neither do I. Isabel feels that her father's stroke cleanses her sin and is 'the mechanism of forgiveness'. What is the nature of her sin?

MG: Betraying her father.

DCC: The relationship between Isabel and her father is emotionally incestuous. They are 'connected by flesh'; her sexual relationship with David is a kind of punishment because her father is *not* jealous; she says that she has 'borne the impress of his body all my life'; she keeps Margaret from her father and is jealous that he has sent her money, written to her and sent her Christmas presents; Isabel's angry at Eleanor's confession that she had sexual fantasies about her father; Isabel says: 'I loved him more than anyone else'; her father says: 'I love you more than I love God. I love you more than God loves you.' What part does this play in the motion of Isabel's life?

MG: I do want to say that there is something overwhelming about their love for one another, and not quite right. Romantic and compelling as it is, there's no way for her to be an adult as long as her father is alive. So although the relationship is very attractive, because it is so all-consuming, it is in some sense damaging to her. It is not healthy. But she manages to survive it because there is that love there. Another writer that I love is Tillie Olsen and one of the messages of Tillie Olsen that has been very instructive to me is that even 'warped' love is somehow life-giving and in the end it will probably come out okay. Love, any passionate attachment, is all to the good. I do believe that in some sort of very primitive way.

DCC: The church has always discriminated against women. When the Second Vatican Council was called, Catholic women were not invited to attend, even though wives of non-Catholic clergy were. Representatives of all the major religious denominations, including Jews, non-Christians, atheists and Communists were invited. Stories abounded about the woman journalist who was asked to leave 'lest her presence defile the pope'; about women forbidden to receive Communion at mass along with the men in Vatican city; about Barbara Ward, the internationally known economist, whose proposition for something practical to be done about poverty and injustice in the world was accepted but *she* was not allowed to speak to the bishops from the council floor because she was a woman. In *The Company of Women*, Father Cyprian warns Felicitas 'Not to be womanish', but to be the opposite, which is orthodox. What do you mean by orthodox?

MG: I guess it is conforming to an ideal which is traditional and ancient. It would also be the perception of men in power, their ancient perception of what the ideal was. This idea of the orthodox is anti-modern and anti-modernist. It values authority over individual freedom and happiness.

DCC: In your excellent article on Archbishop Lefebvre, I had the feeling that the modern world disappoints you. It is Kresge's, not Balmain's. Is there a world where words like 'sublime', 'miracle', 'mystery', 'immutability', and 'the impossible', are realized and compatible with 'certainty' and 'authority'?

MG: Probably, but it would be such an awful world that it would cut out so much of the human and I would never want to live there. I prefer a state of longing for imaginary worlds because people do such terrible things in the search for certainty and sublimity. You could say that's what the Nazis were looking for. That really is the root of totalitarianism. I think one must hunger for that and not try to put it into practice. But as a hunger it makes you much more interesting.

DCC: The bulk of the world's literature describes women in relation to men, and describes them in relation to one another as rivals for men. You have said about your novel *The Company of Women* that you 'want to be talking about women and their spiritual mentors, and the female habit of abdicating responsibility for their inner lives to the men – priests, lovers – who in one way or another compel them'. Could you clarify that?

MG: I think we've always thought that anything not rooted in the flesh is the realm of men. If a woman had aspirations to be anything other than that which is rooted in the flesh, she had to go to a man for it. And he would tell her what she was really like. She would never go to another woman because she was mucking around in the same 'unsublime' area. And this habit of women asking a man, 'tell me what I'm like', and believing him against all sorts of evidence, and then being willing to radically change their lives, is a very big pattern in everyone from professors and students, to husbands and wives, to the Manson family; it just seems to have very strong ramifications. Women believe that men have all the interesting data in some way. I hope it's changing now.

12 Julio Cortázar

DCC: Interviewing has been both praised and damned. . . . How do you feel?

JC: I'll tell you very frankly, that in a general way I don't like interviews. I mean I don't like oral interviews. It's the same as addressing an audience. I feel that I wasn't born for that; I was born to write. Language, literature, and words, belong to the written form. I'm only really happy when I sit alone, facing my typewriter. In the last ten years I have done two or three hundred interviews. Most of them have not been about literature but about political issues, all the Latin American problems, and so on. So at the beginning I was rather terrified by interviews; I had a kind of block that made it very difficult for me even to think, let alone to speak. When I was working in the Bertrand Russell Tribunal and journalists came before or after the sessions to ask for some opinions from the members of the Tribunal, I understood that I couldn't ask them to leave their questions in written form and send my answer by the mail. I had to, as the French say, take my courage with both hands and try to answer. Well, I learned little by little and today an interview is not a problem for me. But I want to go to the centre of your question. I'll tell you that an interview is, for me, more or less what a sonata is. I mean a sonata for two instruments, let's say for violin and piano. The sonata will sound very beautiful, and the two people involved in the interview will express the feeling of a Beethoven or a Brahms when it's played equally well by the piano and the violin. If one is good and the other is not good, the sonata is a failure. Interviews look more or less like that to me. So the personality of the interviewer is very important when I have to answer his or her questions. If I discover that the interviewer is not a person with whom I can have a dialogue, then I feel very disappointed, I answer mechanically and the result is that the sonata is very weak. In our case, I am very

Julio Cortázar (*photograph: Trevor Clark*)

impressed by your questions. I'm not so sure that I will be able to answer all of them but the questions prove to me that Diana Cooper-Clark is very sensitive, very intelligent in that her questions were not improvised just to make an interview but were the result of a long knowledge of Latin American literature and my own books.

DCC: Thank you. Jean Franco has stated that in Latin America, 'the view that the artist can in any way change or modify society through his art has gradually been abandoned by the majority'. Do you agree?

JC: I'm not so pessimistic as Jean Franco. Of course, I don't think the way the Romantic poets, Shelley, for instance, did, that the poet is a kind of reformer of human destiny, and that a good writer has an immense influence on his readers. I am far from believing that. But in Latin America I have witnessed in these last fifteen years the clear and well-proven influence that certain creative work has had on the historical process of many of the Latin American peoples. The period which started in 1955, more or less, and lasted ten years, that movement which was called the 'boom' by some critics, had a tremendous influence in Latin America. I think I am well placed to judge that because my own books were part of that so-called 'boom' and became widely read in all Latin America. I began to receive hundreds, and later thousands, of letters, not from critics and other intellectuals, just letters from the common reader, from the man who had bought one of my novels or collections of short stories and wanted to establish a dialogue with me, and who wanted to put questions, to make criticisms, to accept or to reject. Little by little I began to discover that a few writers of different nationalities, Peruvians, Colombians, Argentinians, and so on, were having a deep influence in the awareness of the Latin American reality. Many people were trying to find this awareness but for different reasons were unable to reduce it to a system of clear ideas. It happened that people like Carlos Fuentes, Vargas Llosa or García Márquez established new perimeters for them in which certain deep elements of the Latin American reality were seen, felt and expressed for the first time from the depths, and not just through the mere imitation of European models. Of course, all this is very little when you think of the political side of history, when you think of El Salvador, Argentina, or Chile. Everything we intellectuals say or do seems futile, compared with the material and economic forces that are in play in Latin America. One should not forget that when the dictatorships in Argentina, Uruguay and Chile took power, they forced all intellectuals into exile creating such a situation for them that they had to die, or leave the country. I think that this is one example among many other proofs, that the dictators were afraid of the influence of certain writers, painters and musicians on their people. Perhaps the most horrible but at the same time the most symbolic thing that a dictatorship did in this context happened the day when the Chilean soldiers cut the hands off Victor Jara in the national stadium in Santiago. That was for me an awful and clear symbol of the fear that the dictator always has of the artist, of the intellectual. The hands of Victor Jara made music in his guitar and his voice was a voice loved by the Chilean people.

DCC: That is very sad. It seems a travesty to deviate. Lawrence Ferlinghetti describes himself as an acrobat who defies death on the high wire by 'performing entrechats . . . and other high theatrics'.

> For he's the super realist
> > who must perforce perceive
> > taught truth
> > before the taking of each stance or step
> in his supposed advance
> > > toward that still higher perch
> > where Beauty stands and waits
> > > with gravity
> > > > to start her death-defying leap

[Number 15, in *A Coney Island of the Mind* (New Directions Books, 1958)]

Do you ever see yourself this way?

JC: Oh no, I don't see myself as an acrobat like Ferlinghetti. I always see myself as an amateur, as though I'm not a professional. An acrobat is a professional symbolically. I'm just an amateur writer who has his fun and his pleasure writing novels and short stories and sometimes poems. Intellectual work is never performed before the public. This does not mean that I don't like the notion of an audience, that is to say the notion of readers. The reader is absolutely, essentially, my notion of my own work; but the work in itself, the fact of sitting down to write a novel or a short story has nothing of the performance of an acrobat. The acrobat is seen by an audience and that is not my case. My audience is invisible; my readers are there but not when I'm working.

DCC: People have talked about writers in many different

ways. William Faulkner said that, 'if a writer has to rob his mother he will not hesitate; the "Ode on a Grecian Urn" is worth any number of old ladies'. Graham Greene and Sylvia Plath felt the same way. Do you?

JC: Selfishness is one of the components of literary activity. If you're not selfish to a certain degree you can't work, you can't concentrate; but I don't agree with this notion of almost absolute selfishness that some people attribute to the great intellectuals, to the great creators. I think that the selfishness of a poet or a writer is quite insignificant if you compare it to the general selfishness that prevails in economic matters or matters of property, houses, land and all that.

DCC: You once said: 'I wrote *Hopscotch* as I did to enable the reader to grow very angry and independent and to hurl my book out the window if he chose.' Is this a cruel relationship as someone suggested?

JC: No, I think that the writer must be compared to a surgeon. Good literature acts like a kind of mental knife in the mind and sensibility of a reader. It's exploring new regions of the perception and the comprehension of the world and sometimes the journey is difficult to make and it hurts. In that sense, when I was writing *Hopscotch*, I felt that I could hurt many of my readers. I wanted them to be hurt because I felt that surgery was a necessity but that's not a notion of cruelty – with a surgeon it's not cruel.

DCC: In *A Change of Light*, one of your narrators says despairingly: 'I know that what I'm writing can't be written.' Am I right in feeling that you sometimes share this notion?

JC: It's quite true, Diana. So many times I feel when writing that there are things that can't be written, and perhaps that is literature, to do your best, to try to write the impossible. Perhaps literature is a second version of an impossible first version of something we dreamt of writing and we couldn't.

DCC: I wonder if this would make interpretation pointless. One of Carlos Fuentes' characters may well have been speaking for him: 'every human being has the right to take a secret to the grave with him; every storyteller reserves the right not to clear up mysteries; in order that they may remain mysteries; and anyone whom this displeases may ask for his money back'. Given that you are probably plagued with questions to please interpret your books, would you agree with that statement?

JC: I quite agree with Carlos Fuentes. I have been plagued many times by critics and readers who ask for the explanation of things. I'll tell you an anecdote. When I first came to France and I published some of my short stories (what I call fantastic stories), I was amused to discover that many French readers were disappointed with the fantastic stories because they'd like a final explanation. They have a more geometrical and Cartesian mind in France. I can remember a very well-known French writer who told me rather timidly after reading one of my short stories, 'well, I like it very much, it is alright but why don't you add a little footnote explaining what really happened at the end'. I laughed and he was a little ashamed. I should add that there are two kinds of writers: one is the writer that honestly is the first not to know what happens to some of his characters, in some of his plots, in some of his books. I think I belong to this category. When I finish a short story, it's finished in its written form. I have no explanation to offer because I don't have an explanation, except the one that the short story suggests, perhaps clearly, perhaps hiddenly; but there's also another kind of writer. I don't like these, the ones who play with false difficulties, false enigmas, false complications, false mysteries. I don't go along with this because it's very easy to discover to which one of the two categories a good writer belongs.

DCC: Willa Cather detested the idea that the writer had demons, that their gifts and visions were part of childhood traumas and neuroses. But you don't seem to feel that way. Writing can exorcise the burden of certain thoughts, feelings, nightmares, and neurotic products. Mario Vargas Llosa has also said that 'the writer is an exorcist of his own demons'.

JC: I just think that Freud and Jung were right. We have a subconscious, not only of personal traumas, childhood memories and all kinds of negative and positive forces, but I think too, like Jung, that we inherit a kind of collective unconscious and that we writers are speakers for these forces which not only belong to us as persons but that belong to the race, to the collectivity. There are forces that sometimes try to manifest themselves through novels, short stories, music, and paintings.

DCC: You have commented several times that you write when you find yourself haunted by an obsession which reaches crisis level. Margery Safir suggests that the author's stance in the moment of writing parallels his protagonist's stance in his moment of transgression.

JC: It's true that for a writer like me, an obsession can be a reason and even a theme for literature. I began writing short stories and these stories were a kind of exorcism. I didn't realize at the time that I was writing them to get rid of obsessions, manias, neuroses that disturbed me in my youth. I discovered that after writing a short story about a little neurotic state that state disappeared in me and I felt quite well. That was the day when I knew that I had been exorcising a hidden negative force in myself and I was very thankful to literature for that discovery. Margery Safir's observation is true too because if you're writing about a neurosis in an open or a disguised form, you suffer it at the very moment when you are writing. You are possessed by your neuroses. If you weren't, I suppose that the story would be very weak.

DCC: Is it more accurate to say that you 'compose' your books rather than 'write' them?

JC: Music has always been very important to me and the notion of rhythm is crucial to my appreciation of a style. When I write, the sentences don't come only with an intellectual meaning, a need to express something, but every sentence comes to me from a certain beat, a certain rhythm. I could use the word 'passion' to express this feeling. If a sentence doesn't have this kind of balance, this musical movement, I feel that there is something lacking. The paradox is that I feel in such cases that it is also lacking in intellectual meaning. I haven't expressed exactly what I wanted to express, and I have to look it over and sometimes subtract or add some elements in the sentence, not for euphonic reasons, just for rhythmical reasons. Then I feel that the intellectual meaning, the communication that sentence conveys is there and it is there because the rhythm is there.

DCC: You have experimented with what you call 'rotting writing'. Are categories such as book, sequence, character, plot, also 'rotting'?

JC: There are many fixed elements in what people call 'writing' that are for me 'rotting writing'. Some writers take too much to categories, rules, syntax and all kinds of things which in themselves are necessary as rhetoric until you begin to take the means for the end and at that moment everything begins to be 'rotting writing'. If a writer sticks too much to preconceived notions such as style, syntax, the propriety of words and constructions, he is going headlong to a kind of rotting writing in my opinion. You have to 'break' in order to 'construct' in literature; if you don't break anything in your passage through the language, through what you are doing, you won't build anything real. In that sense, the musical impulse, what I call the 'swing' or the 'rhythm', is essential: that's my real axe, that's the weapon in which I make some progress in the page I am writing.

DCC: I'm interested in synaesthesia which seems to reflect what you've just said. Feelings, sounds (music), and thoughts could become fields of colour and shape. In *Hopscotch*, for instance, the sound of someone climbing a stair makes a drawing of that stair in La Maga's ear. In the nineteenth century, the poet, Alfred de Musset, was experimenting with translating music into words; Chopin was trying to translate colour into music (e.g. gold would be soprano and blue would be bass); and Delacroix was trying to translate music into colour. What is the advantage of synaesthesia?

JC: Of course, one should quote Baudelaire's sonnet, 'Les Correspondences', and one should go far back in time to Kirschner, a German monk who tried to create a music which corresponded to the scale of colours and put colour in music and vice versa. I think Kirschner had imagined that music should be performed with the projection by magic lanterns of the colours that corresponded to the given sounds. This is more or less scientific but what do poets do since the most ancient times? All metaphors are generally an alliance of a mixture of different sensations. To speak of the sea which has the colour of wine (that's Homer, I think in *The Odyssey*) is an effort to apply a visual notion to another object which is generally considered blue or green. I think that Homer was the first to see an immense wine-coloured sea and this metaphor or image you could find in the whole course of the poetry tradition. I don't have a good memory for poems but I know that I've read hundreds and hundreds of images in which the poet is translating the visual into auditory sensations or the auditory into tactile sensations. The poet uses the five senses but interchanges them to give more richness to the poetic image. The advantage of synaesthesia is that it has an aesthetic beauty; it opens the possibility of breaking the barriers of the different senses to touch things with your ear or to listen with your hand or to smell with your eyes. Another advantage in breaking the barriers of the five senses is that it gives a man the feeling that reality can be explored, not only by each physical sense restricted by its capacities, but also by the sensitive possibilities of synaesthesia.

DCC: Your love of music is obvious. In 'The Pursuer', Johnny Carter, a jazzman modelled after Charlie Parker, sees a second reality through his jazz music. It has been suggested that your writing technique resembles a jam session which takes off from fixed and stable forms, often complex and elaborate, on which you build your creative improvisations. Do you write similarly to the way that you play your trumpet?

JC: Yes, and how! When I discovered jazz in the thirties, I knew that jazz musicians never played by musical notation but that they liked to improvise their solos. For me, it was one of the most beautiful and profound lessons on creative liberty. I was very young when I decided that my own writing (since I couldn't be a musician, because I wasn't gifted enough) would try to improvise as a jazz musician does. But we shouldn't mistake the meaning of the word 'improvisation'. I don't mean a formless improvisation like that of a child when he is just whistling without form, without limits, without a given melody. My idea of improvisation was to be free in a form, free in a structure like a jazz musician is. When a musician improvises on 'Tea for Two' or 'Solitude' or 'I Can't Give You Anything But Love, Baby', of course, he has to keep in his head all the melodic bridges, the melodic successions that make that melody and not another melody. In that sense, literature would be an improvisation on a given form and that given form would be to tell a story, to develop a poem, or to write a novel. The form would be there and I should adjust to that form but once *inside* that form I would proceed with the utmost liberty, with the utmost improvisation.

DCC: In *Ultimo round*, you acknowledge Mallarmé's work on the idea that meaning lies in the articulation of what is between the signs, in the gaps and intervals created by them. The reader would fill in the empty spaces. That reminded me of Ralph Ellison's *Invisible Man*. He has a wonderful scene in the beginning of the novel. A prizefighter is boxing a yokel. Yet the yokel wins because he simply stepped inside of his opponent's sense of time. This leads to the invisible man's discovery of 'a new analytical way of listening to music. The unheard sounds came through, and each melodic line existed of itself, stood out clearly from all the rest, said its piece and waited patiently for the other voices to speak. That night I found myself hearing not only in time, but in space as well.' That's what you were just talking about and I must say jazz does that to me.

JC: That is a very beautiful and difficult idea. An Indian metaphysical thinker said that more or less. When you look at two separate objects and you begin to look at the gap between the two objects and you concentrate your attention in that gap, in that void between the two objects, then at one moment, you see reality. It is a beautiful intuition indeed that is parallel to Mallarmé's idea about silence. I love Mallarmé very much and it's because he was the poet of silences. When he says of a woman that she's the 'musicienne du silence', this is wonderful for me because in the absence of sound she's making her music, she is the musician of silence. Mallarmé found reality in silence, in everything which is absent. There's another sonnet by Mallarmé in which he's thinking of the ancient Amazons who used to cut off one of their breasts in order to use their bow and arrows more efficiently. When he's speaking to a woman, he's not seeing her real breast but the empty space in the Amazon's chest. I haven't read Ralph Ellison's *Invisible Man* [I sent him a copy] but it had to be a very beautiful book by the example you've given me of the prizefighter who loses his fight against the yokel because his opponent has another sense of time. I've seen it in real boxing, and you know I love boxing very much. I've seen an Argentinian boxer, who was a very good one, lose a fight against an old Mexican boxer who couldn't punch him, who had no more strength but had all the technique that was needed to change the sense of time of his opponent. All the blows of the Argentinian were lost in the air. You see it's really a good example of what I feel about jazz, the values of silences, the music which is not heard music. I feel it as well as you. There is another beautiful example; it's the music of Anton Webern. Just as Mallarmé was the poet of silence, Webern was the musician of silence. Some of his very short works consist of more silence than notes. It is a silence that is so deep, so charged with feeling and meaning that finally it's the real music. Webern knew that very well and used silence as a part of his music.

DCC: According to Roland Barthes, writing becomes *real* writing when it prevents the reader from answering the question 'Who is speaking?' The act of reading has been changed by the act of writing in this century. In the nineteenth-century novel there was a closed structure (I don't wholly agree with this), whereby the novelist determined everything, and the reader was dished up the whole meal. You have talked about the reader–accomplice, the reader who discovers his own fictionality, his possible authorship. The reader is thereby required to perform the narrator's traditional function. I find this very exciting. Readers have always participated in the feelings of the characters but now we can try to share the author's act of writing. You have written that the reader will be a 'travelling companion . . . , provided that the reading will abolish reader's time and substitute author's time. Thus the reader would be able to become a co-participant and co-sufferer of the experience through which the novelist is passing, at the same moment and in the same form.' But I wonder about the ability of the reader. Is it a question of brains or sensibility? Many people find your books difficult (even quite sophisticated readers, but maybe if they weren't so sophisticated they'd understand better; like La Maga in *Hopscotch*). I agree with what you are saying, and I feel that the reader should be as committed as the writer, but I still have reservations.

JC: Many times when I felt a little discouraged, I used to say to myself that all that I wrote in *Hopscotch* about the reader as an accomplice, a fellow traveller, was perhaps a kind of wishful thinking. But as time passes, I'm convinced of the contrary. In all these years when I travelled in Latin America and I met my readers in the most different circumstances, the street, cafés, hotels, etc., I discovered that I was right, that I had many, many accomplice–readers, and perhaps more than that. The word 'co-participant', would be more true, because many of these people who came to speak to me (in general very young people), were co-participants with my own work. Of course, there were differences, there were misunderstandings, but that is a part of the most beautiful interaction that can take place between a writer and his reader. I discovered that in Nicaragua, Cuba or Argentina, there were a lot of co-participants in current literature. They don't read all that the conventional reader reads, they don't read only to accept or reject, but they take part in the battle, they take part in what is happening in the book, and in a way they are rewriting it in their minds. They change it lots of times but it is very exciting and very surprising. I agree with you that the reader should be as committed as the writer. In Latin America, a reader which I respect is a reader as committed as the writer. If he is not so, he is just a reader of knowledge, a reader of short stories. He's a hedonist who looks for his pleasure, which is very, very beautiful but I think in Latin America some of us are writing for another kind of enjoyment of literature. A more fruitful, a more useful, a committed literature.

DCC: In 1979, you said that your readers came from the bourgeoisie or the intelligentsia. Has this changed?

JC: Well, not very much. I think that most of my readers come from the upper classes in the cultural and economic sense because my books aren't easy, and I know that my short stories and my novels are more accessible to a highly cultured person than to a worker. But at the same time I could add that in Latin America, great, great progress has taken place. There are lots of readers who don't belong to the university world but they are avid and very good readers of literature and they are perfectly able to enter into my universe or Fuentes'. or García Márquez's without any perceptible difficulty. The difficulties will always lie exclusively with the intellectuals. For instance, a young reader in Nicaragua came to me and asked me, 'Why do you put sentences in English in that short story? I don't understand English.' He was right in his way but I explained to him that the only way to express what that short story wanted to express were those sentences in English. It is his job as a reader now to look for an explanation of those sentences.

DCC: Your use of the Doppelgänger, the double, in your short stories and your novels, has been discussed over and over. But I'm especially interested in the way in which the reader and the narrator become doubles. The reader is both observer and observed, the reader joins the pattern described in *Hopscotch*, as 'paravisiones', the experience of feeling oneself as oneself and yet as another at one and the same time. The reader is drawn into the text as his consciousness expands.

JC: It's difficult for me to know how the reader's consciousness can expand. On the other hand, I can say that this feeling of 'doubleness', of Doppelgänger, has been in me all my life. Since I was a child, to double, to be myself and others, to feel myself in others, not only other men or other women, but other things, other objects, has been very familiar to me. I remember very well that I used to explain that to my school fellows when I was a child and of course they looked at me as if I were crazy, and in a way I was and I am, but for me to be single is not the whole reality. I'm at least double, and sometimes I feel that I'm not only myself but all that surrounds me. In a way that coincides with the more philosophical idea of Ortega y Gasset when he said that 'man is man and what surrounds him'. Of course, if you want to give that a cultural rather than a philosophical idea, then it would be John Donne's declaration that 'no man is an island'. In my case it is not so philosophical, it's rather a sensitive thing. I think that every poet, and John Keats knew that better than anyone, is able to transfer himself, to put himself into other things. When Keats wrote, 'when I see a sparrow playing in a courtyard, I am the sparrow, I'm playing in the courtyard', he was saying much better than I, what I feel every day when I'm in the street; when I see a beautiful child, I am that child for a second. I share his feelings, the way he's enjoying his life, then I can see a beautiful girl or perhaps an ugly girl and I'm that girl, beautiful or ugly. I share a way of seeing what in my own way I was seeing differently a few seconds before. Well, that capacity of being myself and others has been a great help in my writing, because as soon as I imagine a character, I'm that character. As soon as I see a house, an imaginary house, I'm not only in that house but I become part of the house itself, its atmosphere, all that the house contains. If all that can expand the reader's consciousness I'd be very glad. I hope it is true because many times people have told me that what they read in my books has made them richer, and I believe that they were telling the truth.

DCC: I know that the critic does not often help the writer but can the critic help the reader? Or should the reader be on his or her own with little or no help from the author or the critic?

JC: I'll be very definite in my answer. I know a lot of writers who hate critics. I've been always a great pal with critics, provided that I approve beforehand their kind of criticism, their approach, not only to my work, but to literature in general. For instance, in Latin America, I love very much the criticism made by people like Angel Rama or Davi Arrigucci to name only two, because there are others, but they come to my mind now because I feel they not only have the utmost capacity to criticize but they have a deep sensibility. They can be a Doppelgänger of the old folks they are writing about [*laughs*]. When I feel that a critic is not only looking at my work from an outside critical point of view but he's ready to plunge ahead and share my own experience to decide later if he likes it or not, then I'm with that critic. I feel a friend of his and I think that what he writes about myself or other writers is very helpful for the creator. Critics have taught me a lot about myself and I say this not only out of false modesty, but because I really believe it. I'm speaking not only of professional critics because sometimes I find criticism in private letters from unknown correspondents who say very sensible and intelligent things about my work. I discover lots of mistakes and I'm very grateful for people who are able to show me the right way. I have here in my house a lot of unpublished theses written by young people in the American, German or French universities about my short stories or novels and some of them taught me a lot about my own job. So my relationship with critics and criticism is highly positive. On the other hand, I cannot stand a critic who before criticizing a book prepares his own outline, frame or creed in which he wants the book to fit, and if the book doesn't satisfy his requirements then it's a bad book. I think that's a great mistake and it's a direct result of pedantry. That kind of critic is always a pedant; they know the truth, they are the owners of the truth and we, the authors, should adjust to that truth. I can give names because I'm not ashamed to do it. For instance, Manuel Pedro González, who was always opposed to my work, never found a valid argument to sustain his opposition, simply because he decided that since I was trying to experiment with language and experiment with the texture and the architecture of the novel, I was falling into a capital sin. According to his ideas, the novel should be this way, 'ABCDE', and the short story too. So since my own work didn't adjust to his point of view then I was a very bad writer. Well, I always thought that González was a very bad critic.

DCC: Much has been said about the mixture of fantasy and reality in Latin American literature and most certainly in your writing. Literature seems to have the tools for this (interior monologues, free association, dreams, counterpoint, circular time, simultaneous and pre-active narration, the labyrinth, the fragmentation of chronological time, the use of myths, multiple points of view, the slow-up, the fade-out, the close-up, the flashback, etc.). Is it possible to capture this on the critical level? Does criticism have a vocabulary or a structure to do this at the present time? Or will a new way of seeing, a new vocabulary have to be created?

JC: I think that it is a question you should ask the critics. I really don't know if critics and criticism have a vocabulary or a structure to coincide with all the experiments we writers are trying to do. But to put it with some humour I'd say that many critics go ahead of creators because they prepare creeds and schemes and categories as a spider making its web to catch the flies, and the flies are the novelists and the short-storytellers [*laughs*]. In a way you can say that critics place themselves after the work of creation; they don't try to impose norms or vocabularies or creeds but at the same time when there's very experimental work, critics are taken a little aback sometimes. Sometimes they seem to be surprised and I understand that very well because as a reader I can be surprised too with experimental writing that I'm not able to grasp at first reading. I know that it may take a long time for readers and critics in general to enter into the new universe that somebody has just charted and discovered. I think that one of the best examples in Latin America has been that of José Lezama Lima. His work in Cuba and in the whole of Latin America was so much ahead of what was being written in the same period by other writers that of course readers and critics were taken by surprise and many mistakes were made and many silly things were said about Lezama Lima's work. I must have made mistakes myself when I read his writing. For me, it was very difficult to enter into some of the developments Lezama Lima made because I was looking for a rationale, for an intellectual development of the ideas, of the theme, of the treatment of the subject, and it was a mistake, because to enter his world you had in a way to be like Lezama Lima, to give yourself over to a world in which ideas, feelings, sensations, intuitions and culture in its most refined acceptation would merge in a whole way of expressing newness and discoveries. You can't ask the impossible of critics. You can't ask the impossible of someone who tries to understand a book which is not very understandable in the first stage and which may take a long time to understand. Ask James Joyce's critics [*laughs*].

DCC: Would you say that you are writing fiction which is also literary criticism? Writers such as Iris Murdoch and John Fowles are.

JC: I don't think that I'm writing that kind of fiction. I could say that the literary criticism that one could find in my fiction is literary criticism addressed to myself. In my own way I'm always criticizing myself and trying to correct things and to show myself a new path, new ways, new articulations and combinations of language, in order to go ahead and discover a new little patch of creative land. But I don't like to mingle literary criticism with creation because I think that the two are contradictory. When you create fiction, you have to be terribly free; you need an awful liberty to go on. If you stop looking around, even looking into yourself, and you become complacent, you are bound to fail, I think.

DCC: Some writers believe that criticism can become an art itself. A Canadian poet, Eli Mandel, has written that criticism is a novel. Do you agree?

JC: No, but I've seen some critical essays that in a way were novels. They went their own way so broadly, so freely, and they took such a distance from the book they were speaking of that they became a kind of original creation which had little to do with the work criticized. That could be very beautiful indeed. When Jean Paul Sartre criticized Baudelaire, the book had very little to do with the real Baudelaire or his poetry. It was Sartre's book and had a validity which belonged to Sartre's genius. But I think those are always exceptions. Finally, a critic must be a critic just as a creative writer must be a creative writer. This merging of criticism and creative work doesn't often give good results. Perhaps it could be useful to make a distinction between a criticism of literature and a criticism of reality as a whole because in that case all creative writers are critics. The man who wrote *Tristram Shandy* or the man who wrote *Ulysses* or the man who wrote *Hopscotch* was trying to understand, to affirm and deny, different aspects of the whole reality. In that sense I think that the greatest literature has always, or almost always, been a critical literature. When it comes to the critic of literature, then I think that the creator sets himself apart from the professional critic and goes his own way.

DCC: Critics are fond of 'influences' in a way that writers are not. You have said: 'I am not talking of "influences", a horrible professional word clung to desperately by those who cannot find the true keys to genius, I am talking of deep participation, of brotherhood on an essential plane . . . .'

JC: I never accepted the idea of 'influence' as a kind of servitude that some critics try to impose in their criticism of others. They finally deny the very idea of originality. Some critics don't accept an author if they are not able to demonstrate that the author was influenced by Flaubert, etc. They seem to think that the literary world is the result of a kind of collage, a patchwork, made of different influences combined in a new form. That's absolutely false; that's not true of good literature. Influences, for me, are something much deeper; they are brotherhoods. You see, when I suffered as a child, the influence of Edgar Allan Poe and the influence of the Romantic poets and novelists were a brotherhood. Those influences didn't force me to do things in such or such a way; they were there, keeping me company but I was absolutely free. I could have taken directions given by books I had read but those influences were not obliging me in a given direction. So I've never been afraid of saying which were the major influences in my own work. On the contrary, every time I can discover another influence I'd forgotten, I'm very, very happy. I'll always remember the day I discovered the influence that Jule Laforgue, the French poet, had in my way of looking at certain things; love, for instance. That day I felt that Laforgue was there, not guiding, not obliging me, but simply accompanying me in the way I'd like to be near the young people of the future when I'm dead. I don't want to make my possible influence a compulsive force. I want to be there like a friend, a companion, being near and helping if necessary.

DCC: That's a lovely idea. In a discussion of your writing, Sara Castro-Klarén declared that she did not intend to trace the influences on your work. She felt that 'the problem then is not to search for a hidden, determinant source, but rather to establish a coherent aesthetic backdrop against which one may ascertain the direction to which both the name-dropping and the experimentation point'. For her, the direction is surrealism, which you seem to reject (you said it is 'not a school but a *Weltanschauung*') as similar and also the direction of pataphysics.

JC: My statement that surrealism was not a school but a *Weltanschauung* contains all that I think and especially that which I feel. Surrealism is never an influence on a writer but a manner of 'being', literally speaking. A writer can be influenced by André Breton, by Artaud, etc., but in essence you are not influenced by surrealism, you *are* surrealist, you were born surrealist or a pataphysician. Then given that manner of 'being' which, let's call it surrealism, becomes your *Weltanschauung*, in a very natural way you join the surrealist literary camp. Of course, you like writers who see the world in a similar way as you are seeing it. But they do not influence you. You were seeing the world in a surrealist way before you learned that Artaud, Breton, or Dali had a similar *Weltanschauung*. I think that's the difference between surrealism and other literary schools which are really influences. Surrealism is not an influence; you cannot become a surrealist, you have to be surrealist beforehand. It has to live with you in your blood; it's a vision, it's an interior liberty which expresses in written form a certain way of choosing your themes and handling them.

DCC: The same critic wrote an article called 'Ontological Fabulation: Toward Cortázar's Theory of Literature'. Do the words 'ontological fabulation' or 'theory of literature' make any sense to you?

JC: It is true that a fable is related to myths. Many fables, many myths, are born from ontological foundations. They belong to the inner self of mankind. A good critic can discover that some themes, some subjects, chosen by a writer as a pure invention, can, in fact, respond to deeper reasons and touch ontological foundations. In some of my short stories, for instance, critics saw what a scientist like Jung called the 'collective unconscious'. I think that they were right. Perhaps a writer, myself in this case, believes that he is simply telling a story, his story, but in fact he is telling the deep story which embraces perhaps all the past, all the heritage of the human race.

DCC: Manuel Pedro González, whom you consider a bad critic, Ignacio Iglesias and Guillermo de Torre, among others, question the positive aspects of the 'new novel', citing its over-emphasis of form and technique, and its 'babelismo idiomatico'. Kessel Schwartz feels that Latin American writers of the new novel prefer self-realization to communication; that they are evolving into a new kind of aesthetic élite, which seeks to hide rather than to convey. The critic Arnold Chapman has written that your 'invitation to the sport of do-it-yourself storytelling is nearly irresistible, even though it may prove sometimes too stimulating for sound critical judgement, and sometimes also leaves doubt as to what, exactly, the novel narrates. One might ask whether the inventor or manufacturer of a literary Scrabble should be given credit for all the combinations the players may put together.' What is your response?

JC: This amuses me because I can see how critics like Manuel Pedro González and Guillermo de Torre are taken aback, disconcerted, and angry when they face all kinds of genuinely experimental literature. It seems incredible to me how most of the critics and even the good critics are *behind* what is really happening in the literary scene. As soon as somebody tries to expand the usual literary activity, the result is refusal by the critic to accept this experimentation and try to reduce it to a formal exercise. For instance, Mr Kessel Schwartz says that the Latin American writers are seeking to hide rather than to convey which in my opinion is a big mistake because if anything has been conveyed these last twenty years it has been through our literature, through its better exponents. People who are doing experiments, such as Fuentes, García Márquez and myself, have conveyed a lot of meaning and a lot of messages to our readers. When a critic begins to speak about hiding, perhaps what has happened is that the thing is hidden from him because he is applying a certain kind of perimeter. The novel evades him and that's why Schwartz thinks that the writer is hiding instead of conveying.

DCC: *A Manual for Manuel* raised 'a lot of dust' to use your words. One reaction was, 'how could a writer whose reputation was made on novels that glorified the aesthetic, uncommitted life, write a novel that argued for political commitment?' Any thoughts on that reaction?

JC: If the political commitment is there in *A Manual for Manuel*, then literature is there too and it is more literature than politics. By that I mean that when I wrote that book I believed and I'd go on believing that an honest writer sincerely committed to the peoples of Latin America can convey political meaning without sacrificing the literary value of his work. Well, once you say that you realize that the problem is very complicated because literature and politics are not good friends. The writer then becomes a referee in a boxing match. We are between the two boxers, politics and literature, trying to make a good fight while they are trying to destroy each other by good or bad means. That's why the referee has to be there to control and prevent fouls and low, low punches. I don't know if it's a good comparison but now that I have made it, I'm rather proud of it because I love boxing very much as you probably know. I think it also reflects the real situation for *A Manual for Manuel*. I stood in the middle of the ring at my left was the will to write a real novel and if I could a good novel. On the other hand, there was the need to convey a political message and more exactly a moral, ethical and ideological message especially to my Argentinian readers. When I wrote that book, Argentina was beginning that period of torture, violence, killings, and murder that took the country to the sad state in which it is today. Sometimes the political urge made me write pages and pages that I then had to destroy because they were completely out of the novel context. They were rather a pamphlet than a narrative. On the other hand, sometimes I was simply a novelist writing and all the playful part of the book took the upper hand and I was so happy describing all the antics of my characters. You know that I have a small specialty in inventing characters who are all the time performing most strangely. Well, that's my pleasure and in a way I am like that so I just write what I live myself. The problem was a problem of balance and when I finished *A Manual for Manuel* I didn't care about the criticisms. Many people dislike the book simply because they dislike the political ideas in it. So for them it was very disagreeable to read a novel which in itself was amusing for them but conveyed a message that they rejected. Well, that was exactly my intention and I was very happy for these negative criticisms. Of course, there were many readers who read the book and who understood very well both the novel and the message. I continue to believe that it is an imperfect book because it was written under pressure. It was the first time I had decided to write a book very quickly because for political reasons the book had to be published on a given date before the presidential elections in Argentina. That made me work in an unnatural way because I'm very lazy; I work when I like. *A Manual for Manuel* was a forced work and I feel it when I read it. I'd like to change a lot of things, which is impossible now.

DCC: Is *A Manual for Manuel* a variation on *Hopscotch* rather than a radical departure from it?

JC: I agree completely with you because *A Manual for Manuel* is simply a variation on *Hopscotch* from the literary point of view. The content is quite different because *Hopscotch* didn't convey a political message; if any it was a metaphysical message. I wasn't interested in politics at the time. *A Manual for Manuel* is, let's say, a political book in general terms. But when I began to write *A Manual for Manuel* my problem, as I told you before, was to balance the political and literary aspects of the book. That was new for me, and it was very difficult. I risked a total failure if I couldn't grasp the contradictory elements and balance them in the best possible way. So if I had tried, as I always try when I begin a new story, to experiment in language, in the construction, in the building of the book, that would have given me a lot of additional problems and difficulties that I was sure that I wouldn't be able to surpass. Therefore, I took a more conservative position concerning the writing of the book. I just wrote in a way that I already knew which was the style of *Hopscotch*. It's a very natural way for me because I simply tell things the way they are happening in my imagination and then everything becomes fluent. In *Manuel* I didn't try to invent new possibilities. I used the play, the verbal tricks, that were already in *Hopscotch* and that reappeared in *Manuel*. I made a closed circuit of the characters in both books; there is a kind of club when the reader finds them at the same time. Everybody is there in a few pages and then the action begins and follows when all the characters have been presented like in a cocktail party when you meet twenty people in twenty minutes.

DCC: In Muriel Spark's book *The Mandelbaum Gate* the central character dismissed the *nouveau roman* as 'repetition, boredom, despair, going nowhere for nothing'. Do you agree with those who feel that the theory of the '*nouveau roman*' is more interesting than the actual fiction?

JC: Yes, I continue to believe so. I've read only a few *nouveau roman* which could have really interested me for one reason or another. But when those writers wrote about their point of view, their theory, they clarified a lot concerning modern literature. I am also very thankful to these people for trying to destroy the traditional pyschological novel which was a kind of endemic malady in French literature. It continues in a way because psychological novels are the most popular, the most read. There are hundreds of them written and published every year in France but the *nouveau roman* showed all the weaknesses of this kind of literature and I think that the best writers now write psychological novels with a sharper self-criticism than before.

DCC: Do you sometimes have a huge joke at the expense of learned critics who find hidden meaning where nothing at all was intended?

JC: Yes, of course. Every writer has a great laugh sometimes when he's been told what he meant in one of his novels or short stories and he knows very well that it is not true. The writer knows that the reader or the critic has applied a meaning that was completely alien to his thoughts. I have many, many examples of that but I'll just tell you one. When I wrote one of my first short stories which is called 'Casa Tomada' and it was published in Buenos Aires, two critics discovered that this short story was an allegory. The couple of characters who were expelled little by little from their house were according to those critics the image of the real Argentinian people who were being expelled by 'the dark forces of Peronism'. I had a good laugh when I read that one because never in my life had I thought of such a meaning.

DCC: Alternatively, even though many writers do not agree, you have said that you learn a lot about yourself from critics: 'there are many interpretations that I believe to be either completely or partially accurate. Thus, they show me pieces of my own mosaic, or my unknown unconscious. They show me my nocturnal self, nocturnal in the psychological sense, and in that sense I'm very grateful for that kind of interpretation.' Could you expand that?

JC: This is a very good question for me because it gives the reverse side of what I was just saying: the positive explanations that a critic can give of some aspects of a work that the writer doesn't know, and is unable to understand. I would add that this is for the best because if I had a clear consciousness of what I'm writing, I think I'd be a very unhappy man and probably a very poor writer. It seems so irrational but I can't imagine one hundred per cent rational writing. I can't imagine myself going to my typewriter with a plan fully prepared where everything is more or less in place and things will happen according to a mental schedule. I know perfectly well that there are good writers who work in that way but my approach is different. When I don't know what I'm going to do, then that is the time I write best. Somebody is behind me and he's simply giving me all that my hands are writing. This doesn't mean that I work in a kind of somnambulistic state. I'm quite conscious of what I'm doing while I'm doing it and I can very well stop a sentence, cut a page and begin again and so on. I'm guiding my work but when I say that I'm guiding my work, the work itself is another thing. I am the pilot of a ship but a pilot who doesn't know where the ship has to go. He just guides the ship in order to avoid the coast or an obstacle and that's all. Other than that he doesn't know where the ship is going and where the trip is going to finish. Some critics wrote books or articles demonstrating in a very cool and convincing way a lot of motivations of what I call my nocturnal life (and I mean by that all that comes from the deep when I begin to write a story, especially a short story). This all comes from complexes, neuroses, and angst in the existential sense. The critics were able to dissect this and to find the roots. I know a Jungian interpretation of some of my short stories and when I read it I was frightened because I had to accept the explanation. I had to accept that this short story was reflecting very clearly, even in the name of the characters, one given complex. And of course when I wrote that story, and I remember very well when and how I wrote it, I never thought of complexes. I gave the characters the first name that came to my head. Now, it seems that the names came to my head because I was already in a subconscious state and I was trying to express that nocturnal part of myself. That frightens me a bit because if you think about it metaphysically, you discover that if those critics are right, then a writer is *not* a free man. He thinks that he is writing freely but, in fact, he is obeying his subconscious. In Jungian terms, he's a part of the collective subconscious so he's a prisoner of a very, very complex and immense heritage that makes him simply a scribe who must once again put a myth in a new written form. But what counts finally is not to let yourself believe that you're not free because it's not true. When you write a new short story or a new novel you're absolutely free and you take pleasure in the freedom that writing gives. Critics come later to prove that in a Jungian way you are not free but as a writer you don't care about that because you felt free when you wrote.

DCC: The Chilean novelist José Donoso has written that for Latin Americans the novel has suddenly been transformed into *the* artistic form *par excellence*. The novel, he feels, has advanced suddenly to the first rank to occupy the favoured position previously occupied by poetry. If you agree, how do you account for this?

JC: Yes, he's right. The novel has advanced to that rank. Yet we should take into account that a lot of current poetry is not written in the form of poems but is put into novels and becomes a part of these novels. It's quite a modern phenomenon. In my opinion it started in the twenties. For instance, there is Hermann Broch's novel *The Death of Virgil*, which for me is a great, great poem and at the same time it's a narrative. You shouldn't forget that *The Odyssey* and *The Iliad* are at the same time novels as well as poems. The form is a poem and the content is a novel; it is a narrative. Actually now this is reversed; the form is prose but the content of many novels is deeply poetic. So all these belong to the banishing of traditional categories and the appearance of hybrid forms, new forms, composed forms, in which poetry merges with prose to give new ways of expressing new sensibilities. All this is highly positive for me and I don't like people who continue to believe that poetry has always to be a poem or it won't be poetry.

DCC: A long time ago, you wrote that poetry is 'the fulfilment of the self . . . its absolute embodiment and its entelechy'. Do you still feel the same? Why is this more so than with the novel?

JC: There seems to be a misunderstanding here, Diana, because in my case I'd never compare the novel with poetry in a general sense because even if they are both forms of verbal expression they are quite different not only in form but in scope. So to ask me if poetry is more fulfilling than the novel, or vice versa, would be like asking me to establish a scale of values between a symphony and a sonata; both are music but you can't compare a sonata with a symphony. They've been born with quite a different scope in their limits and their possibilities and they don't admit any comparison except in the form of mere analogies. The basic problem in this case is that you could define the novel as an open form while great poetry is always a closed form and starting from this first essential difference all the rest is different too.

DCC: You have said that 'English is the language of poetry.' Why?

JC: If I said that English is the language of poetry, I don't think that I was saying it in an exclusive way. That would be to deny other languages of poetry. Of course, poetry goes where it wants and where it can. But I happen to believe, and to feel, that English is one of the most musical languages, for my ear in any case. Its formal possibilities provide an opening which other languages like French, for instance, which is stricter in its syntax, don't always give. When I speak of the musicality of English, I'm not only speaking of its euphonic quality but also of the harmony that pervades an English poem, a kind of internal rhythm based on, I don't know, measures of time in the language. English is the language of poetry for me because when I wrote that sentence I was thinking of verses such as 'Season of mists and mellow fruitfulness' or any other poems from the great Keats.

DCC: At the risk of yet again not quoting you correctly, you have also said that part of your prose is thought of, seen and written poetically? In what way?

JC: It *is* another possible misunderstanding that must be cleared. Yes, of course, I said that part of my prose is thought of, seen and written poetically but what I mean when I say that is that I happen to write a good part of my work, especially the short stories, in the state of mind wherein logic is abandoned. There is another kind of thought, if you may call it a thought, that takes place intuitively. It is almost the physical kind of thought that is there when you write a poem. That is to say that all the logical exigencies of reality, such as two plus two make four, are not valid and many of my short stories tend to prove that two plus two may make five or three, in certain given circumstances. In that way I write poetically because poetry doesn't care about logic in its best moments.

DCC: In your article on the short story you compared the novel to the movies. They both have an open order, a detailed and rounded structure in which many frames or puzzle pieces eventually deliver a finished story to the viewer. Are there any other similarities?

JC: There *are* other similarities, especially the one concerning time. A novel takes a long time to be read and a movie to be seen; a short story is like a very short movie in which everything has to be condensed, rounded and finished up. I think always of a sphere, a circle, when I think of the short story. A novel is open and a movie has one-hour-and-a-half to two hours to develop. So the forms coincide. The author, the creator has all this time to develop situations, to create bifurcations, flashbacks, to complete things on the spot or later on; these are some of the things that a short story or a short movie can't do. Of course, you can find some other similarities. For instance a novel and a movie provide ample space to present and develop a lot of characters, situations, inter-reactions, and inter-relations. You are able to create very complex situations, you can describe things or make a narrative which covers perhaps a few years, and sometimes even whole centuries. This really couldn't be done in a short story.

DCC: Jean Ricardou made an interesting remark about the novel: 'the novel ceases to be the writing of a story to become the story of a writing'.

JC: This corresponds to the new critical view of literature. In France, it is called the New Criticism, and even structuralism. I only agree in part with that because if when you write a novel you forget that you are writing a story and you only concentrate on the story of writing, there's a danger always waiting there. The novel ceases to be a novel in the ordinary sense and becomes a kind of essay or a philosophical meditation or a way of conveying ideas, just expressed through a story. I'm old-fashioned in that sense and many other senses and, for me, a novel must be above all a story. It must contain a story. Of course, the beauty, the value and the meaning of that story depends on all the other elements that novelists can add to it. If it is just for the story's sake, then you have the best sellers. It's just a story but when Tolstoy writes he's telling one of the greatest stories in literature and at the same time he's making it sustain a whole philosphy of life, a whole philosophy of human relationships; so it takes on a new dimension. If a novel can only be reduced to the story it narrates, it doesn't go very far; but when a novel can only be reduced to the writing part of it, when it is a kind of exercise of style or a mere experimentation in a new style, in a new use of language, then, it becomes defective. Many modern novels which are based on Jean Ricardou's idea can be great books, very, very great books. They can be full of discoveries about the writing of the book but do we have the right to go on calling them novels? I'm not so sure. I can't read them like a novel; I can read such a book with the greatest interest, but it's the same interest that applies to a good book on anthropology, or a good book on philosophy, or a good book on scientific matters. For me, it has ceased to be a novel but, of course, times are changing and those books not only are valid but they are fascinating. The danger is that we go on making comparisons for new things and trying to define and develop ideas concerning the new forms of literature and at the same time we keep using the old words, the old categories of short story, novels etc. We should try to find new words for new things and, of course, this has always been very difficult.

DCC: I agree. In a sense, writing distorts and violates life by stopping life through imposing form on it. Severo Sarduy has said that the type of literature which is transgressive is that literature which does not write *about* something, but actually *is* something. Your novels are like this for me.

JC: I fully agree with Sarduy's point of view and I'm very, very happy that you find that my novels are like this for you. My hope when I write a novel or a short story is that the story is not *about* a plot, *about* something I invented or that happened and that I am treating in a literary way. My hope is that the result of what I have written will have a kind of autonomous existence, even, if I may say so, a kind of independent essence; a thing which is valid by itself. I suppose this is only a hope, I don't know how far I or other writers can achieve that, but if I didn't write in that hope I think that my writing would be traditional writing with not much interest.

DCC: Your novel *62: A Model Kit* has been called an 'anti-novel'. Are the words 'anti-novel' or the 'new novel' just as restrictive as the word 'novel'?

JC: This is a synthesis of your questions and my answers. It's above all a matter of vocabulary, and of terms. Critics, readers and even writers are talking of 'anti-novel' or 'counter-novel' or 'new-novel' simply because the word 'novel' is in a way an obsolete word for the new literature some of us are trying to do. They simply show these new currents that tried to use the form called 'novel', that is to say a long narrative, giving it a new scope, new possibilities of the language and simply changing many traditional laws concerning literature and the narrative form. Those words, 'anti-novel' or a 'new-novel', will awaken in the sensitive reader a new attitude before he or she begins to read that book. When you buy a book that is called an 'anti-novel' you couldn't begin to read it as though you were reading a Victor Hugo novel or a Dickens novel. You will know that the writer tried new forms and looked for new horizons. If you are aware of all that, you are helping the writer. You are working at his side and that helps you as a reader to enter into the deep sense and meaning of that book, and that helps enormously to find its real value. Of course, there are many writers who are not genuine in that sense and they present their books under a cloak of experimentation. They decide to tell a story beginning in the future and finishing in the past and they make all kinds of reversals. Often the reader will discover in the second chapter that all that is quite artificial, they are telling the same old story but they are simply changing the way of presenting it to the reader. When it is genuine it has sense, but in many cases you quickly discover that they have very few things to say, so they apply artifical methods to embezzle their readers.

DCC: I have heard so many terms, interpretations, and definitions of reality. With reference to Latin American literature, I most often hear about 'magic realism', 'superrealism' and 'surrationalism'. Do these terms have any meaning for you?

JC: I read every day the same words you speak of, 'magic realism', 'supperrealism', 'surrationalism', and there's another word which many critics use; it is the old word 'Baroque'. They define all Latin American literature as baroque literature. This is partly true because we write in a richer way, that is to say any given narrative situation is explored with the greatest possibilities of the language and the imagination. A French novelist would explain this in a few sentences, which has its merits but has its disadvantages too because reality is so rich and so full of possibilities and bifurcations. Latin American novelists tried to explore all the possibilities. You only have to read Asturias or Carpentier. By the way it was Alejo Carpentier who always applied the word 'baroque' to Latin American literature. The baroque in the plastic arts, painting and architecture was that fear of the void that the artist and the sculptor and the architect tried to fill with convolutions, adornments, and curls and forms and volumes, because they couldn't stand that void which for me is wonderful. You find it in Gothic art, those empty, big, beautiful naves of Gothic churches in which the air, the space, is king but it is king because there's a wonderful form surrounding it and limiting it. The baroque is afraid of this open space, and tries to eliminate it. The novelist tries to eliminate it with words, well, not exactly words, but by trying to multiply all the ramifications of a given situation so that when a character speaks with another or acts in this or that way, a Latin American novelist will try, in general to explore all the possibilities of this dialogue, of this action. That can give marvellous results, that can give perhaps the best of Carpentier, Asturias and one who is especially dear to me, José Lezama Lima. On the other hand, in Argentina, without imitating the European models, we are more sober in our ways of presenting reality and we hope nevertheless to apprehend this reality in its essence. So when I hear words like 'magic realism' or 'superrealism', I'm not really convinced that this could be applied on the whole to Latin American literature.

DCC: I have some awareness of what you mean. I won't articulate beyond two quotes from your writing. In your short story 'The Pursuer', the protagonist searches for 'a reality that escapes every day'. And in *A Manual for Manuel* we are told that 'you can't measure reality in terms of confusion or order'.

JC: This is trying to express a deep feeling in myself because I couldn't imagine reality in binary terms. I think that we apprehend one immediate reality and most people stop there and accept that reality, which they grasp in two ways; the first is the way they receive as a heritage from the past through education and examples, and the other way is the reality they grasp through their senses and their mind, which is always pragmatic. If you begin to find that everything is a problem, everything is an enigma, everything is a mystery, life becomes very difficult. Man is an economical animal. His intelligence is a selective intelligence, that's why logic was invented. Logic helps to make a choice in reality and informs us why this is blood, this is a chair, this is my brother; but as soon as you look at just your hand for more than one minute, suddenly you begin to discover something that I would call a mystery. This incredible thing that is one part of your body terminates in five fingers which are touching space. But what is this limit and why this limit? Why do I finish here instead of finishing two yards further on or why don't I simply not have hands at all? This notion of mystery has been my own life since I was a child. The problem for my parents, friends and teachers was that I questioned everything. When they said, 'you have a hand with five fingers', the first thing I would say was always, 'why five and not four or six, and why a hand and what is a hand?' And that is a supreme mystery. There's the mystery of the matter that makes us a body but it's a very special kind of a body because it's not the body of a tree or a body of a caterpillar. All this is very childish indeed but children have often this sense of mystery. The real writer and the real poet and the real artist is the man who keeps the child alive in himself.

DCC: Time is an important part of our sense of reality. Virginia Woolf, in *Orlando*, states: 'An hour, once it lodges in the queer element of the human spirit may be stretched to fifty or a hundred times its clock length; on the other hand, an hour may be accurately represented by the timepiece of the mind by one second.'

JC: Virginia Woolf's quotation is wonderful. Time is one of the biggest mysteries for a man who doesn't accept the time his clock is showing him. You remember, of course (because you know my work better than myself), that part in 'The Pursuer', when Johnny Carter discovers in the Paris Métro that two minutes could be half an hour in his mind because when he's in a state of distraction between two Métro stations he imagines things that in a normal time could take half an hour and suddenly he discovers that the Métro has only gone from one station to another and by the clocks that takes exactly two minutes. So when one is aware of the elasticity of time, you can't accept the usual notions of time. Why should I accept the usual notion of space as it is given to us; why should I accept the dictionary definition of a table or a cat or a wall or a man?

DCC: I've often felt the same way. Horacio, in *Hopscotch*, needs to 'apprehend unity in the midst of plurality'.

JC: The need that Horacio represents in *Hopscotch* corresponds to what I've been trying to say. People like Horacio and myself happen to be deeply anguished and deeply frightened by the sense of mystery that we face with the smallest things in the reality that surrounds us. We're trying to discover the mystery of the hand, the mystery of the chair, so finally a moment arrives in which there's a kind of thirst for the opposite, that is to say a notion of unity. This permanent plurality of things drives you to madness upon reflection, because the human mind biologically has not developed to the point where we can accept an infinite plurality which finally dissolves the reality in which we are. So the opposite idea is born: the notion of unity. Horacio and I feel that there must be a state to attain and which we have not attained. Mankind has not attained that state of mind or feeling of *Weltanschauung* wherein we have harmony, a deep unity with nature, with reality that is located in the inner self, in the most deep and central region of our divided and broken modern self. That's why Horacio speaks so often of that search for a centre, that search for a metaphysical place in which all contradictions would be resolved, in which all the plurality of the reality would take their real dimensions and be seen as we see now the leaves of a tree. But it would have to be the total tree which contains all the leaves in one central harmony which is the tree itself.

DCC: Laughter seems to be important to our sense of ourselves. You have suggested that the world is not only absurd, but it may be a figment of the imagination from whose chains humour and parody may free you.

JC: If I suggested before that the world is absurd, today I would say rather the opposite: it is not the world that is absurd, it is we who are absurd. We are absurd in a world that we don't know exactly as it is simply because we are absurd. If we could find a way to annihilate our own absurdity in many senses of the word, then I think that the word would take its real image and would perhaps give us that centre of unity and harmony that we were speaking of. But for the time being, weapons like laughter and humour are perhaps the possibilities we have that are less absurd than a certain seriousness, a certain believing in things that are given to us in a certain form. To use humour in life and literature and to laugh in life and literature is not absurd; it is perhaps one of the only sound things that we have at our disposal. Perhaps I'm mistaken but every time that humour is applied by myself or I read some humour applied by a writer in a given situation, I feel a kind of illumination. Humour is always like a light which is breaking the obscurity around us. Real humour is not absurd. On the contrary, just by taking a thing and looking at it from the other side and discovering the possibility of applying humour in this unusual examination of the thing, you are doing a very useful thing because you are discovering new aspects of reality that are too often frozen by logic, by intelligence, by reflection, by laws, and by dictionaries.

DCC: You have said, 'I don't write for my readers. I throw myself like a good toreador in front of the bulls, without thinking of money or fame. I love the game and the beauty of writing.' I know how a toreador might get killed, but how might you?

JC: I could be killed if I gave no thought to my reader waiting on the other side of my work and if one day the readers decided that my writing wasn't the kind of reading they wanted or they needed. I must say without false modesty that that has not been the case up to now. On the contrary, my readers are many and scattered across the whole world and especially in Latin America. I know I have wonderful readers everywhere, readers that belong to all social classes, all cultural levels, which makes me very happy because I hate 'class writers', 'upper or lower class' writers and all that. So for the time being I don't think I will be killed for literary reasons; I might be killed for political reasons. I'll go on writing in the first place for myself but at the same time having a deep respect and a deep love for the readers who are waiting somewhere to read new books, mine and others. I write as if I have my typewriter on a bridge and I was looking at the other end of the bridge. But the bridge is very, very large so I can't see distinctly to the other side; however I know there are men, women, and even children there and that what I am doing is going to go across the bridge and reach the other people. I'll have their responses, good, bad, understanding, misunderstanding, it doesn't matter; the thing that counts is that there is a bridge and, for me, literature is building bridges in mankind, stretching bridges from one man to another, from writer to reader. Perhaps that is the only thing a writer can do and I'm happy to be able to make some bridges from time to time.

Index